W9-AEY-268

THE KING LEAR PERPLEX

Wadsworth Guides to Literary Study

Maurice Beebe, General Editor

THE
KING LEAR
PERPLEX

EDITED BY HELMUT BONHEIM
UNIVERSITY OF CALIFORNIA, SANTA BARBARA

WADSWORTH PUBLISHING COMPANY, INC.
BELMONT, CALIFORNIA

© 1960 by Wadsworth Publishing
Company, Inc., Belmont, California.
All rights reserved. No part of this
book may be reproduced in any
form, by mimeograph or any other
means, without permission in writing from the publisher.

First Printing, May 1960
Second Printing, January 1961
Third Printing, December 1962

L.C. Cat. Card No.: 60-9978

Printed in the United States of
America

Manufactured by American Book–
Stratford Press, Inc.

PREFACE

So much has been written on *King Lear* that the student coming to a study of the play is likely to be overawed by the sheer weight of previous comment. All too often he despairs of so much as even beginning to discover and understand the best of what has already been said; and he is likely to think that even if he could overcome this first obstacle, he would then find it impossible to add anything of his own to the *King Lear* "perplex." This book is intended to help the student overcome both of these obstacles. It offers the reader key portions of a discussion in which many of the finest critical minds of three centuries have participated. And that discussion is not over. I am confident that this book will raise for the alert student as many questions as it settles and therefore encourage additional thought and research on a work of literature that can never be exhausted.

Just as the critics quoted use earlier critics for help, even if only as whipping boys, the student who comes to this book from a fairly fresh reading of the play will in turn use the insights of his predecessors. He will find that more remains to be done. Although our wonder at Shakespeare's achievement may be no greater than the wonder which Johnson or Coleridge so eloquently expressed, we have the benefit of their insights as well as of our own.

In selecting material, I have tried to keep a balance between the best and the most representative. Although those readers who prefer to approach the material by major themes and problems may do so easily with the help of a topical index provided at the end of this volume, the selections are arranged chronologically to give the student a sense of historical development. He will discover that the play has said different things to different generations. Modern readers will find some of the early critics naïve and ignorant, but no more so than many of our present-day commentators will seem in a century or two. Although the reader is spared the most blatant extremes of the ridiculous, he is not spared all. If he is alert, he will recoil here and there at specters of bad logic, narrowness, unjustified self-confidence, and downright lapses of taste. He will find that before Coleridge almost no critic discussed the play in any detail, and that it was another hundred years before the nineteenth century emphasis on character gave way to the kinds of exploration we have come to take for granted—hard looks at Elizabethan conventions behind the play, at the philosophy, language, and imagery which are, together with character, aspects of

v

the complex work of art we admire. Of the chief schools and styles of critical approach to *King Lear* represented here, some have fallen into general disrepute or are simply out of fashion; now in disrepute, for example, is the first selection in this book, Nahum Tate's revision of the play, which held the English stage for 150 years. The reader must therefore discriminate critically in using the material here collected. But if he finds weak spots in some of the criticism, he will also find information applied with resourcefulness and perceptiveness, often with a wisdom that has been directed at few other works of literature.

I cannot pretend that there is any real substitute for digging up the material for one's self, experiencing the delight of stumbling onto an occasional oasis in the hot wastes of critical discussion. But only months of reading in the best libraries will begin to cover the thousands of pages here reduced to under two hundred. This compression has forced me to exclude entirely some worthy discussions of the play and mercilessly to extract the gist of others. To compensate for the numerous exclusions and excisions, I have included a fairly extensive bibliography which lists not only additional criticism, but also certain technical or scholarly matters outside the bounds of this book: sources, editions, dating, textual emendations, staging problems, relation to other works, and so on. This bibliography is arranged by topics, and most of the entries are briefly annotated.

For the convenience of those who wish to use this book as a guide to literary study, I have left the selections as true to their originals as is practicable. Editing has tended to remove comment irrelevant to the objectives of this collection, excessive or repetitive quotations from the play, and scholarly, historical, and biographical matters. The spaced ellipses (. . .) are mine, as opposed to the unspaced ellipses (...) of the originals. Unnecessary footnotes are omitted, and those remaining renumbered. Where the bracketed number, which indicates original pagination, would have fallen in the middle of a word because that word was divided between two pages, the number has been set at the end of that word. And since students are already sufficiently confused about matters of punctuation, I have normalized the most extreme vagaries to accepted American usage, but have otherwise made every attempt to be faithful to the original, even to the extent of reproducing little inconsistencies and currently unacceptable quirks of style. I have not altered all quotations to conform to one edition of the play. Only a few obvious errors have been silently corrected.

The student in search of an essay topic will find the index designed for his need, and the excerpts themselves can serve as models of what may be done. Then if he wishes to explore beyond the present selections he would do well to consult the most searching critics further, to whose extended commentaries excerpting cannot do justice: notably H. N. Hudson, A. C. Bradley, Harley Granville-Barker, R. B. Heilman, G. Wilson Knight, W. H. Clemen, William Empson, and

D. G. James. If material for a longer study is wanted, the student can turn to the annotated bibliography. The best student will inevitably rely on the play itself and on his own sense of it for primary source material, but he will find that true originality, in criticism as in literature and the arts, almost certainly presupposes a knowledge of what others before him have accomplished.

H. B.

CONTENTS

Preface . . . . **v**

Part One

THE *KING LEAR* PERPLEX: SELECTED CRITICISM . . 1

most famous of romantic critics

most famous 20th criticism

absurdities, utilitarian viewpoint

Part Two

THE *KING LEAR* PERPLEX: SELECTED CRITICISM

> *Duff-Muggli, who now may be quoted by very kind arrangement* . . . *, first called this kind of paddygoeasy partnership the ulykkhean or tetrachiric or quadrumane or duck and drakes or debts and dishes perplex.* . . . —*James Joyce:* FINNEGANS WAKE

Nahum Tate

From "The History of King Lear" [1687].
London, 1745.

SCENE, *A Prison*

LEAR *asleep, with his Head on* CORDELIA'S *Lap.*

CORD.   What Toils, thou wretched King, hast thou endur'd
To make thee draw, in Chains, a Sleep so sound?
Thy better Angel charm thy ravish'd Mind
With fancy'd Freedom; Peace is us'd to lodge
On Cottage Straw. Thou hast the Beggar's Bed,
Therefore should'st have the Beggar's careless Thought.
And now, my Edgar, I remember thee:
What Fate has seiz'd thee in this general Wreck
I know not, but I know thou must be wretched,
Because Cordelia holds thee dear.
O Gods! A sudden Gloom o'er-whelms me, and the Image
Of Death o'er-spreads the Place.—Ha! Who are there?

Enter CAPTAIN *and Officers with Cords.*

CAPT.   Now, Sirs, dispatch; already you are paid
In Part, the Best of your Reward's to come.

LEAR.   Charge, charge upon their Flank, their last Wing halts.
Push, push the Battle, and the Day's our own.
Their Ranks are broke, down with Albany.
Who holds my Hands?—O thou deceiving Sleep,
I was this very Minute on the Chace;
And now a Prisoner here.—What mean the Slaves?
You will not murder me? [65]

CORD.   Help, Earth and Heaven!
For your Souls sake, dear Sirs, and for the Gods.

OFF.   No Tears, good Lady; no pleading against Gold and **Prefer-**
ment.
Come, Sirs, make ready your Cords.

CORD.   You, Sir, I'll seize,
You have a human Form, and if no Prayers
Can touch your Soul to spare a poor King's Life,

3

If there be any thing that you hold dear,
By that I beg you to dispatch me first.

CAPT.   Comply with her Request; dispatch her first.

LEAR.   Off Hell-Hounds, by the Gods I charge you spare her;
'Tis my Cordelia, my true pious Daughter;
No pity?—Nay, then take an old Man's Vengeance.

*Snatches a Partisan, and strikes down two of them;
the rest quit* CORDELIA, *and turn upon him.*

Enter EDGAR *and* ALBANY.

EDG.   Death! Hell! Ye Vultures, hold your impious Hands,
Or take a speedier Death than you wou'd give.

CAPT.   By whose Command?

EDG.   Behold the Duke, your Lord.

ALB.   Guards, seize those Instruments of Cruelty.

CORD.   My Edgar, Oh!

EDG.   My dear Cordelia! Lucky was the Minute
Of our Approach; the Gods have weigh'd our Suff'rings;
W'are past the Fire, and now must shine to Ages.

GENT.   Look here, my Lord, see where the generous King
Has slain two of 'em.

LEAR.   Did I not, Fellow?
I've seen the Day, with my good biting Faulchion
I cou'd have made 'em skip: I am Old now,
And these vile Crosses spoil me; out of Breath,
Fie, oh! quite out of Breath, and spent.

ALB.   Bring in old Kent; and, Edgar, guide you hither
Your Father, whom you said was near; [*Exit* EDGAR.
He may be an Ear-Witness at the least
Of our Proceedings. [KENT *brought in here.*

LEAR.   Who are you?
My Eyes are none o'th'best, I'll tell you streight;
Oh Albany! Well, Sir, we are your Captives,
And you are come to see Death pass upon us.
Why this Delay?—Or is't your Highness's Pleasure [66]
To give us first the Torture? Say ye so?
Why here's old Kent and I, as tough a Pair
As e'er bore Tyrant's Stroke.—But my Cordelia,
My poor Cordelia here, O pity—

ALB.   Take off their Chains.—Thou injur'd Majesty,
The Wheel of Fortune now has made her Circle,
And Blessings yet stand 'twixt thy Grave and thee.

LEAR.   Com'st thou, inhuman Lord, to sooth us back
To a Fool's Paradise of Hope, to make
Our Doom more wretched? Go to, we are too well
Acquainted with Misfortune, to be gull'd
With lying Hope; no, we will hope no more.

ALB.   I have a Tale t'unfold, so full of Wonder
As cannot meet an easy Faith;
But by that Royal injur'd Head 'tis true.

KENT.   What wou'd your Highness?

ALB.   Know, the noble Edgar
Impeach'd Lord Edmund, since the Fight, of Treason
And dar'd him for the Proof to single Combat,
In which the Gods confirm'd his Charge by Conquest;
I left ev'n now the Traitor wounded mortally!

LEAR.   And whither tends this Story?

ALB.   'Ere they fought,
Lord Edgar gave into my Hands this Paper;
A blacker Scroll of Treason and of Lust,
Than can be found in the Records of Hell;
There, Sacred Sir, behold the Character
Of Goneril, the worst of Daughters, but
More vicious Wife.

CORD.   Cou'd there be yet Addition to their Guilt!
What will not they that wrong a Father do?

ALB.   Since then my Injuries, Lear, fall in with thine,
I have resolv'd the same Redress for both.

KENT.   What says my Lord?

CORD.   Speak, for methought I heard
The charming Voice of a descending God.

ALB.   The Troops, by Edmund rais'd, I have disbanded;
Those that remain are under my Command.
What Comfort may be brought to chear your Age,
And heal your savage Wrongs, shall be apply'd;
For to your Majesty we do resign [67]
Your Kingdom, save what Part yourself confer'd
On us in Marriage.

KENT.   Hear you that, my Liege?

CORD.   Then they are Gods, and Virtue is their Care.

LEAR.　Is't possible?
Let the Spheres stop their Course, the Sun make halt,
The Winds be hush'd, the Seas and Fountains rest;
All Nature pause, and listen to the Change.
Where is my Kent, my Cajus?

KENT.　Here, my Liege.

LEAR.　Why I have News that will recall thy Youth:
Ha! Didst thou hear't, or did th'inspiring Gods
Whisper to me alone? Old Lear shall be
A King again.

KENT.　The Prince, that like a God has Pow'r, has said it.

LEAR.　Cordelia then shall be a Queen, mark that:
Cordelia shall be a Queen; Winds catch the Sound,
And bear it on your rosy Wings to Heav'n—
Cordelia is a Queen.

Re-enter EDGAR *with* GLOSTER.

ALB.　Look, Sir, where pious Edgar comes,
Leading his Eyeless Father. O my Liege!
His wond'rous Story well deserves your Leisure;
What he has done and suffer'd for your Sake,
What for the fair Cordelia's.

GLOST.　Where's my Liege? Conduct me to his Knees, to hail
His second Birth of Empire: My dear Edgar
Has, with himself, reveal'd the King's blest Restauration.

LEAR.　My poor dark Gloster.

GLOST.　O let me kiss that once more scepter'd Hand!

LEAR.　Hold, thou mistake'st the Majesty, kneel here;
Cordelia has our Pow'r, Cordelia's Queen.
Speak, is not that the noble suff'ring Edgar?

GLOST.　My pious Son, more dear than my lost Eyes.

LEAR.　I wrong'd him too, but here's the fair Amends.

EDG.　Your Leave, my Liege, for an unwelcome Message.
Edmund (but that's a Trifle) is expired.
What more will touch you, your imperious Daughters,
Goneril and haughty Regan, both are dead,
Each by the other poison'd at a Banquet:
This, dying, they confess'd.[68]

CORD.　O fatal Period of ill-govern'd Lives!

LEAR.　Ingrateful as they were, my Heart feels yet
A pang of Nature for their wretched Fall.—

But Edgar, I defer thy Joys too long:
Thou serv'dst distress'd Cordelia; take her crown'd,
Th' imperial Grace fresh blooming on her Brow;
Nay, Gloster, thou hast here a Father's Right,
Thy helping Hand t'heap Blessings on their Heads.

KENT. Old Kent throws in his hearty Wishes too.

EDG. The Gods and you too largely recompence
What I have done; the Gift strikes Merit dumb.

CORD. Nor do I blush to own myself o'er-paid
For all my Suff'rings past.

GLOST. Now, gentle Gods, give Gloster his Discharge.

LEAR. No, Gloster, thou hast Business yet for Life;
Thou, Kent, and I, retir'd to some close Cell,
Will gently pass our short Reserves of Time
In calm Reflections on our Fortunes past,
Cheer'd with Relation of the prosperous Reign
Of this celestial Pair; thus our Remains
Shall in an even Course of Thoughts be past,
Enjoy the present Hour, nor fear the last.

EDG. Our drooping Country now erects her Head,
Peace spreads her balmy Wings, and Plenty blooms.
Divine Cordelia, all the Gods can witness
How much thy Love to Empire I prefer!
Thy bright Example shall convince the World
(Whatever Storms of Fortune are decreed)
That Truth and Virtue shall at last succeed.
[*Ex. Omnes.*] [69]

Joseph Warton

From *The Adventurer* [1753, 1754]. Volume
IV. London, 1778.

General criticism is on all subjects useless and unentertaining;
but is more than commonly absurd with respect to Shakespeare, who
must be accompanied step by step, and scene by scene, in his gradual
developments of characters and passions, and whose finer features
must be singly pointed out, if we would do complete justice to his

genuine beauties. It would have been easy to have declared, in general terms, "that the madness of Lear was very natural and pathetic;" and the reader might then have escaped, what he may, perhaps, call a multitude of well-known quotations: but then it had been impossible to exhibit a perfect picture of the secret workings and changes of Lear's mind, which vary in each succeeding passage, and which render an allegation of each particular sentiment absolutely necessary. [No. 116, December 15, 1753, 93]

Madness being occasioned by a close and continued attention of the mind to a single object, Shakespeare judiciously represents the resignation of his crown to daughters so cruel and unnatural, as the particular idea which has brought on the distraction of Lear, and which perpetually recurs to his imagination, and mixes itself with all his ramblings. . . . [No. 122, January 5, 1754, 140]

. . . this drama is chargeable with considerable imperfections. The plot of Edmund against his brother, which distracts the attention, and destroys the unity of the fable; the cruel and horrid extinction of Glo'ster's eyes, which ought not to be exhibited on the stage; the utter improbability of Gloster's imagining, though blind, that he had leaped down Dover cliff; and some passages that are too turgid and full of strained metaphors, are faults which the warmest admirers of Shakespeare will find it difficult to excuse. I know not, also, whether the cruelty of the daughters is not painted with circumstances too savage and unnatural; for it is not sufficient to say, that this monstrous barbarity is founded on historical truth, if we recollect the just observation of Boileau,

Le vray peut quelquefois n'etre pas vraisemblable.

Some truths may be too strong to be believed. [*Ibid.*, 148]

$$\star\!\!\!\!\star$$

Charlotte Lennox

From *Shakespear Illustrated*. Volume III. London, 1754.

The King of France . . . [287], charm'd with the Virtue and Beauty of the injured Cordelia, marries her without a Portion.

Shakespear does not introduce this Prince till after the absurd

Trial Lear made of his Daughters Affection is over. The Lover who is made to Marry the disinherited Cordelia on account of her Virtue, is very injudiciously contrived to be Absent when she gave so glorious a Testimony of it, and is touch'd by a cold Justification of her Fame, and that from herself, when he might have been charm'd with a shining Instance of her Greatness of Soul, and inviolable Regard to Truth.

So unartfully has the Poet managed this Incident, that Cordelia's noble Disinterestedness is apparent to all but him who was to be the most influenced by it. In the Eyes of her Lover she is debased, not exalted; reduced to the abject Necessity of defending her own Character, and seeking rather to free herself from the Suspicion of Guilt, than modestly enjoying the conscious Sense of Superior Virtue.

Lear's Invective against her to the King of France is conceived in the most shocking Terms. . . .[288]

a Wretch, whom Nature is asham'd Almost t'acknowledge hers.

Well might the King of France be startled at such Expressions as these from a Parent of his Child; had he been present to have heard the Offence she gave him to occasion them, how must her exalted Merit have been endeared to him by the extream Injustice she suffered; but as it is, a bare Acquittal of any monsterous Crime, is all the Satisfaction she can procure for herself; and all the Foundation her Lover has for the Eulogium he afterwards makes on her. [Quotes Cordelia's speech asking Lear to acquit her of "vicious blot."]

From this Speech of Cordelia's, and Lear's Answer, France collects Matter for extenuating [289] a supposed Error in his Mistress, not for Admiration of her Worth.

FRANCE.

Is it but this? a Tardiness in Nature,
Which often leaves the History unspoke,
That it intends to do.

Yet a Moment after, without knowing any more of the Matter, he lavishes the warmest Praises on her Virtues, and offers to make her (loaded as she is with her Father's Curses, and deprived of the Dower he expected with her) Queen of France. This Conduct would be just and natural, had he been a Witness of her noble Behaviour; but doubtful as it must have appeared to him in such perplexing Circumstances, 'tis extravagant and absurd.

Shakespear has deviated widely from History in the Catastrophe of his Play; the Chronicle tells us, that King Lear having been dispossessed by his rebellious Sons in Law of that Half of the Kingdom which he had reserved for himself, and forced, by repeated Indignities from his Daughters, to take Refuge in France, was received with great Tenderness by Cordelia, who prevailed upon her Husband to attempt his Restoration; accordingly an Army of Frenchmen pass'd over into Britain, by which, the Dukes of Cornwal and Albany being defeated, King Lear was restored to his Crown, died in Peace two Years after, and left his Kingdom to Cordelia. In Shakespear the Forces of the two wicked Sisters are victorious, Lear and the pious Cordelia are taken Prisoners, she is hanged in Prison, and the old King dies with Grief. Had Shakespear followed the Historian,[290] he would not have violated the Rules of poetical Justice; he represents Vice punished, and Virtue rewarded; in the Play one Fate overwhelms alike the Innocent and the Guilty, and the Facts in the History are wholly changed to produce Events, neither probable, necessary, nor just.[291]

$$\rightthreetimes$$

Samuel Johnson   *says much of play can be explained by putting it in context with the age*

From "Notes on the Plays" [1765]. *Johnson on Shakespeare,* ed. Walter Raleigh. London: Oxford University Press, 1952.

In Shakespeare's best plays, besides the vices that arise from the subject, there is generally some peculiar prevailing folly, principally ridiculed, that runs thro' the whole piece. Thus, in the *Tempest,* the lying disposition of travellers, and in *As you like it,* the fantastick humour of courtiers, is exposed and satirised with infinite pleasantry. In like manner, in his play of *Lear,* the dotages of judicial astrology are severely ridiculed. I fancy, was the date of its first performance well considered, it would be found that something or other happened at that time which gave a more than ordinary run to this deceit, as these words seem to intimate, *I am thinking, brother, of a prediction I read this other day, what should follow these eclipses.* However this be, an impious cheat, which had so little [155] foundation in nature or reason, so detestable an original, and such fatal consequences on the manners of the people, who were at that time strangely besotted with it, certainly deserved the severest lash of satire.[156]

So blasphemous a delusion . . . it became the honesty of our poet to expose. But it was a tender point, and required managing. For this impious juggle had in his time a kind of religious reverence paid to it.

It was therefore to be done obliquely; and the circumstances of the scene furnished him with as good an opportunity as he could wish. The persons in the drama are all pagans, so that as, in compliance to custom, his good characters were not to speak ill of judicial Astrology, they could on account of their religion give no reputation to it. But in order to expose it the more, he, with great judgment, makes these pagans Fatalists; as appears by these words of *Lear,*

> By all the operations of the orbs,
> From whom we do exist and cease to be.

For the doctrine of fate is the true foundation of judicial Astrology. Having thus discredited it by the very commendations given to it, he was in no danger of having his direct satire against it mistaken, by its being put (as he was obliged, both in paying regard to custom, and in following nature) into the mouth of the villain and atheist. . . .[157]

I know not well why Shakespeare gives the Steward, who is a mere factor of wickedness, so much fidelity. He now refuses the letter, and afterwards, when he is dying, thinks only how it may be safely delivered.[158]

The Tragedy of *Lear* is deservedly celebrated among the dramas of Shakespeare. There is perhaps no play which keeps the attention so strongly fixed; which so much agitates our passions and interests our curiosity. The artful involutions of distinct interests, the striking opposition of contrary characters, the sudden changes of fortune, and the quick succession of events, fill the mind with a perpetual tumult of indignation, pity, and [159] hope. There is no scene which does not contribute to the aggravation of the distress or conduct of the action, and scarce a line which does not conduce to the progress of the scene. So powerful is the current of the poet's imagination, that the mind, which once ventures within it, is hurried irresistibly along.

On the seeming improbability of Lear's conduct it may be observed, that he is represented according to histories at that time vulgarly received as true. And perhaps if we turn our thoughts upon the barbarity and ignorance of the age to which this story is referred, it will appear not so unlikely as while we estimate Lear's manners by our own. Such preference of one daughter to another, or resignation of dominion on such conditions, would be yet credible, if told of a petty prince of Guinea or Madagascar. Shakespeare, indeed, by the mention of his Earls and Dukes, has given us the idea of times more civilised, and of life regulated by softer manners; and the truth is, that though he so nicely discriminates, and so minutely describes the characters of men, he commonly neglects and confounds the characters of ages, by mingling customs ancient and modern, English and foreign.

My learned friend Mr. Warton, who has in the *Adventurer* very minutely criticised this play, remarks, that the instances of cruelty are too savage and shocking, and that the intervention of Edmund destroys the simplicity of the story. These objections may, I think, be answered, by repeating, that the cruelty of the daughters is an historical fact, to which the poet has added little, having only drawn it into a series by dialogue and action. But I am not able to apologise with equal plausibility for the extrusion of Gloucester's eyes, which seems an act too horrid to be endured in dramatick exhibition, and such as must always compel the mind to relieve its distress by incredulity. Yet [160] let it be remembered that our authour well knew what would please the audience for which he wrote.

The injury done by Edmund to the simplicity of the action is abundantly recompensed by the addition of variety, by the art with which he is made to co-operate with the chief design, and the opportunity which he gives the poet of combining perfidy with perfidy, and connecting the wicked son with the wicked daughters, to impress this important moral, that villany is never at a stop, that crimes lead to crimes, and at last terminate in ruin.

But though this moral be incidentally enforced, Shakespeare has suffered the virtue of Cordelia to perish in a just cause, contrary to the natural ideas of justice, to the hope of the reader, and, what is yet more strange, to the faith of chronicles. Yet this conduct is justified by the Spectator, who blames Tate for giving Cordelia success and happiness in his alteration, and declares, that, in his opinion, *the tragedy has lost half its beauty.* Dennis has remarked, whether justly or not, that, to secure the favourable reception of Cato, *the town was poisoned with much false and abominable criticism,* and that endeavours had been used to discredit and decry poetical justice. A play in which the wicked prosper, and the virtuous miscarry, may doubtless be good, because it is a just representation of the common events of human life: but since all reasonable beings naturally love justice, I cannot easily be persuaded, that the observation of justice makes a play worse; or, that if other excellencies are equal, the audience will not always rise better pleased from the final triumph of persecuted virtue.

In the present case the publick has decided. Cordelia, from the time of Tate, has always retired with victory and felicity. And, if my sensations could add any thing to the general suffrage, I might relate, that I was [161] many years ago so shocked by Cordelia's death, that I know not whether I ever endured to read again the last scenes of the play till I undertook to revise them as an editor.

There is another controversy among the criticks concerning this play. It is disputed whether the predominant image in Lear's disordered mind be the loss of his kingdom or the cruelty of his daughters. Mr. Murphy, a very judicious critick, has evinced by induction of particular passages, that the cruelty of his daughters is the primary source of his distress, and that the loss of royalty affects him only as

a secondary and subordinate evil; He observes with great justness, that
Lear would move our compassion but little, did we not rather consider
the injured father than the degraded king.[162]

> *this is where he gets*
> *our compassion, but*
> *the build-up of Lear is*
> *1st + foremost that of a*
> *King — his lost of royalty*
> *affects him more in my opinion*

Henry Mackenzie

From *The Mirror,* Number 100, April 22,
1780. *The Mirror: A Periodical Paper.* London: W. Strahan, 1793. Pp. 327-334.

In two of *Shakespeare's* tragedies are introduced, at the same time,
instances of counterfeit madness, and of real distraction. In both plays
the same distinction is observed, and the false discriminated from the
true by similar appearances. *Lear's* imagination constantly runs on the
ingratitude of his daughters, and the resignation of his crown; and
Ophelia, after she has wasted the first ebullience of her distraction [328]
in some wild and incoherent sentences, fixes on the death of her father
for the subject of her song:

> "They bore him bare-fac'd on the bier—
> "And will he not come again?
> "And will he not come again?" &c.

But *Edgar* puts on a semblance as opposite as may be to his real
situation and his ruling thoughts. He never ventures on any expression, bordering on the subjects of a father's cruelty, or a son's misfortune. *Hamlet* in the same manner, were he as firm in mind as *Edgar,*
would never hint any thing in his affected disorder, that might lead to
a suspicion of his having discovered the villany of his uncle; but his
feeling, too powerful for his prudence, often breaks through that
disguise which it seems to have been his original, and ought to have
continued his invariable purpose to maintain, till an opportunity
should present itself, of accomplishing the revenge which he medi-
tated.[329]

Shakespeare's genius attended him in all his extravagancies. In
the licence he took of departing from the regularity of the drama, or
in his ignorance of those critical rules which might have restrained
him within it, there is this advantage, that it gives him an opportunity
of delineating the passions and affections of the human mind, as they

exist in reality, with all the various colourings which they receive in the mixed scenes of life; not as they are accommodated by the hands of more artificial poets, to one great undivided impression, or an uninterrupted chain of congenial events. It seems therefore preposterous, to endeavour to *regularize* his plays at the expence of depriving [333] them of this peculiar excellence, especially as the alteration can only produce a very partial and limited improvement, and can never bring his pieces to the standard of criticism, or the form of the *Aristotelian* drama. Within the bounds of a pleasure-garden, we may be allowed to smooth our terraces and trim our hedge-rows; but it were equally absurd as impracticable, to apply the minute labours of the *roller* and the *pruning-knife,* to the nobler irregularity of trackless mountains and impenetrable forests.[334]

✕

Charles Lamb

we become Lear
the mind of Lear is what is great
Lear identifies with heaven
Lear has to die

From "On Shakespeare's Tragedies" [1808]. *The Complete Works In Prose And Verse Of Charles Lamb.* London: Chatto and Windus, 1875.

But the Lear of Shakespeare cannot be acted. *nor can the storm* The contemptible machinery by which they mimic the storm which he goes out in, is not more inadequate to represent the horrors of the real elements, than any actor can be to represent Lear: they might more easily propose to personate the Satan of Milton upon a stage, or one of Michael Angelo's terrible figures. The greatness of Lear is not in corporal dimension, but in intellectual: the explosions of his passion are terrible *a play of minds* as a volcano: they are storms turning up and disclosing to the bottom *the physical is not imp.* that sea his mind, with all its vast riches. It is his mind which is laid *stripping* bare. This case of flesh and blood seems too insignificant to be thought *theme* on; even as he himself neglects it. On the stage we see nothing but corporal infirmities and weakness, the impotence of rage; while we read it, we see not Lear, but we are Lear,—we are in his mind, we are *empathy* sustained by a grandeur which baffles the malice of daughters and storms; in the aberrations of his reason, we discover a mighty irregular power of reasoning, immethodized from the ordinary purposes of life, but exerting its powers, as the wind blows [261] where it listeth, at will upon the corruptions and abuses of mankind. What have looks, or tones, to do with that *Lear's* sublime identification of his age with that of the heavens themselves, when in his reproaches to them for conniving at the injustice of his children, he reminds them that "they themselves are old"? What gesture shall we appropriate to this? What has the voice or the eye to do with such things? But the play is beyond all art, as the tamperings with it show: it is too hard and stony; it must have love-scenes and a happy ending. It is not enough that Cordelia is a daughter, she must shine as a lover too. Tate has put his hook in the nostrils of this Leviathan, for Garrick and his followers, the show-men of the scene, to draw the mighty beast about more easily. A happy ending!—as if the living martyrdom that Lear had gone through, —the flaying of his feelings alive, did not make a fair dismissal from the stage of life the only decorous thing for him. If he is to live and be happy after, if he could sustain this world's burden after, why all this pudder and preparation,—why torment us with all this unnecessary sympathy? As if the childish pleasure of getting his gilt robes and sceptre again could tempt him to act over again his misused station,— as if at his years, and with his experience, anything was left but to die.[262]

William Hazlitt

Shakes. caught up in this himself
things which are sacred are torn apart
Lear personifies this

From *Characters of Shakespear's Plays* [1817]. *The Complete Works of William Hazlitt.* Volume IV. London and Toronto: J. M. Dent and Sons, Ltd., 1930.

We wish that we could pass this play over, and say nothing about it. All that we can say must fall far short of the subject; or even of what we ourselves conceive of it. To attempt to give a description of the play itself or of its effect upon the mind, is mere impertinence: yet we must say something.—It is then the best of all Shakespear's plays, for it is the one in which he was the most in earnest. He was here fairly caught in the web of his own imagination. The passion which he has taken as his subject is that which strikes its root deepest into the human heart; of which the bond is [257] the hardest to be unloosed; and the cancelling and tearing to pieces of which gives the greatest revulsion to the frame. This depth of nature, this force of passion, this tug and war of the elements of our being, this firm faith in filial piety, and the giddy anarchy and whirling tumult of the

*upside
down
world*

thoughts at finding this prop failing it, the contrast between the fixed, immoveable basis of natural affection, and the rapid, irregular starts of imagination, suddenly wrenched from all its accustomed holds and resting-places in the soul, this is what Shakespear has given, and what nobody else but he could give. . . .

Othello

The character of Lear itself is very finely conceived for the purpose. It is the only ground on which such a story could be built with the greatest truth and effect. It is his rash haste, his violent impetuosity, his blindness to every thing but the dictates of his passions or affections, that produces all his misfortunes, that aggravates his impatience of them, that enforces our pity for him. The part which Cordelia bears in the scene is extremely beautiful: the story is almost told in the first words she utters. We see at once the precipice on which the poor old king stands from his own extravagant and credulous importunity, the indiscreet simplicity of her love (which, to be sure, has a little of her father's obstinacy in it) and the hollowness of her sisters' pretensions. . . .[258]

. . . a happy ending has been contrived for this play, which is approved of by Dr. Johnson and condemned by Schlegel. A better authority than either, on any subject in which poetry and feeling are concerned, has given it in favour of Shakespear, in some remarks on the acting of Lear, with which we shall conclude this account: [quotes Charles Lamb's rejection of Tate's revision.] [270-271]

happy ending

Samuel Taylor Coleridge

From *Lectures and Notes on Shakspere* [1818], collected by T. Ashe. London: George Bell and Sons, 1890.

It was not without forethought, nor is it without its due significance, that the division of Lear's kingdom is in the first six lines of the play stated as a thing already determined in all its particulars, previously to the trial of professions. . . . The strange, yet by no means unnatural, mixture of selfishness, sensibility, and habit of feeling derived from, and fostered by, the particular rank and usages of the individual;—the intense desire of being intensely beloved,—selfish, and yet characteristic of the selfishness of a loving and kindly nature

alone;—the self-supportless leaning for all pleasure on another's breast;
—the cravings after sympathy with a prodigal disinterestedness, frustrated by its own ostentation, and the mode and nature of its claims;—
the anxiety, the distrust, the jealousy, which more or less accompany
all selfish affections, and are amongst the surest contradistinctions of
mere fondness from true love, and which originate Lear's eager wish
to enjoy his daughter's violent professions, whilst the inveterate habits
of sovereignty convert the wish into claim and positive right, and an
incompliance with it into crime and treason;—these facts, [329] these
passions, these moral verities, on which the whole tragedy is founded,
are all prepared for, and will to the retrospect be found implied, in
these first four or five lines of the play. They let us know that the
trial is but a trick; and that the grossness of the old king's rage is in
part the natural result of a silly trick suddenly and most unexpectedly
baffled and disappointed.

. . . observe the matchless judgment of our Shakspere. First, improbable as the conduct of Lear is in the first scene, yet it was an old story
rooted in the popular faith,—a thing taken for granted already, and
consequently without any of the effects of improbability. Secondly, it
is merely the canvas for the characters and passions,—a mere occasion
for . . . the incidents and emotions. Let the first scene of this play
have been lost, and let it only be understood that a fond father had
been duped by hypocritical professions of love and duty on the part
of two daughters to disinherit the third, previously, and deservedly,
more dear to him;—and all the rest of the tragedy would retain its
interest undiminished, and be perfectly intelligible. The accidental is
nowhere the groundwork of the passions, but that which is catholic,
which in all ages has been, and ever will be, close and native to the
heart of man,—parental anguish from filial ingratitude, the genuine-
ness of worth, though coffined in bluntness, and the execrable vileness
of a smooth iniquity.[330]

. . . from Lear, the *persona patiens* of his drama, Shakspere passes
without delay to the second in importance, the chief agent and prime
mover, and introduces Edmund to our acquaintance, preparing us
with the same felicity of judgment, and in the same easy and natural
way, for his character in the seemingly casual communication of its
origin and occasion. From the first drawing up of the curtain Edmund
has stood before us in the united strength and beauty of earliest manhood. Our eyes have been questioning him. Gifted as he is with high
advantages of person, and further endowed by nature with a powerful
intellect and a strong energetic will, even without any concurrence of
circumstances and accident, pride will necessarily be the sin that most
easily besets him. But Edmund is also the known and acknowledged
son of the princely Gloster: he, therefore, has both the germ of pride,

and the conditions best fitted to evolve and ripen it into a predominant feeling. Yet hitherto no reason appears why it should be other than the not unusual pride of person, talent, and birth,—a pride auxiliary, if not akin, to many virtues, and the natural ally of honourable impulses. But alas! in his own presence his own father takes shame to himself for the frank avowal that he is his father,—he has "blushed so often to acknowledge him that he is now brazed to it!" Edmund hears the circumstances of his birth spoken of with a most degrading and licentious levity,—his mother described as a wanton by her own paramour, and the remembrance of the animal sting, the low criminal gratifications connected with her wantonness and prostituted [332] beauty, assigned as the reason, why "the whoreson must be acknowledged!" This, and the consciousness of its notoriety; the gnawing conviction that every show of respect is an effort of courtesy, which recalls, while it represses, a contrary feeling;—this is the ever trickling flow of wormwood and gall into the wounds of pride,—the corrosive *virus* which inoculates pride with a venom not its own, with envy, hatred, and a lust for that power which in its blaze of radiance would hide the dark spots on his disc,—with pangs of shame personally undeserved and therefore felt as wrongs, and with a blind ferment of vindictive working towards the occasions and causes, especially towards a brother, whose stainless birth and lawful honours were the constant remembrancers of his own debasement, and were ever in the way to prevent all chance of its being unknown, or overlooked and forgotten. Add to this, that with excellent judgment, and provident for the claims of the moral sense,—for that which, relatively to the drama, is called poetic justice, and as the fittest means for reconciling the feelings of the spectators to the horrors of Gloster's after sufferings,—at least, of rendering them somewhat less unendurable;—(for I will not disguise my conviction, that in this one point the tragic in this play has been urged beyond the outermost mark and *ne plus ultra* of the dramatic)— Shakspere has precluded all excuse and palliation of the guilt incurred by both the parents of the base-born Edmund, by Gloster's confession that he was at the time a married man, and already blest with a lawful heir of his fortunes.[333]

[margin note: Gloucester the blinding most tragic part — assuages wrongs to Edm. somewhat]

. . . in this tragedy the story or fable constrained Shakspere to introduce wickedness in an outrageous form in the persons of Regan and Goneril. He had read nature too heedfully not to know, that courage, intellect, and strength of character, are the most impressive forms of power, and that to power in itself, without reference to any moral end, an inevitable admiration and complacency appertains, whether it be displayed in the conquests of a Buonaparte or Tamerlane, or in the foam and the thunder of a cataract. But in the exhibition of such a character it was of the highest importance to prevent the guilt from passing into utter monstrosity,—which again depends on the presence or absence of causes and temptations sufficient to account for the wickedness, without the necessity of recurring to a thorough fiendishness of nature for its origination. For such are the appointed relations of intellectual power to truth, and of truth to goodness, that it becomes both morally and poetically unsafe to present what is admirable,—what our nature compels us to admire—in the mind, and what is most detestable in the heart, as coexisting in the same individual without any apparent connection,[334] or any modification of the one by the other. . . . in the present tragedy, in which [Shakespeare] was compelled to present a Goneril and a Regan, it was most carefully to be avoided;—and therefore the only one conceivable addition to the inauspicious influences on the preformation of Edmund's character is given, in the information that all the kindly counteractions to the mischievous feelings of shame, which might have been derived from codomestication with Edgar and their common father, had been cut off by his absence from home, and foreign education from boyhood to the present time, and a prospect of its continuance, as if to preclude all risk of his interference with the father's views for the elder and legitimate son:—

He hath been out nine years, and away he shall again.

Act i. sc. 1. . . .
   There is something of disgust at the ruthless hypocrisy of her sisters, and some little faulty admixture of pride and sullenness in Cordelia's "Nothing;" and her tone is well contrived, indeed, to lessen the glaring absurdity of Lear's conduct, but answers the yet more important purpose of forcing away the attention from the nursery-tale, the moment it has served its end, that of supplying the canvas for the picture. This is also materially furthered by Kent's opposition, which displays Lear's moral incapability [335] of resigning the sovereign power in the very act of disposing of it. Kent is, perhaps, the nearest to perfect goodness in all Shakspere's characters, and yet the most individualized. There is an extraordinary charm in his bluntness, which is that only of a nobleman arising from a contempt of overstrained courtesy; and combined with easy placability where goodness of heart is apparent. His passionate affection for, and fidelity to, Lear act on our feelings in Lear's own favour: virtue itself seems to be in company with him.[336]

Kent

   [Act I] sc. 3. The Steward should be placed in exact antithesis to Kent, as the only character of utter irredeemable baseness in Shakspere. Even in this the judgment and invention of the poet are very observable;—for what else could the willing tool of a Goneril be? . . .
   [Act I] sc. 4. In Lear old age is itself a character,—its natural imperfections being increased by life-long habits of receiving a prompt

obedience. Any addition of individuality would have been unnecessary and painful; for the relations of others to him, of wondrous fidelity and of frightful ingratitude, alone sufficiently distinguish him. Thus Lear becomes the open and ample play-room of nature's passions.

> KNIGHT.   Since my young lady's going into France,
> Sir; the fool hath much pin'd away.

The Fool is no comic buffoon to make the groundlings laugh,— no forced condescension of Shakspere's genius to the taste of his audience. Accordingly the poet prepares for his introduction, which he never does with any of his common clowns and fools, by bringing him into living connection with the pathos of the play.[337]

The monster Goneril prepares what is necessary, while the character of Albany renders a still more maddening grievance possible, namely, Regan and Cornwall in perfect sympathy of monstrosity. Not a sentiment, not an image, which can give pleasure on its own account, is admitted; whenever these creatures are introduced, and they are brought forward as little as possible, pure horror reigns throughout. In this scene and in all the early speeches of Lear, the one general sentiment of filial ingratitude prevails as the main spring of the feelings;—in this early stage the outward object causing the pressure on the mind, which is not yet sufficiently familiarized with the anguish for the imagination to work upon it.

> GON.   Do you mark that, my lord?
> ALB.   I cannot be so partial, Goneril,
> To the great love I bear you.
> GON.   Pray you, content, . . .

Observe the baffled endeavour of Goneril to act on the fears of Albany, and yet his passiveness, his *inertia;* he is not convinced, and yet he is afraid of looking into the thing. Such characters always yield to those who will take the trouble of governing them or for them. Perhaps, the influence of a princess, whose choice of him had royalized his state, may be some little excuse for Albany's weakness.[338]

Edgar's assumed madness serves the great purpose of taking off part of the shock which would otherwise be caused by the true madness of Lear, and further displays the profound difference between the two. In every attempt at representing madness throughout the whole range of dramatic literature, with the single exception [339] of Lear, it is mere lightheadedness, as especially in Otway. In Edgar's ravings Shakspere all the while lets you see a fixed purpose, a practical end in view;—in Lear's, there is only the brooding of the one anguish, an eddy without progression.

All Lear's faults increase our pity for him. We refuse to know them otherwise than as means of his sufferings, and aggravations of his daughter's ingratitude.[340]

Act iii. sc. 4. O, what a world's convention of agonies is here! All external nature in a storm, all moral nature convulsed,—the real madness of Lear, the feigned madness of Edgar, the babbling of the Fool, the desperate fidelity of Kent—surely such a scene was never conceived before or since! Take it but as a picture for the eye only, it is more terrific than any which a Michel Angelo, inspired by a Dante, could have conceived, and which none but a Michel Angelo could have executed. Or let it have been uttered to the blind, the howlings of nature would seem converted into the voice of conscious humanity. This scene ends with the first symptoms of positive derangement; and the intervention of the fifth scene is particularly judicious,—the interruption allowing an interval for Lear to appear in full madness in the sixth scene.[341]

How beautifully the affecting return of Lear to reason, and the mild pathos of these speeches prepare the mind for the last sad, yet sweet, consolation of the aged sufferer's death! [342]

$$\rightarrow\!\!\!\times\!\!\!\leftarrow$$

I. Ray

From "Shakespeare's Delineations of Insanity." *American Journal of Insanity*, III (1847), 289-332.

In the tragedy of King Lear, Shakespeare has represented the principal character as driven to madness by the unexpected ingratitude of his daughters; or more scientifically speaking, he has represented a strong predisposition to the disease as being rapidly developed under the application of an adequate exciting cause. It is no part of his object to excite curiosity by a liberal display of wildness and fury, nor awaken our pity by the spectacle of a mind in ruins, and unconscious of its wretchedness. He aimed at [291] dramatic effect by opening the fountains of sympathy for a being of noble nature and generous impulses, cruelly despoiled of the highest endowment of man, but not so far as to lose all trace of his original qualities, or cease for a moment to command our deepest respect. In Lear, we have an individual of a hot and hasty temper, though endowed with strong and generous passions, of a credulous and confiding disposition, governed by impulses rather than deliberate judgment, rendered impatient of restraint or contradiction by the habit of command, with a nervous temperament strongly susceptible of the vexations of life, and moreover, with all these moral infirmities aggravated by old age. With these simple elements of character is mingled and assimilated more or less of mental derangement, with equal regard to pathological propriety and dramatic effect. And so nicely adjusted are the various elements of sanity and insanity, and so admirably do they support and illustrate one another, that we are not surprised in the progress of the action, by violent contrasts; and we feel at last as if it were the most natural thing in the world that Lear should go mad, and precisely in the way represented by the poet. Mad as he becomes, the prominent attributes of his character are always to be seen. Through the whole play, he is the same generous, confiding, noble hearted Lear. In short, assuming Lear to be an historical portrait instead of a poetical creation, we should say there existed in his case a strong predisposition to insanity, and that if it had not been developed by the approach of old age, or the conduct of his daughters, it would have been by something else. His inconsiderate rashness in distributing his kingdom among his children, his disinheriting the youngest for the fearless expression of her feelings, and his banishment of Kent for endeavoring to recall him to a sense of his folly,—all indicate an ill-balanced mind, if not the actual invasion of disease. This view of the case is confirmed by the conversation between the sisters, immediately after the division of the kingdom. . . .[292]

The development of the early stage of Lear's insanity, or its *incubation* as it is technically called, is managed with masterly skill, the more surprising as it is that stage of the disease which attracts the least attention. And the reason is that the derangement is evinced not so much by delusions or gross improprieties of conduct, as by a mere exaggeration of natural peculiarities, by inconsistencies of behavior, by certain acts for which very plausible reasons are assigned though they would never have been performed in a perfectly sound state of mind, by gusts of passion at every trifling provocation, or by doing very proper things at unseasonable [293] times and occasions. With his own free will and accord he gives away his kingdom, but finds it difficult to sink the monarch in the private citizen. . . .

The conduct of the daughters faithfully exhibits the strong tendencies of human nature. No doubt their patience was severely tried,—such a trial as only the mildest temper [294] joined with the firmest principle could enable them to stand successfully. Wanting these, however, his irregularities are met with reproaches and restrictions, instead of kind and conciliating measures; an explosion follows, and in mutual hate and anger they separate. To their heartless natures such conduct may not have appeared like unmitigated ingratitude towards a father who had loved and cherished them as the very idols of his heart, but to be founded on provocation that seemed to justify their behavior. Such is the ingratitude of the world, ever coupled with some shallow pretence of wrong or indignity sustained, and often presenting the fair, outside show of a worthier feeling. In the daughters' treatment of their father, Shakespeare strips off the thin disguises of conventional morality, and lays bare that heartless selfishness which is ever ready to sacrifice to momentary ease and gratification, the tenderest sympathies of our nature. It is fearful to think how often the case of Lear and his daughters is paralleled in actual life, and it is this very commonness of the fact that prevents us from regarding it as a curious monstrosity fitted to excite but a momentary horror, and imparts a deep, moral interest to the representation of the poet.[295]

While pondering upon past scenes, he is conscious that his mind has sustained a fearful shock; and as is often the case in such circumstances, he has a vague presentiment of the sad, fatal result.

But when the conviction is forced upon him that Regan even goes beyond her sister in ingratitude, he utters a wail of heartfelt wretchedness and lofty indignation, ending with another foreboding of the impending calamity. "O, fool, I shall go mad." [296]

There is now obviously a degree of incoherence and absurdity in the thoughts that race through his mind, though they are never destitute of that grandeur and boldness of expression indicative of his lofty and noble nature. The idea of the thunder cracking nature's moulds and destroying the germs of the race, contained in his invocation to the elements, is a little too fanciful for even a figure of poetry. In a similar strain he charges the elements with conspiring with his daughters against his old white head, and soon after imagines that the Gods have raised the storm for the purpose of finding out their enemies. This is crazy enough, no doubt, but his apostrophe to sinners of various kinds, that immediately follows, is both correctly and beautifully expressed. He seems to be fully aware that his thoughts are deviating from the right track, and exclaims that his "wits begin to turn." The predominant idea follows him into the next scene, and ever and anon intrudes upon his reflections, though he always recoils from it with a kind of horror, as if conscious it had the power to deprive him of his reason. "O, that way madness lies." Unable as the insane are to perceive their own insanity, yet this apprehension of its approach so frequently repeated by Lear usually occurs during its incubation. While still able to control his mental manifestations, the patient is tortured with anticipations of insanity, but when he actually becomes so insane, that the most careless observer perceives the fact, then he entertains the most complacent opinion of his intellectual vigor and soundness. And yet this is one of the nicer traits of insanity which the ordinary observer would hardly be supposed to notice. But Shakespeare was no ordinary observer, and this, I imagine, explains the cause of his preeminence in certain parts of his art.

The appearance of Edgar who is feigning madness in order to avoid his enemies again excites Lear's predominant [297] idea, and fixes it permanently in his mind. The former's ragged, wretched, degraded condition he can attribute to nothing but filial ingratitude, and he pours out curses on Edgar's unnatural daughters. He is no longer able to correct the errors of his own judgment; reason exercises but a feeble control over his conclusions, and scarcely a gleam of light struggles through the darkness that envelopes his soul. The predominant idea, however, has not yet relinquished its hold, and still gives direction to his thoughts. The very images of his daughters appear before him in visible forms, glowering upon him with looks of scorn and hate. . . .

The scene on the heath between Lear, Edgar, and the fool, has not its like, we may safely say, in the whole range of English dramatic literature. No less a genius than Shakespeare's would have ventured to bring together, face to face, three such difficult characters,—one actually mad, one falsely pretending to be so, and the third a fool; and yet in the successful management of such discordant and intractable materials, he has given a fresh instance of his wonderful skill. Nothing could have seemed more likely to disappoint and displease, than to bring the noble hearted Lear, staggering under the shock of his daughters' ingratitude, with blasted heart and bewildered reason, into such strange companionship; and yet who can finish this scene, without feeling that he has read a new chapter in the history of mental disease, of most solemn and startling import? The sight of another in rags and wretchedness, reveals to Lear [298] a deeper depth of agony in his own soul. He sees in the stranger only another victim of filial ingratitude—the counterpart of his own case—and Edgar's weak and blighted condition forewarns him of his own approaching fate. Its first effect, as we have already observed, is to produce a shower of curses on Edgar's unnatural daughters, and the next to draw him towards his fellow sufferer by that kind of sympathy which, irrespective of social condition, is awakened by mutual affliction. In this play of wild and discordant fancies the fool mingles his humors, which fall on the ear like sounds of jollity and mirth ascending from a house of mourning. The successful management of such deep masses of light and shade, whether in poetry or painting, requires the master-hand of a Shakespeare, or a Rembrandt.

Thus far the progress of Lear's insanity is represented with the closest fidelity to nature. It is not more different from the disease as daily observed, than Lear's moral and intellectual constitution, when in health, was different from ordinary men's. At every interview reason has seemed to have lost somewhat of its control; the mental excitement has been steadily increasing, until now having reached its height, he is singing, dancing and capering through the fields, fantastically decorated with weeds and flowers, looking, acting and talking like a madman. His perceptive organs are deceived by hallucinations, and his discourse, though tinctured with his natural shrewdness and vigor of thought, is full of incoherence and incongruity. In short he is now what is called *raving*. In the representation of this condition, we have another instance of Shakespeare's unrivalled powers of observation. To ordinary apprehension, the raving of a maniac is but an arbitrary jumble of words and phrases between which no connecting threads can be discerned. But in fact, discordant and heterogeneous as they may appear, they are nevertheless subjected to a certain law of association, difficult as it may be frequently to discover it. . . .[299]

In the first scene in which Lear makes his appearance after becoming stark mad, his mind is solely occupied with images formed under the influence of the intense excitement of the internal perceptive organs. He, at first, fancies himself in a battle, and then as engaged in the sports of archery and falconry. Something reminds him of Goneril, and then succeed to one another by a natural association the ideas of a white beard, of the flattery of his courtiers, and of the detection of their deceptions. When Gloster hears his voice and asks if it be not the King's, Lear replies, "Aye, every inch a king." Visions of his royal state then pass before his eyes, and he is reminded of the criminals he pardoned, and the crimes they committed, and thence by a natural transition, he is led to some caustic reflections on the frailties of woman. Another remark of Gloster turns his mind to the examples of self-righteousness and self-deception, servility and time-serving with which the world abounds, and in a strain of bold, indignant sarcasm, he lashes the [302] vices to which poor human nature is especially prone. All this is exceedingly natural. It is not uncommon to meet with madmen of the most wild and turbulent description, mixing up their ravings with the shrewdest remarks upon men and things, and the keenest and coolest invective against those who have incurred their displeasure. The poet, perhaps, has used the utmost license of his art in the present instance; but if few madmen have exhibited so much matter mingled with their impertinency, as Lear, it may be replied in justification, that few men are endowed like Lear with such a union of strong passions and natural shrewdness of understanding.

Here endeth the madness of Lear. By his youngest daughter he is placed in the charge of a physician whose medicines throw him into a deep sleep from which and his madness together, he awakes as from a dream. The manner of his recovery displays the poet's consummate skill that could delineate the most touching and beautiful traits without violating the strictest regard to facts. Lear, at first knows not where he is, nor where he has been; he scarcely recognises his own friends, and almost doubts his own identity. . . .

A faint idea of recent events now occurs to him, and he says to Cordelia,

> Your sisters
> Have, as I do remember, done me wrong.

A more faithful picture of the mind at the moment when it is emerging from the darkness of disease into the clear atmosphere of health restored, was never executed than this [303] of Lear's recovery. Generally, recovery from acute mania is gradual, one delusion after another giving way, until after a series of struggles which may occupy weeks or months between the convictions of reason, and the suggestions of disease, the patient comes out a sound, rational man. In a small proportion of cases, however, this change takes place very rapidly; within the space of a few hours or a day, he recognises his true condition, abandons his delusions, and contemplates all his relations in an entirely different light.

The management of Edgar's simulation strikingly evinces the accuracy and extent of Shakespeare's knowledge of mental pathology. In placing the real and the simulated affection side by side, he has shown a confidence in his own skill which the result has perfectly justified. In no other way could the fidelity of his delineations have been subjected to a severer ordeal. We are left in no doubt as to his views of what is and what is not genuine insanity; and by holding before us an elaborate picture of each, he enables us to compare them together, and to judge of his success for ourselves. In these pictures he has availed himself of no equivocal traits; the touches of his pencil are of that strong and decided character that admits but a single meaning. Not more true to nature is the representation of Lear writhing under the stroke of real insanity, than is that of Edgar playing upon the popular curiosity with such shams and artifices as would most effectually answer the simulator's purpose. . . .[304]

We cannot dismiss this play without a passing notice of the Fool, in whose character Shakespeare has shown that his observation of mental impairment was not confined to one or a few of its forms. . . . They who find fault with the poet for infusing too much wisdom into the folly of his fools, may well take a lesson from him in certain [305] branches of psychological study. In the present instance, he knew . . . that a very obvious degree of intellectual deficiency is frequently accompanied by considerable shrewdness of observation and practical sagacity. . . .[306]

H. N. Hudson

From *Lectures on Shakspeare.* Volume II. New
York: Baker and Scribner, 1848.

As, in actual life, men in the exercise of present virtues often incur
the evils consequent upon their former vices; so, in Lear, the perverse
self-willed habit of preferring lip-service and glib-tongued flattery to
silent obedience, as a test of love, is visited upon him in the hypocrisy
and ingratitude of his daughters; and, in Gloster, the vices of his youth
and his criminal levity in talking about them, are visited upon him
in the light-hearted, gamesome treachery and subtlety of his natural
son. Yet both the sufferers are justly represented as men "more sinned
against than sinning." For here again, as in actual life, the vices of
some are the occasion of still greater vices in others; while, as if to cut
off all excuse from the more vicious, the same occasion is seen minister-
ing to the noblest and loveliest virtue; the goodness of Cordelia and
Edgar being only tried and purified by the self-same causes that operate
to deprave Goneril, Regan and Edmund. . . .[226]

There is no accounting for the conduct of Goneril and Regan but
by supposing a thorough fiendishness of nature, a very instinct and
impulse of malignity. With but little of soul, and with that little
concentrated in the head, they have no heart to guide and inspire their
understanding, and but just enough of understanding to seize occasions and frame excuses for their heartlessness. . . . They seem to
have something within that turns the very milk of humanity into
venom, which all the wounds they inflict are but occasions for casting.
No atmosphere of delight can abide their presence; an unmitigated
horror uniformly attends their coming. Regan's reply to her father's
"I gave you all," "and in good time you gave it," displays a wantonness
and intrepidity of malice which fairly chills and stiffens the blood in
our veins.

To alleviate the improbability of such treatment of their father,
Goneril and Regan are brought forward in other relations. But degrees of kin bring no difference of cruelty; perhaps, indeed, such a
causeless malice does not admit of degrees, but seizes indifferently on
all opportunities to vent itself. Selfishness reigns in them to such an
extent as to make all objects seem equidistant from self; and Edmund
is the only person in the play who is wicked enough and energetic
enough in his wickedness, to interest their feelings. It is difficult to

think of them otherwise than merely as instruments of [228] the plot; not so much ungrateful persons as personifications of ingratitude. . . .

The improbability of their conduct towards the king was perhaps the greatest difficulty involved in the subject, and gave occasion for the subordinate plot and persons of the drama. By thus exhibiting them in other connections the poet was enabled to soften down that improbability, so as to keep it from sticking out into our faces and breaking the illusion. Some critics, indeed, have censured this plot as an impertinence and embarrassment to the main one: forgetting, apparently, that to deepen and prolong any feeling some diversion is necessary; and that a certain harmony and proportion of objects and emotions is required to give any one of them an appropriate effect. Edmund's independent concurrence with Goneril and Regan in wickedness looks as if Satan were let loose upon the world for a season, and had set the elements of evil astir in many hearts at the same time. "Unnaturalness between the child [229] and the parent, dissolutions of ancient amities, divisions in state, banishment of friends, and nuptial breaches," seem, sure enough, the order of the day. Thus our feelings are balanced and braced by a co-operation of many objects in one effect. Besides, the agreement of the sister-fiends in filial ingratitude might of itself seem to imply some sisterly attachment between them. To complete, therefore, their frightful deformity of character, they must show, that the same principle which unites them against their father, will upon the turning of occasion divide them against each other. Accordingly, that their sympathy springs only from a concurrence of interest, appears in that a conflict of interests breeds in them the deadliest antipathy. As they are rendered mutually aidant by a common hate, so they are rendered mutually hostile by a common love; as if on purpose to show, that there is nothing in them but selfishness, nor even a place to put any thing else; and that "natures which contemn their origin" are utterly incapable of good in any form or towards any object whatever.

In Edmund they find a character worth the fighting for; and that they should now be as restless and reckless to thwart as they previously were to aid one another, is but the natural carrying [230] out of their character. In no other way, perhaps, could their transition from apparent sympathy to real antipathy be effected without abating their claims to execration. For, even to have hated each other from love of any body but a villain and because of his villany, had seemed a degree of virtue. Thus we are let to see, that whether they are drawn together or drawn asunder, still it is from an appetite for sin; that if they unite, it is to do evil, and if they divide, it is to do the same. It is a significant fact, that their passion for Edmund grows out of his treachery to his father; as though they saw in his proceedings an apology for their own; from his similarity of conduct inferred a congeniality of mind; and selfishly caught at his audacious criminality as an earnest of protection to themselves. It is worthy of remark, also, that they are both of the self-same mind and metal; indeed they are so much alike in character, that we can scarce distinguish them as individuals; seem almost too much like repetitions of each other to be realities. All of which but makes them the fitter for the work they are to do; for their sameness of treatment renders it the more galling and insupportable, by causing it to seem the result of a set purpose, a conspiracy coolly formed and unrelentingly pursued. . . .[231] . . . while [Edmund's] personal advantages are such as naturally generate pride, his disgraces of fortune are equally adapted to generate guilt from pride. . . .[232] the kindly influences of human relationship and household ties,—influences so creative as corroborative of virtuous tendencies,—are turned into their contraries. He feels himself the victim of a disgrace for which he is not to blame; which he can never hope to outgrow; which no degree of personal worth can ever efface; and from which he sees no escape but in the pomp and circumstance of worldly power. His consciousness of fine abilities makes him ambitious of a corresponding sphere; his sense of undeserved reproach inspires him with a feeling of injustice; and his ambition easily twists the seeming injustice into a license for seeking by any means the sphere he wants.[233]

Nevertheless he does not, like Goneril and Regan, perpetrate or meditate any gratuitous crimes. There is no spontaneous, purposeless wickedness in him; he nowhere sins merely for the sake of sinning, but for certain definite external objects and rewards. In a word, he is not one of those who "will not serve the Lord if the devil bid them;" he does not prefer evil on its own account, even though it make against his interest. Nay, he does not so much commit crimes, as devise accidents and then commit his cause to them; not so much makes war upon morality, as bows and smiles and shifts her out of the way, that his wit may have free course. He [237] deceives others without scruple indeed, but then he does not consider them bound to trust him; and tries to avail himself of their credulity or criminality without becoming responsible for it. Flirting and coquetting with fortune, and seeking rather to elude than to invade the laws of morality, he but practises a sort of careless, lighthearted, frolicsome villany, as if it were to give room for his wit that the world was made so wide. He is indeed a pretty bold experimenter; but that is because he has nothing to lose if he fail, and much to gain if he succeed. Nor does he attempt to disguise from himself, or gloss over, or anywise palliate his designs, but boldly confronts and stares them in the face, as though assured on sufficient external grounds and reasons whereby to justify or excuse them. Nor is he inaccessible to the relentings and compunctions of nature, only his ambitious desires have for the present silenced them; hence, when the certainty of death has killed off his ambition, his humanity unexpectedly gushes forth, and he "means to do some good despite of his own nature."

Edmund's strength and acuteness of intellect, unsubjected as they are to the moral and religious sentiments, of course exempt him from the superstitions that prevail about him. . . .[238]

The first words in the play inform us, that the division of the kingdom has been resolved upon, the terms of the division arranged, and the several portions allotted, before the beginning of the action. . . .[242] The trial of professions, therefore, is obviously but a trick of the king's, to surprise his children into expressions which filial modesty and reverence would else forbid. . . .[243]

. . . there is, withal, an appearance of obstinacy and sullenness in Cordelia's answer, as if, because her sisters had said much and meant nothing, she would therefore mean much and say nothing, and so resent the old man's credulity to their lies by refusing to tell him the truth. But the fact is, Cordelia cannot, if she wills, talk much about what she is, and what she intends. For there is a virgin delicacy and modesty in all deep and true affection, which makes it shrink from exposure and shun observation. To speak itself out, looks too much like betraying the heart's confidence. . . .[245]

"Of Cordelia's heavenly beauty of soul," says Schlegel, "I do not dare to speak." This is worth all the other criticisms I have seen upon her, put together. Would my plan permitted me to leave her where he has left her; for the best I can say of her will seem, I fear, but desecration of an holy thing. Such a being can be understood only by the feelings of love and respect; and I need not say how incompatible such feelings are with a critical spirit. . . .

That Cordelia, though so seldom seen or heard, is felt throughout the play, has been often remarked, and can hardly have failed to impress every observing reader. I had read the play occasionally for several years before [256] I could fully realize but she was among the principal speakers; and even now, upon taking up the play, I can scarce persuade myself but that the two hours of reading is to be spent chiefly with her; and I always close the book with a feeling of disappointment at having seen and heard her so little; and sometimes even turn back to see if I have not overlooked some passages where she is introduced.[257]

If the best happiness of life consist in forgetting of self and living for others, Kent and Edgar are those of Shakspeare's men whom one should most wish to resemble. Strikingly similar in virtues and in situation, these two persons are, however, widely different in character. Brothers in magnanimity and in misfortune; equally invincible in fidelity, the one to his king, the other to his father; both driven to disguise themselves, and in their disguise both serving where they stand condemned;—Kent, too generous to control himself, is always quick, fiery and impetuous; Edgar, controlling himself even because of his generosity, is always calm, collected and deliberate. . . .[268]

Kent is continually getting himself into trouble in trying to get others out. Blunt, downright, impassioned alike in his sympathies and his antipathies, he pushes right on as regardless of times and occasions as of himself; is as intemperate and reckless in virtue as others are in crime: indefatigable in loyalty and affection, he is present whenever there is suffering to be relieved, or treachery to be defeated. . . . In his impulsiveness, however, Kent can hardly help doing too much: rash, reckless, I might almost say, fanatical in honesty, he often mars what he would mend, hinders where he would help, injures whom [269] he would serve: his noble but indiscreet and ill-timed endeavours to arrest, only go to aggravate Lear's judgment on Cordelia, while at the same time they provoke a similar judgment on himself; and, afterwards, his generous rashness and "saucy roughness" in behalf of the king, while it draws on himself the malice of the sister fiends, only quickens and sharpens their persecution of Lear. Such is Kent's virtue; beautiful indeed, but unavailing. . . .[270]

The scene between Edgar and the eyeless Gloster, where the latter is made to believe himself ascending and leaping from the chalky cliff of Dover, is a remarkable instance of the poet's power to overcome the inherent incredibility of a thing by his opulence of description. Great as is the miracle of Gloster's belief, it is authenticated to our feelings by the array of vivid, truthful imagery that induces it. Thus does Shakspeare, as occasion requires, enhance the beauty of his representation, so as to atone for its want of verisimilitude. When a thing cannot be made beautiful by its truth, he makes it too beautiful not to seem true.

It is well known, that a certain "word-joiner" has favoured the world with a Tatification of this play. In like manner certain others have versified the Psalms for us; and then, as in the case of Shakspeare, a portion of Christendom had a good taste to prefer their versification to the Psalms as God and David wrote them. The chief merit of the Tatified Lear was, that the King and Cordelia came off triumphant; so that the play wound up with a happy catastrophe: or rather, in this arrangement the catastrophe is thrown back into the third or fourth act; so that, instead of a drama beginning at one end and ending at the other, we have a nameless thing beginning at both ends and ending in the middle. And yet Dr. Johnson gave to this miserable work the suffrage of his great name. The gift may drag down the giver; it can never, never raise up the [277] receiver! Tate, however, succeeded in dwarfing and dementing the play, so that the most dull and prosaic mind could relish it; for which cause it has kept and keeps possession of the stage. Why, the catastrophe, as it stands, is the sublimest one in the whole Shakspearian drama. There is an awful beauty in Lear's sighing and gazing his life away over the lifeless form of Cordelia, such as can nowhere else be found; pathos enough to melt the stubbornest heart, and wring tears of confession from insensibility itself. It is the crowning glory of the whole play, which sets the seal to all the glories that have gone before, and without which they are aimless and meaningless. The cutting out of the precious Fool, and the turning of Cordelia into a sort of lovesick intriguante, feigning indifference in order to cheat and enrage her father, and make him abandon her to a forbidden match with Edgar, completes this shameless, this execrable piece of dementation. Tate improve Lear? Set a tailor at work rather to improve Niagara! Withered be the hand, palzied be the arm, that ever dares to touch one of Shakspeare's plays! [278]

$$\asymp$$

A. O. Kellogg

From *Shakspeare's Delineations of Insanity, Imbecility and Suicide*. New York: Hurd and Houghton, 1866.

With great psychological exactness Shakspeare has from the first endowed Lear with those mental peculiarities and eccentricities which experienced medical psychologists recognize at once as the forerunners of confirmed mental disease, but which are usually overlooked by ordinary observers, or not regarded as pathological phenomena, but merely the ebullitions of a temper and disposition naturally fiery and irritable perhaps, and now rendered unbearable through the infirmities incident to age.

This seems to have been the view of Lear entertained by his daughters, as also by those modern critics who, far more ignorant of psychology than the poet who wrote two hundred years before them, have regarded the insanity of Lear as caused solely by the ingratitude and unkindness of his daughters. . . .[17]

All through Scene IV., Act I., we trace a gradual increase of the mental excitement of Lear, rendered worse by the injudicious treatment he receives; and towards the conclusion, after the interview with Goneril, where he is reproached by her for the riotous conduct of his train, and requested to diminish it, which request is accompanied by a threat in case of non-compliance, he becomes quite frantic with rage.[18]

The first intimation Lear himself gives of his own apprehensions of insanity we have at the conclusion of Scene V.

It is one of the most common things in the world to find a man decidedly insane, and yet conscious of his infirmity. A premonition of the impending malady, a certain consciousness that it is approaching,[19] frequently seizes the doomed subject, as is apparent . . . in the case of Lear.

Thus far the whole character is psychologically consistent, and the wonderful skill and sagacity manifested by the great dramatist in seizing upon these premonitory signs, which are usually overlooked by all, even the patient's most intimate friends, and the members of his family, and weaving them into the character of his hero as a necessary element, without which it would be incomplete, like those of inferior artists, is a matter of wonder to all modern psychologists.[20]

If a modern psychological writer, with all the knowledge of our own times at his command, was laboring to convey to the minds of his readers the manner in which insanity is induced in those predisposed by nature to the disease, in order that such persons and their friends might guard against the malady, he could not do better than point out the conduct of Goneril and Regan towards Lear, as set forth in Act II., Scene IV., of the play. All the feelings of his generous nature are outraged and trampled upon. The waywardness manifested as the result of impending disease, meets with none of that forbearance we are accustomed to [21] expect from the native gentleness of woman and the affection of daughters, but selfishness and ingratitude reign supreme in their hearts. Would that this were only an isolated or imaginary case! . . .

. . . on the heath . . .[22] the one absorbing thought, the ingratitude of his daughters, shuts out, as far as he is personally concerned, all idea of physical suffering. It is a well-known fact, that, when the mind is swayed by intense emotions, the sensibility even to intense bodily pain is often completely suspended. The physical endurance manifested by the insane under certain circumstances is truly astonishing,—even delicate females have been known to undergo with impunity what might be supposed sufficient to destroy the most vigorous physical constitution. This fact is most beautifully and concisely set forth by Lear in allusion to the suffering of his companions in the storm upon the heath, when they urge him to take shelter in the hovel. . . .

When the mind's free,
The body's delicate; the tempest in my *mind*
Doth from my senses take all feeling else,
Save what beats there.[23]

. . . perhaps the most ingeniously constructed scene in the whole play is that in which the poet brings together Lear, now an undoubted madman, Edgar, who assumes madness for purposes of disguise and deception, and the Fool. What results are to be anticipated from the operation of the extraordinary psychological machinery, now set in motion by and under the direction of the great artist, none but the master-workman himself can foresee. Here, however, all things work together harmoniously. Everything is consistent. The appearance of Edgar, ragged, forlorn, a miserable picture of wretchedness and woe, serves only, like the elements in the former scene, to arouse the predominant idea in the mind of the madman; and filial ingratitude, nothing else, could have brought him to this state, and recognizing in him [24] a counterpart of himself, his first question is, "Hast thou given all to thy two daughters?"

The warm, sympathetic nature of Lear is strongly aroused by the pitiful object before him, whom he regards as a fellow sufferer from like causes, and though not a king, like himself, he is nevertheless a "philosopher and most learned Theban"; and respectfully craving the "noble philosopher's" company, and essaying to enter into scientific discourse, asks him his studies, and gravely inquires "the cause of thunder." How beautifully true all this is to nature, those who are at all acquainted with insanity can furnish ample testimony; as, also, how admirably the genuine disease contrasts with the counterfeit, with which it is here brought in contact.[25]

. . . Shakspeare [does not give us] any allusion to the rotary chairs, the vomitings, the purgings by hellebore, the showerings, the bleedings, scalp-shavings, and blisterings, which, even down to our own times, have been inflicted upon these unfortunates by "science falsely so-called," and which stand recorded as imperishable monuments of medical folly; but in place of all this, Shakspeare, speaking through the mouth of the Physician, gives us the . . . "means" set forth by the Physician . . . used successfully in the restoration of Lear. He is thrown into a deep sleep, and from this he awakes convalescent.

Here follows another most important consideration, which is not overlooked by this wonderful medical psychologist.

He leaves nothing incomplete, therefore the danger of *relapse* must be taken into consideration, and the means to prevent it are pointed out with his usual truthfulness and accuracy. This we have in the advice given by the Physician to Cordelia. . . .[27]

The late distinguished physician to the insane, Dr. Brigham, . . . says: "Now we confess, almost with shame, that although near two centuries and a half have passed since Shakspeare wrote thus, we have very little to add to his method of treating the insane as thus pointed out. To produce sleep, to quiet the mind by medical and moral treatment, to avoid all unkindness, and when the patients begin to convalesce to guard, as he directs, against everything likely to disturb their minds and cause a relapse, is now considered the best, and nearly the only essential treatment." [28]

$\not\!\times$

Edward Dowden

From *Shakspere: A Critical Study of His Mind and Art* [1875]. New York: Harper & Brothers, 1881.

What was irony when human life was viewed from the outside, extra-mundane point of view becomes, when life is viewed from within, Stoicism. For to Stoicism the mere phenomenon of human existence is a vast piece of unreason and grotesqueness, and from this unreason and grotesqueness Stoicism makes its escape by becoming indifferent to the phenomenon, and by devotion to the moral idea, the law of the soul, which is forever one with itself and with the highest reason. The ethics of the play of *King Lear* are Stoical ethics. Shakspere's fidelity to the fact will allow him to deny no pain or calamity that befalls man. . . . He admits the suffering, the weakness, of humanity; but he declares that in the inner law there is a constraining power stronger than a silken thread; in the fidelity of pure hearts, in the rapture of love and sacrifice, there is a charm which is neither air nor words, but, indeed, potent enough to subdue pain and make calamity acceptable. Cordelia, who utters no word in excess of her actual feeling, can declare, as she is led to prison, her calm and decided acceptance of her lot:

> We are not the first
> Who, with best meaning, have incurred the worst;
> For thee, oppressed king, I am cast down;
> Myself could else out-frown false fortune's frown.

But though ethical principles radiate through the play [231] of *Lear,* its chief function is not, even indirectly, to teach or inculcate moral truth, but rather, by the direct presentation of a vision of human life and of the enveloping forces of nature, to "free, arouse, dilate." . . .[232]

Shakspere "takes ingratitude," Victor Hugo has said, "and he gives this monster two heads, Goneril . . . and Regan." The two terrible creatures are, however, distinguishable.[234] Goneril is the calm wielder of a pitiless force, the resolute initiator of cruelty. Regan is a smaller, shriller, fiercer, more eager piece of malice. The tyranny of the elder sister is a cold, persistent pressure, as little affected by tenderness or scruple as the action of some crushing hammer; Regan's ferocity is more unmeasured, and less abnormal or monstrous. Regan would avoid her father, and, while she confronts him alone, quails a little as she hears the old man's curse pronounced against her sister:

> O the blest gods! so will you wish on me
> When the rash mood is on [235]

. . . Shakspere opposes the presence and the influence of evil not by any transcendental denial of evil, but by the presence of human virtue, fidelity, and self-sacrificial love. In no play is there a clearer, an intenser manifestation of loyal manhood, of strong and tender womanhood. The devotion of Kent to his master is a passionate, unsubduable devotion, which might choose for its watchword the saying of Goethe, "I love you; what is that to you?" Edgar's nobility of nature is not disguised by the beggar's rags; he is the skilful resister of evil, the champion of right to the utterance. And if Goneril and Regan alone would leave the world unintelligible and desperate, there is

> One daughter
> Who redeems nature from the general curse
> Which twain have brought her to.

We feel throughout the play that evil is abnormal; a curse which brings down destruction upon itself; that it is without any long career. . . .

It is worthy of note that each of the principal personages of the play is brought into presence of those mysterious [239] powers which dominate life and preside over human destiny; and each, according to his character, is made to offer an interpretation of the great riddle. Of these interpretations, none is adequate to account for all the facts. Shakspere (differing in this from the old play) placed the story in heathen times, partly, we may surmise, that he might be able to put the question boldly, "What are the gods?" . . .[240]

⎯✕⎯

Francis Jacox

From *Shakspeare Diversions*. New York: Scribner, Welford, and Armstrong, 1875.

Improvers upon Shakspeare banished the Fool in *Lear* from the stage, and in so doing they rendered it impossible, as one of Shakspeare's ablest editors contends, that the original nature of Lear should be understood. For it is the Fool who interprets to us the old man's sensitive tenderness lying at the bottom of his impatience; from the Fool he can bear to hear truth; his jealous pride is not alarmed; and in the depths of [79] his misery, having scarcely anything in the world to love but the Fool, to him Lear clings. Banish the Fool? Who sees not, asks Charles Lamb, that the Fool in *Lear* has a kind of correspondency to, and falls in with, the subjects he may seem to interrupt. . . . Schlegel sees in the Fool, next to Kent, Lear's wisest counsellor, as well as most faithful associate. . . .[80]

It is literally that Lear's heart was breaking, when, with the last gaspings of worn-out nature,—suffocated, struggling ("Pray you, undo this button; Thank you, sir:")—he gave his last look on Cordelia's white dead face, as she lay cold, and still as any stone, in his shrunken, nerveless arms; and wailed forth, as he gazed, that wild, appalling iteration of Never, never, to which Shakspeare has, in perfect pity, and with profoundest pathos, assigned a line complete in itself—a verse in which the word is quintupled into intensified despair. . . .[278]

Has any one ever observed, I wonder,—or did Shakspeare himself consciously intend,—a painful analogy, but by contrast, between this Never of Lear's in the last scene of the last act, and another (quite other) Never of his, in the first of the first? When, in his turbulent wrath at her lack of demonstrative affection, and her resolute abstinence from her sisters' hyperbole of adulation, Lear dismisses Cordelia to a foreign home, it is in these resentfully implacable words:

> Thou hast got her, France: let her be thine; for we
> Have no such daughter, nor shall ever see
> That face of hers again.

So raged the exasperated father in his pride of power. But he was to see that face of hers again. It was to be the first face he should see, and know, on recovering from delirium—when all else that were near of kin to him, had proved themselves less than kind, and, having stripped him of all, were banded together against him. . . .[279]

Algernon Charles Swinburne

From *A Study of Shakespeare* [1876]. London: Chatto and Windus, 1902. By permission of William Heinemann Ltd.

Of all Shakespeare's plays, *King Lear* is unquestionably that in which he has come nearest to the height and to the likeness of the one tragic poet on any side greater than himself whom the [170] world in all its ages has ever seen born of time. It is by far the most Aeschylean of his works; the most elemental and primaeval, the most oceanic and Titanic in conception. . . .

. . . on the horizon of Shakespeare's tragic fatalism we see no . . . twilight of atonement . . . [or] pledge of reconciliation [171]. . . . Requital, redemption, amends, equity, explanation, pity and mercy, are words without a meaning here.

> As flies to wanton boys are we to the gods;
> They kill us for their sport.

The words just cited are not casual or episodical; they strike the keynote of the whole poem, lay the keystone of the whole arch of thought. . . .

. . . in this the most terrible work of human genius it is with the very springs and sources of nature that her student has set himself to deal. The veil of the temple of our humanity is rent in twain. Nature herself, we might say, is revealed—and revealed as unnatural. In face of such a world as this a man might be forgiven who should pray that chaos might come again. Nowhere else in [172] Shakespeare's work or in the universe of jarring lives are the lines of character and event so broadly drawn or so sharply cut. Only the supreme self-command of this one poet could so mould and handle such types as to restrain and prevent their passing from the abnormal into the monstrous: yet even as much as this, at least in all cases but one, it surely has accomplished. In Regan alone would it be, I think, impossible to find a touch or trace of anything less vile than it was devilish. Even Goneril has her one splendid hour, her fireflaught of hellish glory. . . .

On the other side, Kent is the exception which answers to Regan on this. Cordelia, the brotherless Antigone of our stage, has one passing touch of intolerance for what her sister was afterwards to brand as indiscretion and dotage in their father, which redeems her from the charge of perfection. . . .[173]

It should be a truism wellnigh as musty as Hamlet's half cited proverb, to enlarge upon the evidence given in *King Lear* of a sympathy with the mass of social misery more wide and deep and [174] direct and bitter and tender than Shakespeare has shown elsewhere. . . . A poet of revolution he is not, as none of his country in that generation could have been: but as surely as the author of *Julius Caesar* has approved himself in the best and highest sense of the word at least potentially a republican, so surely has the author of *King Lear* avowed himself in the only good and rational sense of the words a spiritual if not a political democrat and socialist.[175]

$$\rightthreetimes$$

Denton J. Snider

From *The Shakespearian Drama: The Tragedies.* Boston: Ticknor & Co., 1887.

It will be noticed that the action of the play lies mainly in the sphere of the Family, and portrays one of its essential relations—that of parents and children. The conflicts arising from this [127] relation involve also brothers and sisters in strife. The domestic side of life is thus torn with fearful struggles, and its quiet affection and repose are turned into a display of malignant hate and passion. Each element is present. There is on the one hand the most heroic fidelity, and on the other the most wanton infidelity. The parents are both faithful and faithless to their relation; so are the children, taken collectively. Such are its contradictory principles, and hence arises the conflict in which the offending individuals perish, since they destroy the very condition of their own existence, namely, the Family. But those who have been true to their domestic relations, and have not otherwise committed wrong, are preserved. It is essentially the story of fidelity and infidelity to the Family.

Still we must note that the action has a tendency to burst the limits of the Family, and to rise into more universal relations. A commonwealth is also involved, Lear is monarch as well as parent, his children, too, are rulers; thus the political element is whirled into the domestic cataclysm, and the wrong of the home becomes the wrong of the government. The classes of society are also infected, as we may see in Gloster; indeed, it is not too much to say that this drama presents a condensed picture out of the World's History; the decline and corruption of a State, and its process of freeing itself from that corruption, through war and tragedy, till final restoration. So the family of Lear, in its domestic limits, is made, by the [128] cunning of the poet, to cast an image of the Universal Family.

The spirit of *King Lear* belongs emphatically to Shakespeare's own time. The play takes its mythical setting from pre-historic Britain, "before the building of Rome," says Holinshed, the chronicler, from whom the poet, in part at least, derived the story. But the drama, as it now stands, reaches to the very heart of the age of the Tudors and Stuarts, and reveals to us the disease of absolute authority, showing how such an authority wrecks society on the one hand, and, on the other, wrecks the monarch who exercises it. In this sense the present drama is historical, and Shakespeare shows himself the poet of the English, and indeed of the whole Anglo-Saxon consciousness, whose history is largely made up of the attempt to put legal limits upon an absolute sovereignty.[129]

And can we not see that Lear and Gloster have made their own Inferno, and have created their own means of punishment? That primal deed of each becomes character, and it becomes environment. Goneril and Regan, and likewise their court, are Lear's own product; even Edgar, disguised as mad Tom, upon whom Lear seems to come by accident, is really a result of this society, and the accident of meeting him is Lear's necessity. . . .[178]

[Cordelia] brings a French army into England, to secure to her father his right, as she says; it is evident that she means to place him again on the throne. She thus assails the highest ethical institution of man— the State; in defending a right, she unwittingly herself commits the greatest wrong.[198] The poet was doubtless patriotic; neither he nor his audience would allow Frenchmen to be victorious in England, and the one who introduced the ancient enemy of the nation would be held the worst of traitors. Moreover, Lear had resigned his power and divided his kingdom; he had no longer any just claim to the crown. Her invasion of the country rouses up against her the head of the State, Albany, who was otherwise favorable both to her and to Lear. But he had to defend his own realm, though he hates his associates and loves those who are fighting against him. Had Cordelia been satisfied with the restoration of her father to his reason and to his family, Albany would have given her both aid and sympathy. However much we may admire her character and regret her fate, however indignant we may be against her two sisters, still we must, in the end, say she did wrong—she violated the majesty of the State. In her affection for parent she attempted to destroy the higher principle for the sake of the lower. The result is, she loses the battle, is taken prisoner, and perishes.

The death of Cordelia is often felt to be unjustifiable, and the play was once altered to suit this feeling. But a true comprehension of the nature of Dramatic Art will vindicate the poet. The end of Tragedy is not that somebody get killed, or even that a villain be brought to justice; it must show the collision of two ethical principles, both of which have validity in the reason of man. The individuals who are the representatives of these [199] conflicting principles are brought into a struggle which admits of no mediation. Both, from one point of view, are in the right; and yet both, from another point of view, are in the wrong. The deeper, more universal thought must decide the conflict and must triumph in the end, for strife cannot be eternal. Cordelia's profoundest impulse is devotion to Family—a very lofty principle of action; but she is led by it into a collision with the State—a still higher principle. Undoubtedly, these two elements ought to be harmonized if possible, but Tragedy means that they cannot always be harmonized, and, hence, the lesser must be subordinated by violence and death.[200]

It may be affirmed very decidedly that Shakespeare makes Cordelia tragic in accord with a conscious principle of his Art. His two chief sources, Holinshed's chronicle and the old play of *Lear* portray her invasion as successful in restoring her father to his throne. The poet must have purposely changed the story in this regard. On what ground? Assuredly not to show the good woman overwhelmed in her goodness; that is not Shakespeare's view of the moral order of things. An innocent person may perish in the world of accident, but not in the ethical world of which Shakespeare gives the picture. Like his tragic [201] characters in general, she is caught in the antithesis of opposing principles; in following one virtue to excess, she violates another; in pursuing one right to an extreme, she falls into wrong. . . .[202]

A history of society in small is shown in the drama; we see how a period gets corrupt and perverted, then how it is purified. A destructive element, a poison is introduced into the body politic, which passes through wrong, convulsion, revolution to restoration. Society is not tragic in Shakespeare, but the individual may be, if he collides with its interest, and persists in his collision. We notice that three men are left, the truly positive men of the play, Albany, Edgar and Kent, who are to build up anew the shattered social organism. Thus the tragedy leaves us hopeful of a purified society, and reconciled with the supreme ethical order, which, we feel, cannot perish, though it, too, has to pass through its periods of corruption and purification.[209]

Bernhard ten Brink

From *Five Lectures on Shakespeare,* tr. Julia
Franklin. London: George Bell & Sons, 1895.

"Lear" is . . . among all Shakespeare's tragedies the most profound. In no other work does the poet present the great world-mystery
in such lofty symbols, with such remorseless truth. The world into
which he introduces us is impelled by wild passion, rude pleasures,
coldly calculating egoism. In the fate of its inhabitants is seen clearly
the hand of Nemesis: the wicked fall victims to their own crimes; but
is there not also revealed the rule of a benign Providence in the
fortunes of Lear, and, above all, in the lot of Cordelia? Or do we,
perhaps, rather receive the impression to [242] which Gloucester lends
words when he says:

> As flies to wanton boys, are we to the gods—
> They kill us for their sport.

The poet does not deny a Providence,—he believes in a divine government of the world,—but he is content to worship in humility the
mystery in which it enshrouds itself. He paints the world as he sees it,
and it appears dark to him; but it is at night that the stars become
visible.

"Nothing almost sees miracles but misery," says Kent; but the
miracle consists in this: that in misery human fortitude is best developed, that virtue, like a lovely lily, springs forth out of the common
slough of depravity. Gloucester only learns to know in his wretchedness the true worth of man and of life, and Lear then first experiences
what love means. The optimism which the poet does not renounce
even in "Lear" is of a [243] purely ethical nature; he appeals to our
conscience. In loud tones he preaches the duty of resigned endurance,
of manly steadfastness, of strenuous moral conduct; he makes us feel
how the Good, totally regardless of any outward success, is in itself a
thing most real, to be striven for above all other things. He strengthens
our faith in virtue and incites us to it in figures like that of Kent, and,
above all, in the gracious and lofty figure of Cordelia; he animates us
with hope in the eventual triumph of the good in this world in the
fortunes of Edgar.

The picture of the world which Shakespeare presents to us is
illuminated in one way in his tragedy, and in another in his comedy;
the deeply religious spirit of the artist is apparent in both—a religious-

ness whose root and essence lie in his moral sense, and which, therefore, does not need to shut its eyes to unpleasant facts. Shakespeare loves life and is penetrated with a sense of its high worth, but yet,[244] like Schiller, he is convinced that life is not the highest good, and he knows that no one can be pronounced happy before his death. To him the best thing on earth is love—self-sacrificing, active; and he feels that it is infinite love which pervades and animates the universe.[245]

A. C. Bradley

From *Shakespearean Tragedy* [1904]. London: Macmillan & Co., Ltd., 1937. By permission of Macmillan & Co., Ltd., St. Martin's Press, A. C. Bradley's representative, and the Macmillan Company of Canada, Ltd.

. . . *King Lear,* as a whole, is imperfectly dramatic, and there is something in its very essence which is at war with the senses, and demands a purely imaginative realisation. It is therefore Shakespeare's greatest work, but it is not what Hazlitt called it, the best of his plays; and its comparative unpopularity is due, not merely to the extreme painfulness of the catastrophe, but in part to its dramatic defects, and in part to a failure in many readers to catch the peculiar effects to which I have referred,—a failure which is natural because the appeal is made not so much to dramatic perception as to a rarer and more strictly poetic kind of imagination.[248]

The oft-repeated judgment that the first scene of *King Lear* is absurdly improbable, and that no sane man would think of dividing his kingdom among his daughters in proportion to the strength of their several protestations of love, is much too harsh and is based upon a strange misunderstanding. This scene acts effectively, and to imagination the story is not at all incredible. It is merely strange, like so many of the stories on which our romantic dramas are based. Shakespeare, besides, has done a good deal to soften the improbability of the legend, and he has done much more than the casual reader perceives. The very first words of the drama, as Coleridge pointed out, tell us that the division of the kingdom is already settled in all its details, so that only the public announcement of it remains. Later we find that the lines of division have already been drawn on the map of Britain (1.38), and again that Cordelia's share, which is her dowry, is perfectly well known to Burgundy, if not to France (11.197,245). That [249] then which is censured as absurd, the dependence of the division on the speeches of the daughters, was in Lear's intention a mere form, devised as a childish scheme to gratify his love of absolute power and his hunger for assurances of devotion. And this scheme is perfectly in character. We may even say that the main cause of its failure was not that Goneril and Regan were exceptionally hypocritical, but that Cordelia was exceptionally sincere and unbending. And it is essential to observe that its failure, and the consequent necessity of publicly reversing his whole well-known intention, is one source of Lear's extreme anger. He loved Cordelia most and knew that she loved him best, and the supreme moment to which he looked forward was that in which she should outdo her sisters in expressions of affection, and should be rewarded by that 'third' of the kingdom which was the most 'opulent.' And then—so it naturally seemed to him—she put him to open shame.

There is a further point, which seems to have escaped the attention of Coleridge and others. Part of the absurdity of Lear's plan is taken to be his idea of living with his three daughters in turn. But he never meant to do this. He meant to live with Cordelia, and with her alone. The scheme of his alternate monthly stay with Goneril and Regan is forced on him at the moment by what he thinks the undutifulness of his favourite child. In fact his whole original plan, though foolish and rash, was not a 'hideous rashness' or incredible folly. If carried out it would have had no such consequences as followed its alteration.[250]

Doubtless we are right when we turn with disgust from Tate's sentimental alterations, from his marriage of Edgar and Cordelia, and from that cheap moral which [251] every one of Shakespeare's tragedies contradicts, 'that Truth and Virtue shall at last succeed.' But are we so sure that we are right when we unreservedly condemn the feeling which prompted these alterations, or at all events the feeling which beyond question comes naturally to many readers of King Lear who would like Tate as little as we? What they wish, though they have not always the courage to confess it even to themselves, is that the deaths of Edmund, Goneril, Regan and Gloster should be followed by the escape of Lear and Cordelia from death.[252]

The improbabilities in King Lear surely far surpass those of the other great tragedies in number and in grossness. And they are particularly noticeable in the secondary plot. For example, no sort of reason is given why Edgar, who lives in the same house with Edmund, should write a letter to him instead of speaking; and [256] this is a letter absolutely damning to his character. Gloster was very foolish, but surely not so foolish as to pass unnoticed this improbability; or, if so foolish, what need for Edmund to forge a letter rather than a conversation, especially as Gloster appears to be unacquainted with his son's handwriting? Is it in character that Edgar should be persuaded without the slightest demur to avoid his father instead of confronting him and asking him the cause of his anger? Why in the world should Gloster, when expelled from his castle, wander painfully all the way to Dover simply in order to destroy himself (IV.i.80)? And is it not extraordinary that, after Gloster's attempted suicide, Edgar should first talk to him in the language of a gentleman, then to Oswald in his presence in broad peasant dialect, then again to Gloster in gentle language, and yet that Gloster should not manifest the least surprise?

Again, to take three instances of another kind: (a) only a fortnight seems to have elapsed between the first scene and the breach with Goneril; yet already there are rumours not only of war between Goneril and Regan but of the coming of a French army; and this, Kent says, is perhaps connected with the harshness of *both* the sisters to their father, although Regan has apparently had no opportunity of showing any harshness till the day before. (b) In the quarrel with Goneril Lear speaks of his having to dismiss fifty of his followers at a clap, yet she has neither mentioned any number nor had any opportunity of mentioning it off the stage. (c) Lear and Goneril, intending to hurry to Regan, both send off messengers to her, and both tell the messengers to bring back an answer. But it does not appear either how the messengers [257] *could* return or what answer could be required, as their superiors are following them with the greatest speed.

Once more, (a) why does Edgar not reveal himself to his blind father, as he truly says he ought to have done? The answer is left to mere conjecture. (b) Why does Kent so carefully preserve his incognito till the last scene? He says he does it for an important purpose, but what the purpose is we have to guess. (c) Why Burgundy rather than France should have first choice of Cordelia's hand is a question we cannot help asking, but there is no hint of any answer. (d) I have referred already to the strange obscurity regarding Edmund's delay in trying to save his victims, and I will not extend this list of examples. No one of such defects is surprising by itself, but their number is surely significant. Taken in conjunction with other symptoms it means that Shakespeare, set upon the dramatic effect of the great scenes and upon certain effects not wholly dramatic, was exceptionally careless of probability, clearness and consistency in smaller matters, introducing what was convenient or striking for a momentary purpose without troubling himself about anything more than the moment. . . .[258]

Nothing enables us to imagine whereabouts in Britain Lear's palace lies, or where the Duke of Albany lives. In referring to the dividing-lines on the map, Lear tells us of shadowy forests and plenteous rivers, but . . . he studiously avoids proper names. The Duke of Cornwall, we presume in the absence of information, is likely to live in Cornwall; but we suddenly find, from the introduction of a place name which all readers take at first for a surname, that he lives at Gloster (I.v.1). This seems likely to be also the home of the Earl of Gloster, to whom Cornwall is patron. But no: it is a night's journey from Cornwall's 'house' to Gloster's, and Gloster's is in the middle of an uninhabited heath. Here, for the purpose of the crisis, nearly all the persons assemble, but they do so in a manner which no casual spectator or reader could follow. Afterwards they all drift towards Dover for the purpose of the catastrophe; but [259] again the localities and movements are unusually indefinite. And this indefiniteness is found in smaller matters. One cannot help asking, for example, and yet one feels one had better not ask, where that 'lodging' of Edmund's can be, in which he hides Edgar from his father, and whether Edgar is mad that he should return from his hollow tree (in a district where 'for many miles about there's scarce a bush') to his father's castle in order to soliloquise (II.iii.) . . .[260]

How is it, now, that this defective drama so overpowers us that we are either unconscious of its blemishes or regard them as almost irrelevant? As soon as we turn to this question we recognise, not merely that *King Lear* possesses purely dramatic qualities which far outweigh its defects, but that its greatness consists partly in imaginative effects of a wider kind. And, looking for the sources of these effects, we find among them some of those very things which appeared to us dramatically faulty or injurious. Thus, to take at once two of the simplest examples of this, that very vagueness in the sense of locality which we have just considered, and again that excess in the bulk of the material and the number of figures, events and movements, while they interfere with the clearness of vision, have at the same time a positive value for imagination. They give the feeling of vastness, the feeling not of a scene or particular place, but of a world; or, to speak more accurately, of a particular place which is also a world.[261]

. . . the secondary plot fills out a story which would by itself have been somewhat thin. . . . the sub-plot simply repeats the theme of the main story. Here, as there, we see an old man 'with a white beard.' He, like Lear, is affectionate, unsuspicious, foolish, and self-willed. He, too, wrongs deeply a child who loves him not less for the wrong. He, too, meets with monstrous ingratitude from the child whom he favours, and is tortured and driven to death. This repetition does not simply double the pain with which the tragedy is witnessed: it startles and terrifies by suggesting that the folly of Lear and the ingratitude of his daughters are no accidents or merely individual aberrations, but that in that dark cold world some fateful malignant influence is abroad, turning the hearts of the fathers against their children and of the children against their fathers, smiting the earth with a curse, so that the brother gives the brother to death and the father the son, blinding the eyes, maddening the brain, freezing the springs of pity, numbing all powers except the nerves of anguish and the dull lust of life.[262]

For Dante that which is recorded in the *Divine Comedy* was the justice and love of God. What did *King Lear* record for Shakespeare? Something, it would seem, very different. This is certainly the most terrible picture that Shakespeare painted of the world. In no other of his tragedies does humanity appear more pitiably infirm or more hopelessly bad. What is Iago's malignity against an envied stranger compared with the cruelty of the son of Gloster and the daughters of Lear? What [273] are the sufferings of a strong man like Othello to those of helpless age? Much too that we have already observed—the repetition of the main theme in that of the under-plot, the comparisons of man with the most wretched and the most horrible of the beasts, the impression of Nature's hostility to him, the irony of the unexpected catastrophe—these, with much else, seem even to indicate an intention to show things at their worst, and to return the sternest of replies to that question of the ultimate power and those appeals for retribution. Is it an accident, for example, that Lear's first appeal to something beyond the earth,

> O heavens,
> If you do love old men, if your sweet sway
> Allow obedience, if yourselves are old,
> Make it your cause:

is immediately answered by the iron voices of his daughters, raising by turns the conditions on which they will give him a humiliating harbourage; or that his second appeal, heart rending in its piteousness,

> You see me here, you gods, a poor old man,
> As full of grief as age; wretched in both:

is immediately answered from the heavens by the sound of the breaking storm? Albany and Edgar may moralise on the divine justice as they will, but how, in the face of all that we see, shall we believe that they speak Shakespeare's mind? [274]

King Lear has been held to be profoundly 'pessimistic' in the full meaning of that word,—the record of a time when contempt and loathing for his kind had overmastered the poet's soul, and in despair he pronounced man's life to be simply hateful and hideous.[275]

But . . . its keynote is surely to be heard neither in the words wrung
from Gloster in his anguish, nor in Edgar's words 'the gods are just.'
Its final and total result is one in which pity and terror, carried perhaps
to the extreme limits of art, are so blended with a sense of law and
beauty that we feel at last, not depression and much less despair,
but a consciousness of greatness in pain, and of solemnity in the
mystery we cannot fathom.[279]

There is nothing more noble and beautiful in literature than Shakespeare's exposition of the effect of suffering in reviving the greatness
and eliciting the sweetness of Lear's nature. . . .[284] but Lear owes
. . . this to those sufferings which made us doubt whether life were
not simply evil, and men like the flies which wanton boys torture for
their sport. Should we not be at least as near the truth if we called
this poem *The Redemption of King Lear,* and declared that the business of 'the gods' with him was neither to torment him, nor to teach
him a 'noble anger,' but to lead him to attain through apparently
hopeless failure the very end and aim of life? One can believe that
Shakespeare had been tempted at times to feel misanthropy and
despair, but it is quite impossible that he can have been mastered by
such feelings at the time when he produced this conception.[285]

The parallel between Lear and Gloster, already noticed, is, up to a
certain point, so marked that it cannot possibly be accidental. Both
are old white-haired men (III.vii.37); both, it would seem, widowers,
with children comparatively young. Like Lear, Gloster is tormented,
and his life is sought, by the child whom he favours; he is tended and
healed by the child whom he has wronged. His sufferings, like Lear's,
are partly traceable to his own extreme folly and injustice,[293] and,
it may be added, to a selfish pursuit of his own pleasure. His sufferings,
again, like Lear's, purify and enlighten him: he dies a better and
wiser man than he showed himself at first. They even learn the same
lesson, and Gloster's repetition (noticed and blamed by Johnson) of
the thought in a famous speech of Lear's is surely intentional. And,
finally, Gloster dies almost as Lear dies. Edgar reveals himself to
him and asks his blessing (as Cordelia asks Lear's):

> but his flaw'd heart—
> Alack, too weak the conflict to support—
> 'Twixt two extremes of passion, joy and grief,
> Burst smilingly.

So far, the resemblance of the two stories, and also of the ways
in which their painful effect is modified, is curiously close. And in
character too Gloster is, like his master, affectionate, credulous [294]
and hasty. But otherwise he is sharply contrasted with the tragic Lear,
who is a towering figure, every inch a king, while Gloster is built on a

smaller scale, and has infinitely less force and fire. He is, indeed, a decidedly weak though good-hearted man; and, failing wholly to support Kent in resisting Lear's original folly and injustice, he only gradually takes the better part. Nor is his character either very interesting or very distinct. He often gives one the impression of being wanted mainly to fill a place in the scheme of the play; and, though it would be easy to give a long list of his characteristics, they scarcely, it seems to me, compose an individual, a person whom we are sure we should recognise at once. If this is so, the fact is curious, considering how much we see and hear of him.[295]

Kent has fortunately expressed our feelings towards [Oswald]. Yet twice we are able to feel sympathy with him. Regan cannot tempt him to let her open Goneril's letter to Edmund; and his last thought as he dies is given to the fulfilment of his trust. It is to a monster that he is faithful, and he is faithful to her in a monstrous design. Still faithfulness is faithfulness, and he is not wholly worthless. Dr. Johnson says: 'I know not well why Shakespeare gives to Oswald, who is a mere factor of wickedness, so much fidelity'; but in any other tragedy this touch, so true to human nature, is only what we should expect. If it surprises us in *King Lear,* the reason is that Shakespeare, in dealing with the other members of the group, seems to have been less concerned than usual with such mingling of light with darkness, and intent rather on making the shadows as utterly black as a regard for truth would permit.

Cornwall seems to have been a fit mate for [298] Regan; and what worse can be said of him? It is a great satisfaction to think that he endured what to him must have seemed the dreadful disgrace of being killed by a servant. He shows, I believe, no redeeming trait, and he is a coward, as may be seen from the sudden rise in his courage when Goneril arrives at the castle and supports him and Regan against Lear (II.iv.202). But as his cruelties are not aimed at a blood relation, he is not, in this sense, a 'monster,' like the remaining three.[299]

[Cordelia] had knowingly to wound most deeply the being dearest to her. He cast her off; and, after suffering an agony for him, and before she could see him safe in death, she was brutally murdered. We have to thank the poet for passing lightly over the circumstances of her death. We do not think of them. Her image comes before us calm and bright and still.

The memory of Cordelia thus becomes detached in a manner from the action of the drama. The reader refuses to admit into it any idea of imperfection, and is outraged when any share in her father's [317] sufferings is attributed to the part she plays in the opening scene. Because she was deeply wronged he is ready to insist that she was wholly right. He refuses, that is, to take the tragic point of view, and when it is taken, he imagines that Cordelia is being attacked, or is being declared to have 'deserved' all that befell her. But Shakespeare's was the tragic point of view. He exhibits in the opening scene a situation tragic for Cordelia as well as for Lear. At a moment where terrible issues join, Fate makes on her the one demand which she is unable to meet. As I have already remarked in speaking of Desdemona, it was a demand which other heroines of Shakespeare could have met. Without loss of self-respect, and refusing even to appear to compete for a reward, they could have made the unreasonable old King feel that he was fondly loved. Cordelia cannot, because she is Cordelia. And so she is not merely rejected and banished, but her father is left to the mercies of her sisters. And the cause of her failure—a failure a thousand-fold redeemed—is a compound in which imperfection appears so intimately mingled with the noblest qualities that—if we are true to Shakespeare—we do not think either of justifying her or of blaming her: we feel simply the tragic emotions of fear and pity.[318]

> LEAR.   So young, and so untender?
> CORD.   So young, my lord, and true.

Yes, 'heavenly true.' But truth is not the only good in the world, nor is the obligation to tell truth the only obligation. The matter here was [320] to keep it inviolate, but also to preserve a father. And even if truth *were* the one and only obligation, to tell much less than truth is not to tell it. And Cordelia's speech not only tells much less than truth about her love, it actually perverts the truth when it implies that to give love to a husband is to take it from a father. There surely never was a more unhappy speech.[321]

$$\text{—}\!\!\!\bigstar\!\!\!\text{—}$$

Leo Tolstoy

From "On Shakespeare and the Drama," tr. V. Tchertkoff. *Fortnightly Review*, LXXXVI (1906), 963-983.

Not to mention the pompous, characterless language of King Lear, the same in which all Shakespeare's kings speak, the reader or spectator cannot conceive that a king, however old and stupid he may be, could believe the words of the vicious daughters with whom he had passed his whole life, and not believe his favourite daughter,

characters are placed in conditions possible only in the Midd[le]
—participating in the drama are kings, dukes, armies, and illegit[imate]
children, and [982] gentlemen, courtiers, doctors, farmers, officer[s, sol-]
[di]ers, and knights with visors, etc. It is possible that such anachr[onisms]
[i]s (with which Shakespeare's dramas abound) did not injure th[e pos-]
[si]bility of illusion in the sixteenth century and the beginning of th[e sev-]
[en]teenth, but in our time it is no longer possible to follow wit[h inter-]
[es]t the development of events which one knows could not tak[e plac-]
[e] in the conditions which the author describes in detail. . . . [983]

✳

Tolstoy

From "On Shakespeare and the Drama," t[rans.]
V. Tchertkoff. *Fortnightly Review*, n[.s.]
LXXXVI (1907), 62-91.

[Re]ading any of Shakespeare's dramas whatever, I was, from the ve[ry first,]
instantly convinced that he was lacking in the most importan[t, or even]
[no]t the only, means of portraying characters—individuality of la[nguage,]
[i.e]., the style of speech of every person being natural to h[is char-]
[a]cter. This is absent from Shakespeare. All his characters spea[k, not]
[th]eir own, but always one and the same Shakespearean pretentio[us, un-]
[u]nnatural language, in which not only they could not speak, b[ut in]
[wh]ich no living man ever has spoken or does speak.

[N]o living men could or can say as Lear says—that he would divor[ce his]
[wi]fe in the grave should Regan not receive him; or that the heave[ns would]
[crack] with shouting; or that the winds would burst; or that th[e wind]
wishes to blow the land into the sea; or that the curled wate[rs wish]
[t]o flood the shore, as the gentleman describes the storm; or th[at it is]
[e]asier to bear one's grief; and the soul leaps over many sufferin[g when]
[?] grief finds fellowship; or that Lear has become childless whi[le I am]
[f]atherless, as Edgar says, or use similar unnatural expressions wi[th which]
the speeches of all the characters in all Shakespeare's dram[as over-flow.]

[A]gain, it is not enough that all the characters speak in a way [in which]
no living men ever did or could speak—they all suffer [62] fr[om a com-]
[com]mon intemperance of language. Those who are in love, who a[re prepar-]
[?] ing for death, who are fighting, who are dying, all alike spe[ak much]
[?] and unexpectedly about subjects utterly inappropriate to t[he oc-]

but curse and banish her; and, therefore, the spectator or reader cannot
share the feelings of the persons participating in this unnatural
scene. [967]

The relations between Gloucester and his two sons, and the feelings of these characters, are as unnatural as Lear's relation to his
daughters, or even more so; and, therefore, it is still more difficult
for the spectator to transport himself into the mental condition of
Gloucester and his sons, and sympathise with them, than it is to do
so into that of Lear and his daughters. [968]

The third act begins with thunder, lightning, a storm, of some
special kind such as, according to the words of the characters in the
piece, had never before taken place. . . .

The second scene of the third act also takes place on the heath,
but in another part of it. Lear walks about the heath and says words
which are meant to express his despair: he desires that the winds
should blow so hard that they should crack their cheeks, and that the
rain should flood everything, that lightning should singe his white
head, and the thunder flatten the world and destroy all germs "that
make ungrateful man!" The fool keeps uttering still more senseless
words. Enter Kent. Lear says that for some reason during this storm
all criminals shall be found out and convicted. Kent, still unrecognised
by Lear, endeavours to persuade him to take refuge in a hovel. At
this point the fool pronounces a prophecy in no wise related to the
situation, and they all depart.

The hovel into which Lear is led turns out to be the same which
Edgar has entered, disguised as a madman, *i.e.*, naked Edgar comes
out of the hovel, and, although all have known him, no one recognises
him—as no one recognises Kent—and Edgar, Lear, and the fool begin
to say senseless things, which continue with interruptions for many
pages. In the middle of this scene enters Gloucester, who also does
not recognise either [972] Kent or his son Edgar, and tells them how
his son Edgar wanted to kill him. [973]

The fourth act is again on the heath. Edgar, still attired as a
lunatic, soliloquises in stilted terms about the instability of fortune
and the advantages of a humble lot. Then there comes to him somehow into the very place on the heath where he is, his father, the
blinded Gloucester, led by an old man. In that characteristic Shakespearean language—the chief peculiarity of which is that the thoughts
are bred either by the consonance or the contrasts of words—Gloucester also speaks about the instability of fortune. He tells the old man
who leads him to leave him, but the old man points out to him that
he cannot see his way. Gloucester says he has no way, and therefore
does not require *eyes*. And he argues about his having stumbled when

he *saw,* and about defects often proving commodities. "Ah! dear son Edgar," he adds, "might I but live to *see* thee in my touch, I'd say I had *eyes* again." Edgar, naked and in the character of a lunatic, hearing this, still does not disclose himself to his father. He takes the place of the aged guide and talks with his father, who does not recognise his voice, but regards him as a wandering madman. Gloucester avails himself of the opportunity to deliver himself of a witticism: " 'Tis the times' plague when madmen lead the blind," and he insists on dismissing the old man, obviously not from motives which might be natural to Gloucester at the moment, but merely in order, when left alone with Edgar, to enact the later scene of the imaginary leaping from the cliff.[974]

In the sixth scene Gloucester again appears with his still unrecognised son Edgar, who (now in the guise of a peasant) pretends to lead his father to the cliff: Gloucester is walking along on level land, but Edgar persuades him that they are with difficulty ascending a steep hill. Gloucester believes this. Edgar tells his father that the noise of the sea is heard; Gloucester believes this also. Edgar stops on a level place, and persuades his father that he has ascended the cliff and that in front of him lies a dreadful abyss, and leaves him alone. Gloucester, addressing the gods, says that he shakes off his affliction, as he can bear it no longer, and that he does not condemn them—the gods. Having said this, he leaps on the level ground and falls, imagining that he has jumped off the cliff. . . . [976]

[Edgar] approaches Gloucester, in the character of yet a different person, and expresses astonishment at the latter not being hurt by his fall from such a dreadful height. Gloucester believes that he has fallen and prepares to die, but he feels that he is alive and begins to doubt that he has fallen from such a height. Then Edgar persuades him that he has indeed jumped from the dreadful height, and tells him that the individual who had been with him at the top was the devil, as he had eyes like two full moons and a thousand noses and wavy horns. Gloucester believes this, and is persuaded that his despair was the work of the devil, and therefore decides that he will henceforth despair no more, but will quietly await death. Hereupon enters Lear, for some reason covered with wild flowers. He has lost his senses, and says things wilder than before. He speaks about coining, about the moon, gives someone a yard, then he cries that he sees a mouse, which he wishes to entice by a piece of cheese. Then he suddenly demands the password from Edgar, and Edgar immediately answers him with the words, "Sweet marjoram." Lear says "Pass," and the blind Gloucester, who has not recognised either his son or Kent, recognises the King's voice.

After this enters Lear with the dead Cordelia in his arms, although he is more than eighty years old, and ill. Again begin Lear's

awful ravings, at which one feels ashamed, as at Lear demands that all should howl, and alternatel delia is dead and that she is alive.

> Had I your tongue and eyes (he says) I'd use th
> That heaven's vault should crack.

Then he says that he killed the slave who hange says that his eyes see badly, but at the same time whom all along he had not recognised.

The Duke of Albany says that he will resign of Lear, and that he will reward Edgar and Ke been faithful to him. At this moment the news is b is dead, and Lear, continuing his ravings, begs tha of his buttons—the same request which he had about the heath. He expresses his thanks for tl look at something, and thereupon dies.

Such is this celebrated drama. However abs my rendering (which I have endeavoured to make ble), I may confidently say that in the original For any man of our time—if he were not under th that this drama is the height of perfection—it wo it to its end (were he to have sufficient patience f convinced that, far from being the height of perf carelessly composed production, which, if it coul to a certain public at a certain time, cannot evok but aversion and weariness. Every reader of our the influence of suggestion will also receive exac from all the other extolled dramas of Shakespea senseless dramatised tales, *Pericles, Twelfth Nig beline, Troilus and Cressida.*

But such free-minded individuals, not i speare worship, are no longer to be found in Every man of our society and time, from the scious life, has been inculcated with the idea genius as poet and dramatist, and that all his of perfection. Yet, however hopeless it may se demonstrate in the selected drama, *King Lear,* characteristic of all the other tragedies and com account of which he not only is not representi art, but does not satisfy the most elementary de by all.[981]

. . . in this, as in the other dramas of Shakes live, think, speak, and act quite unconforma and place. The action of *King Lear* takes pla

occasion, being evidently guided rather by consonances and play of words than by thoughts. They speak all alike. Lear raves exactly as does Edgar when feigning madness. Both Kent and the fool speak alike. The words of one of the personages might be placed in the mouth of another, and by the character of the speech it would be impossible to distinguish who speaks. . . .[63]

In the older drama Leir abdicates because, having become a widower, he thinks only of saving his soul. He asks his daughters as to their love for him—that by means of a certain device he has invented he may retain his favourite daughter on his island. The elder daughters are betrothed, while the youngest does not wish to contract a loveless union with any of the neighbouring suitors whom Leir proposes to her, and he is afraid that she may marry some distant potentate.

The device which he has invented, as he informs his courtier Perillus (Shakespeare's Kent), is this, that when Cordelia tells him that she loves him more than anyone, or as much as her elder sisters do, he will tell her that she must, in proof of her love, marry the prince he will indicate on his island.

All these motives for Leir's conduct are absent in Shakespeare's play. Then, when according to the old drama Leir asks his daughters about their love to him, Cordelia does not say, as Shakespeare has it, that she will not give her father all her love, but will love her husband too, should she marry—which is quite unnatural—but simply says that she cannot express her love in words, but hopes that her actions will prove it. Goneril and Regan remark that Cordelia's answer is not an answer, and that the father cannot meekly accept such indifference; so that what is wanting in Shakespeare, i.e., the explanation of Lear's anger which caused him to disinherit his youngest daughter, exists in the old drama. Leir is annoyed by the failure of his scheme, and the poisonous words of his elder daughters irritate him still more. After the division of the kingdom between the elder daughters there follows in the older drama a scene between Cordelia and the King of Gaul, setting forth, instead of the colourless Cordelia of Shakespeare, a very definite and attractive character of the truthful, tender, and self-sacrificing youngest daughter. While Cordelia, without grieving that she has been deprived of a portion of her heritage, sits sorrowing at having lost her father's love, and looking forward to earn her bread by her labour, there comes the King of Gaul, who, in the disguise of a pilgrim desires to choose a bride from amongst Leir's daughters. He asks Cordelia why she is sad. She tells him the cause of her grief. The King of Gaul, still in the guise of a pilgrim, falls in love with her, and offers to arrange a marriage for her with the King of Gaul, but she says she will marry only a man whom she [64] loves. Then the pilgrim, still disguised, offers her his hand and heart and Cordelia confesses she loves the pilgrim and consents to marry him, notwithstanding the poverty that awaits her. Thereupon the pilgrim discloses to her that he it is who is the King of Gaul, and Cordelia marries him. Instead of this scene, Lear, according to Shakespeare, proposes to Cordelia's two suitors to take her without dowry, and one cynically refuses, whilst the other, one does not know why, accepts her. . . .[65]

However strange this opinion may seem to worshippers of Shakespeare, yet the whole of this old drama is incomparably and in every respect superior to Shakespeare's adaptation. It is so first because it has not got the utterly superfluous characters of the villain Edmund, and unlifelike Gloucester and Edgar, who only distract one's attention; secondly, because it has not got the completely false "effects" of Lear running about the heath, his conversations with the fool and all these impossible disguises, failures to recognise and accumulated deaths; and, above all, because in this drama there is the simple, natural, and deeply touching character of Leir, and the yet more touching and clearly-defined character of Cordelia, both absent in Shakespeare. Therefore, there is in the older drama, instead of Shakespeare's long-drawn scene of Lear's interview with Cordelia and of Cordelia's unnecessary murder, the exquisite scene of the interview between Leir and Cordelia, unequalled by any in all Shakespeare's dramas.

The old drama also terminates more naturally and more in [66] accordance with the moral demands of the spectator than does Shakespeare's, namely, by the King of the Gauls conquering the husbands of the elder sisters and Cordelia, instead of being killed, restoring Leir to his former position.[67]

⊰≻

Ashley H. Thorndike

From *Tragedy*. Boston and New York: Houghton Mifflin Company, 1908. Reprinted by permission of and arrangement with the publishers.

The kernel of the story, Lear's trick and Cordelia's unsatisfactory reply, though possessing a kind of objectivity suitable for the stage, is of itself so absurd and childish as to impede illusion of truth. Its development is full of inconsistency, and the interwoven themes of madness, villany, lust, ambition, family feud, and ideal virtue suggest no break from the Elizabethan canon of tragedy. To the story of Lear and his daughters, Shakespeare added the still more childish parallel story of Gloster and his sons. This common device of a reinforcing sub-plot is here extended to every situation and motive. Even the devoted Kent is balanced by Goneril's faithful creature, Oswald; the inhuman sisters are supported by the machinating Edmund; and, most extraordinary of all, the assumed madness of Edgar becomes an accompaniment for the real madness of Lear. The elaboration of the sub-plot causes an unprecedented complexity of persons and events, and it dislocates the structure. The intense interest which is absorbed in the sufferings of Lear finds itself distracted and dissipated in a medley of incidents so incongruous and so confusing that one wonders how a rational mind could have selected them. The crowded scenes which separate the climax of the third act from the catastrophe assuredly form one of the least happy instances of the Elizabethan habit of introducing [167] a change of interest and a variety of incident in the fourth and fifth acts. Yet the structure of the play, if far from faultless, reveals amazing mastery. The development of the action in the first three acts with the constantly increasing tension of feeling, and the final gathering of all the different actions in the wonderfully condensed catastrophe, are among the greatest achievements of dramatic plotting. Moreover, in spite of his zest for crowded and diversified action, Shakespeare's feeling for unity of emotional effect caused him to omit one motive that modern renovators have never been able to forego. He found a place for battles, villany, childish intrigue, the clown's songs and jests, the plucking out of Gloster's eyes, and the protracted foolery between Edgar and his helpless father, but he refused to admit romantic love into this drama of the madness that separates father and child.

Though Shakespeare chose to involve himself in these manifold difficulties of story and structure, he hardly felt his fetters. No play depends less on mere incident and event. The inconsistencies and confusion of the action are forgotten in the wild turmoil of human passions. Wild, terrible, elementary, brutal, grotesque, or sublime,—everything in the play is touched with the imaginative truth that gives it limitless range of suggestion, applicable to any discord of parents and children or to the most dreadful spiritual torture. Insanity, long a favorite theme of Elizabethan tragedy, and fantastic grotesqueness, often its bane, summon his imagination [168] to its most wonderful creation when the feigning Bedlam counters the mad king mid the jests of the fool and the havoc of the storm. Such a conception could have been attempted only in an age which took its emotions strong and mixed. . . .[169]

. . . evil, here represented by the two fiendish daughters as well as by an intriguing villain, dominates the action, and carries all that is good along with it to destruction. But evil is only one of the forces that cause suffering and ruin. Lear and Cordelia contend against their own imperfections and against chance and circumstance so hostile that they seem directed by gods who sport with men as with flies and loose the fury of the elements to torment their victims. Where else in tragedy are the forces that make for ruin so appalling and so irresistible; and where else are suffering and ruin so dreadful and so complete? The sufferers are powerless. Suffering does not here arouse a Promethean defiance, but it discovers and purifies human virtue. If evil is dominant over the action, Cordelia, Kent, the Fool, and the chastened and purified Lear are dominant in our reflections. The end is not the fall and cessation of all that is good. Even in our dismay at the convulsion which evil may cause, there remains the memory of the perfection of human devotion and love. The final impression must, however, partake of confusion and horror at the blackness and ruthlessness of a moral order that can sacrifice perfect virtue in an effort to free itself from the hideous enormity of evil. This is the tragedy of life as Shakespeare saw it, and the cry of bewilderment and agony seems to come from the poet's own heart. . . .[170]

$$\times\!\!\!\!\times$$

Algernon Charles Swinburne

From *Shakespeare*. London: Oxford University Press, 1909. By permission of the publisher.

The conscious and conscienceless abandonment or self-devotion rather than self-surrender of Goneril and Regan to the instincts which they have just enough of practical intelligence to clothe if not to cover with some show of egotistic reasoning is as natural as the cruelty of their servile ministers; even though lightning and rain be here as relentless as the willing and unwilling agents who nailed Prometheus to the cliff. The unspeakable villainy of Edmund. . . .[65]

Against such a triad of most toad-spotted traitors no less heavenly counterpoise or contrast than could be given only by three such figures as those of Cordelia, Kent, and the Fool, could suffice to establish the ethical balance of the poem, and reconcile the sympathy or even sustain the endurance of the reader. The dramatic skill of the supreme dramatic rather than theatrical artist was never more triumphantly manifest than in the fusion and transfiguration of the stories here so naturally and so cunningly interwoven. To have turned the ugly and unmanageable legend of Cordelia's ultimate suicide in prison into the glory of a martyrdom unmatched for its tragic effect of terror and of pity, to have [66] made its inevitable consequence the agony which now strikes out not the reason but the life of her father, is the supreme feat of Shakespeare as a spiritual craftsman. On the other hand, we cannot honestly overlook the one great and grave oversight or flaw to be found in this tragic work: the sudden and inexplicable disappearance of Lear's only comrade and support in the first horror of his exposure as an outcast to the storm. . . . that the Fool should vanish with the tempest, never more to be thought of or mentioned by Lear or by Cordelia, can be neither explained nor excused by any possible audacity or felicity of conjecture. The most fortunate [67] existence of a text from which two of the most priceless and incomparable scenes in the whole poem were struck out by the villainous editors of the folio precludes us from the otherwise natural and inevitable suspicion that another as brutal and treacherous excision may have deprived us of a third, in which we should have seen the last of the noble poor fellow whose suffering, in common with his own, was the means of his master's conversion from the royal egotism of a wilful and headstrong tyrant to the infinite sympathy of a high-minded and tender-hearted man with all sufferers under social negligence and misrule. In the noblest sense of an ambiguous if not indefinable term, the socialism of the revolutionary if not subversive sympathies which imbue with such thoughtful [68] passion the inspired insanity of the beggared and vagrant king can only rest unrecognized as Shakespeare's own prophetic and fervent faith by the blindest and deafest of misreaders.[69]

$$\rightarrow\!\!\!\chi\!\!\!\leftarrow$$

C. F. Tucker Brooke

From *The Tudor Drama*. Boston: Houghton Mifflin Company, 1911. By permission of and arrangement with the publishers.

. . . the trend of Shakespeare's dramatic practice set increasingly, as his genius developed, toward the utilization of what was accidental and ephemeral in the world around him for the demonstration of universal truth. More and more clearly he seems to have perceived that realism is as little as romance itself the necessary adjunct of a particular time and place; and his greatest realistic play, "King Lear," is a tragedy located, perhaps intentionally, at the farthest distance from the contemporary world. "Lear" is throughout a delineation, not of history or of heroic tragedy, but of the more domestic aspects in the relation of man to man, which each writer can understand only from sympathetic observation of the life before his window and which few have ever been able to reproduce save by means of the closest transcription. In Shakespeare's treatment, King Lear and his daughters lose the vague royal dignity which the earlier anonymous play on the same subject allows them, and become practically bourgeois types; while the kingdom of Britain could [398] be replaced without dramatic loss by a farm. "Macbeth" and "Othello," typical expressions of heroic tragedy, deal with the fate of supernormal figures, nature's aristocrats, overwhelmed by the most tremendous catastrophes: but "King Lear" is a parable of common life possible only for one whose eyes had been long fixed on the low average of human society, and designed to portray the hideous consequences attendant upon the ignoble faults of vulgar self-will and petty ingratitude. Lear, Goneril, Regan, and Cordelia are all fundamentally creatures of the hard actual world; and their egotisms and bickering belong to the same type and have obviously the same source in contemporary observation as dozens of the cynical or satirical scenes in the city comedies of Jonson and Chapman. The unlovely aspects of human society when centred in self and unenlightened by the spark of romantic endeavor, furnished the ordinary seventeenth-century playwright with matter for merriment, or at best for satire; but Shakespeare has here shaped it into tragedy too deep for tears.[399]

⤙✦⤚

John Masefield

From *William Shakespeare* [1911]. New York: Henry Holt & Co., 1927. By permission of the Society of Authors and Dr. John Masefield, O.M.

This play begins at the moment when an established blindness in two men is about to become an instrument of fate for the violent opening of their eyes. The blindness in both cases is against the course of nature. It is unnatural that Lear should give his kingship to women, and that he should curse his youngest child. It is unnatural that Gloucester should make much of a bastard son whom he has hardly seen for nine years. It is deeply unnatural that both Lear and Gloucester should believe evil suddenly of the youngest, best beloved, and most faithful spirits in the play. As the blindness that causes the injustice is great and unnatural, so the working of fate to purge the eyes and restore the balance is violent and unnatural. Every person important to the action is thrust into an unnatural way of life. Goneril and Regan rule their father, commit the most ghastly and beastly cruelty, lust [189] after the same man, and die unnaturally (having betrayed each other), the one by her sister's hand, the other by her own. Lear is driven mad. The King of France is forced to war with his wife's sisters. Edmund betrays his half-brother to ruin and his father to blindness. Cornwall is stabbed by his servant, Edgar kills his half-brother. Gloucester, thrust out blind, dies when he finds that his wronged son loves him. Cordelia, fighting against her own blood, is betrayed to death by one who claims to love her sisters. . . .[190]

Dramatic genius has the power of understanding half-a-dozen lives at once in tense, swiftly changing situations. This power is shown at its best in the last act of this play. One of the most wonderful and least praised of the inventions in the last scene is that of the dying Edmund. He has been treacherous to nearly every person in the play. His last treachery, indirectly the cause of his ruin, is still in act, the killing of Cordelia and the king.[192] He has been stricken down. "The wheel has come full circle." He has learned too late that

> The gods are just, and of our pleasant vices
> Make instruments to plague us.

He can hardly hope to live for more than a few minutes. The death of his last two victims cannot benefit him. A word from him would save them. No one else can save them. Yet at the last minute, his one little glimmer of faithfulness keeps the word unspoken. He is silent for Goneril's sake. If he ever cared for any one in the world, except himself, he may have cared a little for Goneril. He thinks of her now. She has gone from him. But she is on his side, and he trusts to her, and acts for her. He waits for some word or token from her. He waits to see her save him or avenge him. The death of Lear will benefit her. It will be to her something saved from the general wreck, something to the good, in the losing bout. An impulse stirs him to speak, but he puts it by. He keeps silent about Lear, till one comes saying that Goneril [193] has killed herself. Still he does not speak. The news pricks the vanity in him. He strokes his plumes with a tender thought for the brightness of the life that made two princesses die for love of him. When he speaks of Lear, it is too late, the little, little instant which alters destiny has passed. Cordelia is dead. . . .[194]

Sigmund Freud

From "The Theme of the Three Caskets"
[1913]. *Complete Psychological Works.* Volume XII. London: Hogarth Press, 1958. Pp.
289-301. By permission of Hogarth Press and
the Macmillan Co.

. . . in . . . *The Merchant of Venice* . . . a *man* chooses between
three—caskets. If what we were concerned with were a dream, it would
occur to us at once that caskets are also women, symbols of what is
essential in woman, and therefore of a woman herself—like coffers,
boxes, cases, baskets, and so on. . . . now we see that the theme is a
human one, *a man's choice between three women.*

This same content . . . is to be found in another scene of Shakespeare's, in one of his most powerfully moving dramas; not the choice
of a bride this time, yet linked by many hidden similarities to the choice
of the casket in *The Merchant of Venice.* The old King Lear resolves
to divide his kingdom while he is still alive among his three daughters,
in proportion to the amount of love that each of them expresses for
him. The two elder ones, Goneril and Regan, exhaust themselves in
asseverations [292] and laudations of their love for him; the third, Cordelia, refuses to do so. He should have recognized the unassuming,
speechless love of his third daughter and rewarded it, but he does not
recognize it. . . . Is not this once more the scene of a choice between three women, of whom the youngest is the best, the most excellent one?

There will at once occur to us other scenes from myths, fairy tales
and literature, with the same situation as their content. The shepherd
Paris has to choose between three goddesses, of whom he declares the
third to be the most beautiful. Cinderella, again, is a youngest daughter, who is preferred by the prince to her two elder sisters. Psyche, in
Apuleius's story, is the youngest and fairest of three sisters. . . .

In all the stories the three women, of whom the third is the most
excellent one, must surely be regarded as in some way alike if they
are represented as sisters. . . .

But who are these three sisters and why must the choice fall on
the third? . . .[293]

It must strike us that this excellent third woman has in several
instances certain peculiar qualities besides her beauty. They are qualities that seem to be tending towards some kind of unity; we must
certainly not expect to find them equally well marked in every example.
Cordelia makes herself unrecognizable, inconspicuous like lead, she

remains dumb, she 'loves and is silent.' Cinderella hides so that she cannot be found. We may perhaps be allowed to equate concealment and dumbness. These would of course be only two instances out of the five we have picked out. But there is an intimation of the same thing to be found, curiously enough, in two other cases. We have decided to compare Cordelia, with her obstinate refusal, to lead. In Bassanio's short speech while he is choosing the casket, he says of lead (without in any way leading up to the remark):

'Thy paleness moves me more than eloquence.'

That is to say: 'Thy plainness moves me more than the blatant nature of the other two.' Gold and silver are 'loud'; lead is dumb—in fact like Cordelia, who 'loves and is silent.' [294]

If we decide to regard the peculiarities of our 'third one' as concentrated in her 'dumbness,' then psycho-analysis will tell us that in dreams dumbness is a common representation of death.

More than ten years ago a highly intelligent man told me a dream which he wanted to use as evidence of the telepathic nature of dreams. In it he saw an absent friend from whom he had received no news for a very long time, and reproached him energetically for his silence. The friend made no reply. It afterwards turned out that he had met his death by suicide at about the time of the dream. Let us leave the problem of telepathy on one side: there seems, however, not to be any doubt that here the dumbness in the dream represented death. Hiding and being unfindable—a thing which confronts the prince in the fairy tale of Cinderella three times, is another unmistakable symbol of death in dreams; so, too, is a marked pallor, of which the 'paleness' of the lead in one reading of Shakespeare's text is a reminder. It would be very much easier for us to transpose these interpretations from the language of dreams to the mode of expression used in the myth that is now under consideration if we could make it seem probable that dumbness must be interpreted as a sign of being dead in productions other than dreams.[295]

[Freud goes on to cite multiple "evidence from fairy tales that dumbness is to be understood as representing death."] These indications would lead us to conclude that the third one of the sisters between whom the choice is made is a dead woman. But she may be something else as well—namely, Death itself, the Goddess of Death. Thanks to a displacement that is far from infrequent, the qualities that a deity imparts to men are ascribed to the deity himself. Such a displacement will surprise us least of all in relation to the Goddess of Death, since in modern versions and representations, which these stories would thus be forestalling, Death itself is nothing other than a dead man.

But if the third of the sisters is the Goddess of Death, the sisters are known to us. They are the Fates, the Moerae, the Parcae or the Norns, the third of whom is called Atropos, the inexorable.[296]

Lear is an old man. It is for this reason, as we have already said, that the three sisters appear as his daughters. The relationship of a father to his children, which might be a fruitful source of many dramatic situations, is not turned to further account in the play. But Lear is not only an old man: he is a dying man. In this way the extraordinary premiss of the division of his inheritance loses all its strangeness. But the doomed man is not willing to renounce the love of women; he insists on hearing how much he is loved. Let us now recall the moving final scene, one of the culminating points of tragedy in modern drama. Lear carries Cordelia's dead body on to the stage. Cordelia is Death. If we reverse the situation it becomes intelligible and familiar to us. She is the Death-goddess who, like the Valkyrie in German mythology, carries away the dead hero from the battlefield. Eternal wisdom, clothed in the primaeval myth, bids the old man renounce love, choose death and make friends with the necessity of dying.

The dramatist brings us nearer to the ancient theme by representing the man who makes the choice between the three sisters as aged and dying. The regressive revision which he has thus applied to the myth, distorted as it was by wishful transformation, allows us enough glimpses of its original meaning to enable us perhaps to reach as well a superficial allegorical interpretation of the three female figures in the theme. We might argue that what is represented here are the three inevitable relations that a man has with a woman—the woman who bears him, the woman who is his mate and the woman who destroys him; or that they are the three forms taken by the figure of the mother in the course of a man's life—the mother herself, the beloved one who is chosen after her pattern, and lastly the Mother Earth who receives him once more. But it is in vain that an old man yearns for the love of woman as he had it first from his mother; the third of the Fates alone, the silent Goddess of Death, will take him into her arms.[301]

$\times\kern-0.6em\times$

Wyndham Lewis

From *The Lion and the Fox*. New York and London: Chatto and Windus, 1927. By permission of Methuen & Co., Ltd.

Shakespeare is quite conscious of the fact that he is not the servant of a god: nor is he a nihilist without knowing it. As an instance of this the death of Cordelia can be instanced: and an account of this incident quoted to show how this nihilism can be misinterpreted, in the course of a process of "whitewashing."

Professor Bradley draws attention to the "ironic collocation" in *Lear,* where you get the appearance of Cordelia's corpse on the heels of a supplication to "the gods."

> EDMUND. He hath commission from my wife and me
>   To hang Cordelia in the prison, and
>   To lay the blame upon her own despair,
>   That she fordid herself.
>
> ALBANY. The gods defend her!
>
> [*Re-enter* LEAR *with* CORDELIA *dead in his arms.*] [179]

In this "irony" Mr. Bradley sees the "moral" of the whole play. "The *gods,* it seems, do *not* show their approval," he writes, "by defending their own from adversity or death, or by giving them power and prosperity." He implies that in this irony there is no ultimate despair, but rather that it is to be referred to a christian optimism. That does not seem likely, although he uses this theory with success in some other instances of bitter endings. But the punctual arrival of Cordelia, brought in like a Christmas present, so *narquois* and so pat, cannot be anything but what it forces us at once to see it as: an expression of the poet's mockery at the vanity of human supplications, and notions of benevolent powers, of whom we are the cherished children. . . .[180]

$$\succ\!\!\!\prec$$

Alwin Thaler

> From *Shakspere's Silences.* Cambridge, Mass.: Harvard University Press, 1929. By permission of the publisher.

He gives peace, too, and quiet after the tempest, to Lear's fool. Professor Bradley [1] complains that we are left "in ignorance" as to the fate of the fool—that is to say, he objects to the fact that immediately after the storm the fool is allowed (according to his last words in the play) " 'to go to bed at noon' as though he felt he had taken his death," without further or more explicit comment upon Shakspere's part. But to have made too much of the fool's death—if, indeed, he does die— would have been to ignore essential [37] human as well as dramatic distinctions. Some critics [2] still doubt that Lear's last words, "and my poor fool is hanged," are meant for Cordelia. There is no arguing about such a point, but I think it scarcely too much to say that Lear's fool has no more right to these words than Touchstone has to the tears which Jacques weeps for his "poor . . . fools" [3] of the forest. The end must belong to Cordelia. The fool disappears long before, because he has done his work. He has outjested his master's heartstruck injuries in the storm, but he has been a bitter fool withal, a pestilent gall to Lear. Cordelia brings true healing, and so the fool, his occupation gone, disappears. So far as we know, he is faithful to the end—even though his last speech may be, after all, merely a jest to cap Lear's immediately preceding "We'll go to supper i' the morning." [4] In any case, Shakspere probably remembered that he had on his hands not a second Mercutio but a much-loved fool slightly touched in the brain. Perhaps he purposely allowed the fool to drop quietly out of sight because he also remembered that there was another person of the play who *must* go to bed at noon—Cordelia, a daughter and a queen.[5] [38]

Professor Bradley [6] has given sufficient emphasis to the questions that arise if one looks closely at the beginnings of Edmund's intrigue: how Gloucester managed to avoid asking a pointed question or two about the letter ascribed to Edgar; and why Edgar allowed himself to be silently duped,[60] with never a word to his father. Shakspere, after all, answers these objections.

> A credulous father and a brother noble,
> Whose nature is so far from doing harms
> That he suspects none (I.ii.195ff.),—

why should these two stop to ask questions? Edmund's intrigue succeeds because his father and his brother could not have thought of any good reason to suspect him—because it is so absurdly but boldly impossible that no one but himself (at least no one else in his credulous family) could have imagined it. Again, it justifies itself—and the antecedent silences—on the stage because it precipitates the action at such a pace that there is little or no time for afterthoughts. . . .[61]

---

1 Pages 314-315.[37]
2 Alfred Noyes, for example (cf. *Some Aspects of Modern Poetry*, p. 211).
3 *As You Like It*, II.i.22-40.
4 *Lear*, III.vi.90-92.
5 Professor Tolman (*Falstaff and Other Shakespearean Topics*, pp. 93-94) mentions approvingly another explanation of the fool's disappearance—a conjecture (ascribed to Professor Brandl) to the effect that the parts of Cordelia and the fool may originally have been played by the same boy actor. If this was the case, who can say whether it was the cause rather than the effect of Shakspere's conception of the fool's part in the play? At all events, whatever the practical circumstances of the theatre may or may not have contributed to the fool's disappearance (on which point see below, pp. 257ff.), it is *dramatically* right. (Compare, however, W. J. Lawrence's view on this point. Mr. Lawrence, I find, rejects the idea of the doubling in this case.—*Pre-Restoration Stage Studies*, pp. 72-73, 66.) [38]
6 Pages 256ff.[60]

Elmer Edgar Stoll

From *Art and Artifice in Shakespeare: A Study in Dramatic Contrast and Illusion* [1933]. New York: Barnes and Noble, 1951. By permission of Cambridge University Press.

On *King Lear,* which, so far as the underplot is concerned, we have discussed already, we need not dwell. Criticism (as I take it) has not here gone so far astray. What attracted the dramatist was again a striking, but improbable, situation—that of a king, not in his dotage, undertaking to apportion his territory, according to their protestations of affection, among his three daughters, and, because of her laconic honesty, casting off his dearest, only to discover that the others were wholly false and she divinely true. Against the bidding of his heart he disowns her; and in the end his heart is broken by her death. Attempts, indeed, have not been wanting to motive this initial situation, to prove the postulate, to demonstrate what was assumed. Lear has been made out to be on the verge of madness already, like the author himself as he created him; [1] or tyrannical and "compact of vanity," as Stopford Brooke has it, to the point that the critic goes behind the returns, beyond the limits of the play, and bids us "just imagine what those two haughty, high-tempered, icy-minded, very intelligent women had suffered." [2] What can be the point of keeping the audience (and the daughters too) in the dark about such supposititious defects in his nature . . . and also insisting . . . on [138] the admiration and devotion of his friends and retainers? A stage-play is not a riddle, and Shakespeare's least of all. . . . much has been said of the "blindness" of the old King to the inner nature of those about him. . . . Here again what is structure is turned into psychology; what is high-piled drama is flattened into biography, and even autobiography. This is to blur the contrast, to withdraw much of our admiration and sympathy from the heroes and heroines and bestow it on the villains, to set the structure awry, in brief, to rewrite the play. It will no more do to be sympathizing with Goneril and Regan (or counting upon their undiscoverable past) than (though there is precedent for it!) with Iago, or with Claudius; and the terrible violence of the old man before the first scene [139] is over, is owing, undoubtedly, to the uncompromising attitude of Cordelia, in disgust with her sisters, and to the blunt interference of Kent, but primarily and mainly to the dramatic purpose of the dramatist. As Raleigh says of Cordelia, "if she had been perfectly tender and tactful [which, except with her sisters, she elsewhere always is] there would have been no play." Also there would have been none, as we have already seen, had not Lear become so angry. For his wrath

later he has justification, particularly as we remember that he is a king
and a father in the older sense, with rights and privileges nowadays
lapsed or ignored. But he less and less insists on these. His pride and
wilfulness are broken, and he becomes, in the true meaning of the
phrase, as a little child; his reason totters, but his sympathies are
widened, his affections deepened. It is one of the beauties of the
tragedy that he changes; but not so far as from a vain or irascible
"despot" to the Lear we see with the Fool on the heath and with
Cordelia when he has recovered her. Such a change would not even
be psychology, and still less would it be that for coming about *within*
the play.[140]

. . . the dramatist's concern for emotional effect again asserts itself,
though at the expense of character; and is heightened by the aid of the
artifices of music. The violence and variety of the passions call for a
greater violence and variety of expression; and the orchestration that
Mr. Granville-Barker analyses is particularly fine and imposing. The
device of repetition and echoing that we have found in the other great
plays here takes a different form. The King's ravings, the Fool's bab-
blings, and Gloster's murmurings offer continual opportunities to recall the errors and griefs of the past, one's own and others', new and
old. In his feigned madness Edgar, as he whines,

> Through the sharp hawthorn blow the winds,

and, after an interval,

> Still through the hawthorn blows the cold wind,

is far better than any possible stage wind and tree. And instead of the
spaced recurrence of a *leitmotiv*, as here, and [141] in *Othello* and
Macbeth, there is frequently also, in Lear's outcries, an immediate, ham-
mering reiteration; as in

> O! let me not be mad, not mad, sweet heaven;
> Keep me in temper; I would not be mad.
> Hear, Nature, hear! dear goddess, hear!
> Howl, howl, howl, howl! O you are men of stones!
> Thou'lt come no more.
> Never, never, never, never, never.

And that is in keeping with the Titanic vehemence and impulsiveness
of the play. Now though in this there is not necessarily any damage to
character, certainly in the King's volcanic curses, apostrophes, and ravings the representative or mimetic function of dramatic art falls into
abeyance; and at similar cost, but still greater profit, emotional effect
is attained in the dénouement. There, indeed, the musical method is
less apparent than in the *finale* of *Othello* or *Macbeth*. Lear and Cordelia have entered as captives and been sent to prison—to death, as
the Queen (like the audience) expects, but, as the broken King imag-

ines, only to the henceforth uninterrupted happiness of her company. At this point, if ever, in the fitness and fullness of his speeches—

No, no, no, no. Come let's away to prison . . .

and

Upon such sacrifices, my Cordelia . .

drama and lyric meet and merge. Speeches to be spoken, they are all but to be sung. But the King and his daughter then departing, a digression ensues. Albany, on entering, properly requires the captives of Edmund, who answers evasively, in a way that should be alarming: yet, for two hundred and fifteen lines, the attention of everybody on [142] the stage is occupied by other issues, urgent enough, but to Albany and Edgar as nothing in comparison with the fate of Cordelia and Lear. As mere matter of fact the length of the delay makes little difference— Edmund's word to the captain had been "instantly," and of a tragic outcome we are anyway certain enough—but it makes great difference to our emotions. Of the danger we are four times incidentally reminded ere, Kent coming to bid his King and master aye good-night, Albany cries,

Great thing of us forgot!—

and all this, in order that we may be at the highest pitch of anxiety when Lear enters with Cordelia dead, in his arms. The postponement affords a climax, develops a crescendo. As it disposes of the less important issues, continually reminding us of the important, it throws the scene which follows into the high relief which its supreme momentousness demands. And thereby something of the same damage is done to the psychological integrity of Albany and Edgar as to that of Emilia and Banquo, figures alike ancillary and subordinate. Relief, however, is a sculptural expression; and it is of another art that we must be thinking, though of tragedy still, and foremost, as the old man totters in with his burden and his cry.

The climax is held—by another digression. The King, broken and exhausted, presently wanders. He boasts of killing the hangman; vaguely recognizing Kent, he bids him "welcome hither." Albany now, not (as is usual) at the end, takes order for the restoration of the state. But passion recoils. "O, see, see!" and with that piercing note tragedy again has sway:

And my poor fool is hang'd. No, no, no life! . . .[143]

1 J. Dover Wilson, *The Essential Shakespeare*, p. 120. . . .
2 *Ten More Plays of Shakespeare* (1913), pp. 206-7.[138]

John Middleton Murry

From *Shakespeare*. London: Jonathan Cape, 1936. By permission of the publishers.

[The play's] positive theme, as I understand it, is no less than the death of the Self and the birth of Divine Love. That comes to pass in Lear, through absolute isolation, through his becoming 'the thing itself,' through 'madness.'

But in the handling of the theme, I feel that Shakespeare was, if not perfunctory, uncertain. I could almost believe that Shakespeare was on the verge of madness himself when he wrote *King Lear*. . . . in *King Lear*, I find disturbance, hesitation, uncertainty, and a constant interruption of the 'predominant passion.' The major and the minor intensities are continually flagging. The imagination of the theme becomes perfunctory or strained, the imagination of the verse spasmodic. There is weariness, and a flagging of the invention.

It is one of the things which has become, by convention, impossible to say; but *King Lear* makes upon me the impression of the work of a Shakespeare who is out of his depth. He does not really know what he wants to say: perhaps he does not know whether he wants to say anything. One is conscious of the strange sexual undercurrent which disturbs the depths of his 'uncontrolled' [338] dramas—a terrible primitive revulsion against sex, or sexuality, which may have been natural to the imaginative man in the days when the ravages of venereal disease were a new thing in Western Europe. . . . It is some vast upsurge of the animal, destroying humanity, of which Shakespeare is apprehensive: a nonhuman welter of bestiality. . . .[339]

The distinction may be hard to establish objectively, but it is very real to me. It is indeed the difference between the tragic and the diseased vision of life; or again, it is the difference between a despair which engulfs the whole man, and a despair which some part of the man refuses to acknowledge. It seems to me that much of *King Lear* derives from an exaggeration, or exploitation of partial despair. It is a kind of enforced utterance, in a period when—from the ideal point of view—silence was more wholesome and more natural.

A poet of genius creates not how he should, but how he can. I am not saying that it would have been better if Shakespeare had not written *King Lear;* and I wish to safeguard myself in advance against a misinterpretation so preposterous. I am merely demurring to the almost inveterate habit of Shakespeare criticism with regard to the play, which is to represent it as the sublime and transcendent culmination of a 'tragic period.' It is not that, to my mind, at all. It does not belong to the same order as *Hamlet, Othello* and *Macbeth;* or as *Coriolanus* and *Antony and Cleopatra.* It is, in that sequence, an anomaly. Compared to them, it is lacking in imaginative control, it is lacking in poetic 'intensity.' It belongs rather to a group of plays—to which *Timon* and *Troilus* belong—which are the work of a man struggling with an obsession. Amongst these plays it is, indubitably, supreme; but it is with them that it belongs.[342]

Lear's final innocence is not that of a man who has experienced a spiritual revolution through suffering, but that of one who has suffered too much as well. That his final innocence is terrible and wonderful when it comes is beyond dispute. But it is no more than a flash. . . .[347]

To use my own terms, I find *King Lear* lacking in poetic spontaneity. I suspect that this is in the main due to the simple fact that he was attempting the impossible: or rather that he was working against his natural bent, *invita Minerva.* It was not in his natural method to compose a drama as he composed *King Lear.* . . . He was spurring his imagination, which in consequence was something less than imagination.[348]

⸸

Caroline F. E. Spurgeon

main image – human body + mind in anguished movement

From *Shakespeare's Imagery and What It Tells Us.* New York: The Macmillan Co., 1936. By permission of Cambridge University Press.

The intensity of feeling and emotion in *King Lear* and the sharpness of its focus are revealed by the fact that in Shakespeare's imagination there runs throughout only one overpowering and dominating continuous image. So compelling is this that even well-marked different and subsidiary images are pressed into its service, and used to augment and emphasise it.

In the play we are conscious all through of the atmosphere of buffeting, strain and strife, and, at moments, of bodily tension to the point of agony. So naturally does this flow from the circumstances of the drama and the mental sufferings of Lear, that we [338] scarcely realise how greatly this sensation in us is increased by the general "floating" image, kept constantly before us, chiefly by means of the verbs used, but also in metaphor, of a human body in anguished movement, tugged, wrenched, beaten, pierced, stung, scourged, dislocated, flayed, gashed, scalded, tortured and finally broken on the rack.

One can scarcely open a page of the play without being struck by these images and verbs, for every kind of bodily movement, generally involving pain, is used to express mental and abstract, as well as physical facts. I will name only a few of them. Lear, in his agonized remorse, pictures himself as a man *wrenched* and tortured by an "engine," beating at the gate (his head) that let his folly in. Goneril has power to *shake* his manhood; he complains that she has *struck* him with her tongue; the hot tears *break* from him; his heart, he says *will break into a hundred thousand flaws.* Albany wonders how far Goneril's eyes may *pierce.* Gloucester's *"flaw'd heart"* is cracked, and finally it *"burst* smilingly." Kent longs *to tread* Oswald into mortar, and in his heated description of the steward's character, he evokes images of rats *biting* cords, weathercocks *turning,* dogs *following* and geese being *driven.* *" 'Tis worse than murder,"* cries Lear, this *violent outrage* of putting Kent in the stocks, and his emotion on witnessing it *swells* and *climbs,* while the fool adds the picture of a man being dragged along by *holding on* when a great wheel *runs down hill,* and *letting go* only in time to save his *neck being broken.*

So also in scenes not directly concerned with Lear, such as Gloucester's conversations with Edmund, we find the same characteristic. When Edmund, having [339] roused his father's anger against the unwitting Edgar, desires to restrain him from immediate action until he has furnished further proof of the latter's wickedness, he words his argument thus: If you will suspend your indignation until you have "better testimony of his intent, you should *run a certain course;* where, if you *violently proceed against* him, mistaking his purpose, it would *make a great gap* in your own honour and *shake in pieces the heart* of his obedience!" And a little later, Gloucester being indeed shaken to the heart by Edmund's revelations, in the course of ten lines uses these verbs and nouns: *scourged, cools, falls off, divide, cracked, falls from bias, follow disquietly, mutinies, discord, machinations, hollowness, ruinous disorders.*

This use of verbs and images of bodily and generally anguished motion is almost continuous, and it is reinforced by similar words used in direct description, as in the treatment of Gloucester; he is *bound* to a chair, *plucked* by the beard, his hairs are *ravished* from his chin, he is *tied to a stake,* like a bear to *stand the course,* and with his eyes blinded and bleeding, he is *thrust out* of the gates to *smell his way* to Dover.

All through the play, the simplest abstract things are described in similar terms. Even in a scene, pleasant in itself, such as the gentleman's ornate but delightful description of Cordelia's reception of his news

(IV.iii.), this sense of bodily movement and strain is constant. The letters *pierced* her to a demonstration of grief, her passion

> most rebel-like
> Sought to be king o'er her; [IV.iii.15]

it *moved* her, patience and sorrow *strove,* she *heaved* the name of "father" *pantingly forth,* as if it *press'd her heart;* [340] she *shook* the tears from her eyes, and away she *started*

> To deal with grief alone. [IV.iii.33] [341]

✳

John W. Draper

From "The Occasion of *King Lear." Studies in Philology,* XXXIV (1937), 176-185. By permission of *Studies in Philology* and the author.

On the accession of the King in 1603, the company for which Shakespeare was the chief playwright had become the "King's Men"; and so Shakespeare, in effect, had commenced court dramatist; and, only a short time later, in *Macbeth,* he had celebrated the patriotic fervor and the timely popularity of the King that followed on the discovery of the Gunpowder Plot. Years before,[179] in the epilogue of *King Richard III,* he had emphasized the calamities that must arise from rival kings in England: surely, when this theme was paramount in the national consciousness, when the King himself had cited Chronicle history as evidence, a court dramatist, whose company must depend directly on the favor of their royal patron to protect them from the growing attacks of the Puritans—surely such a dramatist, endowed with the shrewdness and sagacity of William Shakespeare, might well develop this same theme in a play that showed the audience the miseries that such a division brought to the king, to the dynasty and so to the whole nation. Indeed, could any well-informed person of that time have seen *King Lear* and not considered it an *exemplum* most aptly fitted to the current situation?

The question of a divided, as opposed to a united, Britain is fundamental in the play. According to Holinshed, and obviously in Shakespeare, Lear is King of all Britain: the play refers to "a British man," the "British powers" as opposed to France, and the quarto of

1608 to the "British party." The dividing of Lear's realm is the first action depicted on the stage, and has every appearance of theatrical significance. At the very beginning of the initial scene, Kent and Gloucester are discussing this "division." After the old King has had his will and disinherited Cordelia, Kent objects, not only to this injustice, but to the whole "hideous rashness," and, according to the folio text, cries out, "Reserve thy state," and later, "Revoke thy gift": apparently, this honest counsellor objects to the division as such, and will risk his head to warn his master. Gloucester, likewise, is horrified that the King has "subscrib'd his power"; and the Fool, who is a sort of chorus, tells Lear with bitterness: "When thou clovest thy crown i' the middle, and gav'st away both parts, thou borest thy ass on thy back o'er the dirt. . . ." And he adds, "thou hast pared thy wit o'both sides, and left nothing i' the middle." The entire plot depends on this division of the kingdom: the quarrels of Goneril and Regan, the disasterous French invasion, the madness and death of Lear, and the distraction of the whole commonwealth that cannot but ensue. Chaos from conflict of authority is the very essence of the play. . . .[180]

The situation of Albany toward the end of the play illustrates the *impasse* to which events have come: he is against his wife because of her cruelties to Lear and Gloucester; but he is perforce also against Cordelia because she has brought a foreign army upon British soil. The skein is so entangled that death is the one way left.

Albany, indeed, has a unique significance in the drama. According to Shakespeare, Lear divided his kingdom into three, and then, after Cordelia's answer, he re-divided her share between the other two, thus leaving two parts in his final division of the realm. Since the island of Great Britain is long and rather narrow north and south, the lines of demarcation must have cut across it east and west, separating it, in the first division, into a southern, a middle, and a northern section. Cordelia's must have been the middle part; for it is later divided between the other two. Thus, in the final division, the two realms of Goneril and of Regan, must roughly have corresponded to England and to Scotland. The titles of the respective husbands bear this out, Cornwall and Albany. Cornwall in ancient times was more extensive than the modern shire; and Lear seems appropriately to have given to this Duke the [181] southern half of his dominions; for Cornwall's capital is the city of Gloucester in the south-central section of the island. Albany then, apparently received the northern half of Britain; and his title at the opening of the play suggests that he was already duke of ancient "Albany," the region north of the Firths of Clyde and Forth, including all the Scottish Highlands. Surely the Elizabethans had enough sense of their historical geography to recognize these names. In more recent times, the Dukedom of Albany dates from 1398; and Mary Queen of Scots in the sixteenth century re-created it in the person of Henry Stuart, Lord Darnley, whom she married. Thus when Shakespeare wrote *King*

Lear, there was a Duke of Albany, and that Duke was James I. Heraldry in the seventeenth century was much too practical and widely known a subject for Shakespeare's audience—at least the courtly part of it—not to guess at this relationship, just as they must have known that Banquo in *Macbeth* was James's reputed ancestor. Is it this glance at Shakespeare's royal patron that made the playwright change the Albany of Holinshed to a character consistently good and virtuous? Is this why, at the conclusion of the play, the distracted kingdom seems to be happily re-united under his sovereign power? At all events, a drama that contrasted England and Scotland separate and miserable over against a united Britain happy and prosperous, must have had a timely meaning; and a Duke of Albany, who after many trials, is apparently left at the end, benign and powerful, in sole possession, to "Rule in this realm and the gored state sustain"—this Duke of Albany was surely not a figure displeasing to the eyes of the contemporary holder of that name and title.[182]

$$\bigstar$$

Robert H. Darby

From "Astrology in Shakespeare's *Lear*." *English Studies*, XX (1938), 250-257. By permission.

In *King Lear*, as elsewhere, Shakespeare seems unconcerned with the more detailed trappings of the "science;" but despite the fact that astrology does not appear in the probable sources,[1] he devotes considerable space to a satirical attack on the popular belief in the system. . . .[251]

The astrologers . . . did but seldom enjoy the untroubled life they so frequently forecast for others: even in early times, skeptics attacked the validity of astral divination; in the Italian Renaissance, astrological belief was often associated with religious skepticism;[2] and, throughout the age of Elizabeth, the controversy still raged. . . .

In 1603, King James arrived in England as the *dux in nomine* of those who opposed judicial astrology: but conviction, not skepticism, motivated James' attack: for, although he allowed the "science" to be "one of the speciall members of the *Mathematicques*," yet he termed it the "Divels schoole". . . .[252]

King James was Satan's "greatest enemy . . . in the world;" [3] and . . . his ideas on witchcraft and astrology were widely known.[4] . . . King James was emphatic in his condemnation of astrology; and his accession to the throne of England meant a marked quickening, on the part of English writers, of interest in witches, demons, and the stars.

Shakespeare definitely and directly employs astrological terms some eighty times; and even more numerous are the implied allusions. Thirty-seven such passages occur in the works generally dated prior to 1600: fifteen, from 1600 to *King Lear;* and, in the play itself, six. . . .[253]

King Lear believes in astrology. Although he swears by various pagan gods, by "the mysteries of Hecate, and the night," yet he reinforces this most pregnant oath "by all the operation of the orbs From whom we do exist and cease to be." Like Edmund, he invokes the goddess "Nature;" similarly, he finds himself betrayed; and the "wrathful skies" of the storm through which he passes—and which he imputes to the power of the "great gods"—would seem to indicate a sort of meteorological astral phenomenon like that in *Julius Caesar* when the dictator is about to be assassinated. Practically all of his followers, moreover, appear to be in accord with Lear's astrological leanings. The faithful Kent, who alone dares oppose the sovereign will, tempers his audacity by likening Lear to some auspicious star; he refers to kings and potentates as "throned and set high" by "their great stars"; and, in speaking of Lear's three daughters, he declares:

It is the stars,
The stars above us, govern our conditions:
Else one self mate and mate could not beget
Such different issues.

Edgar also believes in some system of divine retribution, though perhaps not definitely astrological; in his Tom o' Bedlam disguise, he displays a certain degree of familiarity with the charms of black magic which, according to James I, so often accompanied judicial astrology; and Gloucester readily believes the story of his son's wicked machinations, of "conjuring the moon To stand auspicious mistress." Gloucester, indeed, is thoroughly steeped in astrological lore; and he emphatically voices the popular belief [in Act I, scene ii]. . . .[254]

Most critics concede that *King Lear* probably appeared shortly after the accession of James I; [5] and an examination of the treatment of astrological phenomena would seem to indicate a studied attempt to compliment the king: for, although Shakespeare in his earlier works somewhat reflects the current astrological debate, yet he subjects the pseudoscience to no serious attack; but, in *King Lear,* his attitude changes: here he portrays astrology as a vehicle of villainy in the hands of the profane; and, even to its true believers, a false and traitorous guide. King Lear, notwithstanding his faith in the stars, lives only to lose all faith; his loyal followers, Gloucester, Edgar and Kent, likewise suffer in their sovereign's astrological disaster; and the iconoclast, Edmund, in his downward career, renounces his skepticism for the scant comfort of an utter submission to his fate. Albany alone, of all the major characters, appears to ignore the heavenly signs; and Albany seems to represent King James himself.[6] In an age when artistic expression so generally reflected the ideology of the great and the near-great, the designation of Shakespeare's company as "the King's Men" might in itself be sufficient to warrant a search, in the works of the poet, for the influence of the patron's known opinions and ideals; and especially in a period such as that of 1603-4, in which the plague closed the public theaters most of the time, and in which most of the plays written must therefore have been calculated expressly for court performance, the influence of the courtly taste would appear to be a foregone conclusion. . . .[256]

1 See *The Tragedy of King Lear*, Furness Variorum edition.
2 J. Burckhardt, *Civilization of the Renaissance in Italy*, tr. Middlemore, Vienna, s-d., 6.[252]
3 *Newes from Scotland declaring the Damnable Life and Death of Doctor Fian, a notable Sorcerer* (1591), ed. Harrison, London, 1924, 15.
4 Cf. George Lyman Kittredge, *Witchcraft in Old and New England*, Cambridge [Mass.], 1929, Chapter XVII.[253]
5 See John W. Draper, "The Occasion of *King Lear*," *Studies in Philology*, XXXIV, 2 (April 1937), 176-185.
6 *Ibid.*, 181-182.[256]

✠

Theodore Spencer

From *Shakespeare and the Nature of Man.*
New York: The Macmillan Co., 1942. By
permission of the publisher.

The *unnaturalness* of Goneril and Regan is what Lear cannot bear, as Gloucester cannot understand the apparent unnaturalness of Edgar, and Lear's daughters are fittingly described in those animal images—tigers, wolves, vultures, serpents—which are, as Bradley observes, scattered everywhere through the play.[1] [142]

The unnaturalness, the upsetting of order, which is illustrated by the fact that Goneril and Regan, the children, are dominating Lear, the father, is re-inforced by one of the chief themes which run through the apparently irrelevant speeches and songs of the Fool. The fact is another illustration of how one character or *motif* re-inforces the others. For the Fool is continually referring to things that are upside-down or backside-foremost, or out of the natural order, as things are in Lear's erstwhile kingdom. He says to Lear that, when he divided his realm, "thou borest thine ass on thy back o'er the dirt" (i.4.176); he sings of the cuckoo that bit off the head of its fosterparent (i.4.238); he speaks of the cart drawing the horse (i.4.246); his songs are often a comment on the main situation:

> The man that makes his toe
> What he his heart should make,
> Shall of a corn cry woe,
> And turn his sleep to wake. (iii.2.31)

Such a false sense of values as this is obviously a reflection of Lear's action toward his daughters; Lear, like the man in the song, had mistaken the non-essential for the essential.

Goneril and Regan not only violate natural law by their behavior to their father, they also violate their proper functions as human beings by their lust for Edmund, a lust which ends in murder and suicide, and which makes the description of them as animals doubly appropriate. One violation leads to another.[143]

Man's relation to the gods, the forces that should order him supernaturally, is as much emphasized as his relation to the state that should order him politically and the self-control by reason that should order his own nature. In fact Shakespeare seems in this play deliberately to use the way a man thinks of the gods as an indication of character. All the characters with whom we are meant to sympathize— Lear, Gloucester, Edgar, Kent and Albany—continually appeal to the gods, and in their different ways think of human affairs as controlled by supernatural power. The bad characters, particularly Edmund . . . , are incorrigible individualists and egoists.

Shakespeare emphasizes the distinction as early in the play as he can, in the conversation between Gloucester and Edmund in the second scene of the first act. Gloucester sees everything as [146] conditioned by the heavens, and all the right thinking people in Shakespeare's audience would have agreed with him. But when he leaves the stage, Edmund illustrates the villainy of his own nature, his cynical disregard of correspondences and inter-relations, by taking the opposite point of view from that of his father. . . . Later in the play Kent, an invariably "good" character, directly contradicts this attitude: "It is the stars," he says, "the stars above us, govern our conditions." The contrast is clear throughout.[147]

1 *Shakespearean Tragedy,* p. 266. Shakespeare uses the word "unnatural" 37 times in all his plays; one fifth of these uses is in *Lear.* It is also interesting to note, from a study of the Concordance, that the word "nature" is used a great deal more in the plays written between 1601 and 1608 than in any others—40% of the uses occur in 22% of the plays. It occurs most frequently in *Lear:* 40 times. . . .[142]

–)+(–

Benjamin T. Spencer

From *"King Lear:* A Prophetic Tragedy." *College English,* V (1944), 302-308. By permission.

Lear has further shortcomings, of course; but they are not so basic as his assumption that his "dear goddess nature," has predisposed men to altruism and social justice. His obvious preference for Cordelia, his repeated shows of affection toward her, the "unconstant starts" and "infirmity of his age," all explain, though they do not justify, the treatment that Goneril and Regan are immediately inclined to accord him. They are secondary and symptomatic frailties, not radical defects of character. Yet one other of his tragic weaknesses is pertinent here: his identification of the humane with "all the large effects That troop with majesty." It is the identification which a hundred years ago Thoreau saw insinuating itself into the mind of Western civilization and which he protested as enervating a healthy society. Before the purgatorial heath scenes Lear argues with Goneril that man's life is distinguished from beasts by just such privileges as having a superfluous number of retainers: "allow not nature more than nature needs, Man's life is cheap as beast's." Yet linked to this insistence is a blind indifference to the sufferings of others who lack the bare necessities of life. Somewhat paradoxically, perhaps, after he has seen "unaccommodated man" in his "loop'd and window'd raggedness," Lear is increasingly concerned that the vagabond wretches share in a richness in which he is decreasingly interested. Having shifted his own standard of the humane to an inner quality of mind, he is more generous with external goods. Repentant Gloucester likewise declaims against all "superfluous and lust-dieted" men. . . .[304]

–)+(–

George R. Kernodle

From "The Symphonic Form of *King Lear*."
*Elizabethan Studies and other Essays in Honor
of George F. Reynolds.* Boulder, 1945. Pp.
185-191.

More important in giving a twofold structure to the play than the
balance of Cornwall against Albany is the compact and bold outline of
Part One. From Act I, Scene iii (after the twofold overture), through
Act III, the first part forms a single rising action. It in turn is divided
into two movements, reaching one climax with the thrusting out of
Lear at the end of Act II and another with the thrusting out of Glouces-
ter at the end of Act III. It is a structure of mounting tension, built
by alternation of instruments, contrasts, and counter-movement. From
the time Goneril sets Oswald, the extreme sycophant, on to oppose
Lear, and Lear accepts Kent, the extreme honest man, the fight is on.
The tension begun by Oswald and Kent reaches its first peak with
Lear denouncing Goneril and departing for Regan. Again the minor
instruments take up the theme. Cornwall and Kent confront each other.
There is a quiet moment while Kent reads Cordelia's letter and Edgar
appears in disguise. Then it is time to bring on the main instruments—
Lear facing both Goneril and Regan. The conflict mounts. As he turns
from one to the other, they close in on him. With shorter and shorter
speeches and the staccato repetition of the word *need,* they drive him
to the breaking point. His long impassioned protest at being stripped
of all that makes man better than beast is a full musical arrival—a
recapitulation of the themes of unnatural daughters and the terrors of
the earth. The storm of his anger and madness is taken up by the full
orchestra of backstage thunder, wind, and tempest.[188]

The wicked daughters have triumphed over Lear, but Gloucester
is still to be dealt with. In the third act the rising scenes of Edmund
and Cornwall, leading to the blinding of Gloucester, continue the pattern of the first part and tie together Acts II and III. Act III has an
even more interesting structure than the earlier scenes of Part One—a
structure built on the contrapuntal balance between the three scenes of
Edmund and Cornwall that rise to a terrific climax and the three scenes
of Lear in the storm that start at a climax and get progressively quieter.
When the first scene of Act III has built the storm to a peak, Lear is
brought on, the tempest within equal to that without. The second
tempest scene, Scene iv, is a little quieter; the king is more contempla-
tive and is praying rather than defying the elements. Edgar comes on

with rhythmic incantations and snatches of song. Instead of the trumpet and cymbal of "Strike flat the thick rotundity o' the world," we have the woodwind effect of "Still through the hawthorn blows the cold wind." The third storm scene, Scene vi, is still more subdued: it is under cover, and the storm is in the distant background. After the trial of the joint-stools, the scene is lowered to a whisper, and Lear, exhausted, sleeps.

In contrast to this decrescendo, the alternate scenes—iii, v, and vii—form a bloody and violent crescendo, leading to the blinding of Gloucester, the wounding of Cornwall, and Regan's stabbing of the servant. The first two scenes, rather short, give contrast to the Lear scenes they follow and build up the plot, with Cornwall taking over from Edmund. It is the third, Scene vii, coming just after the Lear scenes have subsided, that carries this crescendo to its climax. Like the end of Act II, the staccato alternation of instruments, with the thrice-repeated "Wherefore to Dover?" leads up to a full musical statement. Gloucester's long speech corresponds to that of Lear at the end of Act II and, like that, is concerned with the theme of unnatural actions that make "man's life as cheap as beast's." Now man's life is lower than beast's. Gloucester's eyes are put out, and, like Lear at the end of Act II, he is thrust out of doors.[189]

$$\times\hspace{-0.5em}\mid\hspace{-0.5em}<$$

J. I. M. Stewart

From "The Blinding of Gloster." *Review of English Studies*, XXI (1945), 264-270. Reproduced by permission of the Clarendon Press, Oxford.

In *The Influence of the Audience on Shakespeare's Drama* Robert Bridges maintains that the blinding of Gloster upon the stage in the third act of *King Lear* notably instances the depraving effect of the playhouse public upon Shakespeare's art. Throughout the plays there is much that must have offended Shakespeare: the abundant obscenity, for example, and the foolish verbal trifling. These were surely imposed upon him by a coarse and stupid audience to whose solicitations he was amenable, and it is likely, therefore, that other of his artistic failures have their explanation here. A stupid audience will also be obtuse, and we must suppose that what seems horrible to us, and seemed hor-

rible to Shakespeare, was deliberately purveyed to these 'wretched beings' as a mere pleasant excitement. Gloster's agony is a 'concession'
made against the dramatist's better judgment.

But of Shakespeare's concessions to the audience there is another
view, summarily stated by Walter Raleigh in the year in which
Bridges's essay was first printed: [1]

> In nothing is Shakespeare's greatness more apparent than in his con-
> cessions to the requirements of the Elizabethan theatre, concessions made
> sparingly and with an ill grace by some of his contemporaries, by him offered
> with both hands, yet transmuted in the giving, so that what might have been
> a mere connivance in baseness becomes a miracle of expressive art.

Raleigh's words read like a vindication of Shakespeare against the
general indictment preferred by Bridges. Can they be felt at all to hold
in the particular instance of Gloster's blinding?

In *King Lear* there is an unusual amount of imagery drawn from
vision and the eyes . . .[264] the use, the abuse and the cheats of
vision are constantly prominent; and this . . . prompts us to apprehend a symbolism of sight and blindness having its culmination in
Gloster's tragedy. The leading significance here has been well pointed
out by Mr. Granville-Barker: [2]

> The larger dramatic value of a meeting between the mad Lear and blind
> Gloster it is surely hard to overrate. What could better point the transcendent
> issue Shakespeare has developed from the two old stories than this encounter
> of the sensual man robbed of his eyes with the wilful man, the light of his
> mind gone out?

Here is a depth in *King Lear* at which the blinding of Gloster, whether
to be represented or not, has appropriateness in the fable; and it is
perhaps worth distinguishing a further depth at which this is, if more
obscurely, so. There is something unmistakably atavic about the play.
. . . Shakespeare drives to his story's immemorial core in drama, and
projects the struggle in that extreme form in which, phylogenetically,
it still exists in the recesses of every human mind. The first anthropol-
ogist to approach *King Lear*—curiously enough, he seems not yet to
have arrived—when he observes how one paternal figure is deprived of
his possessions and wits, and another of his eyes, will certainly aver
that these incidents are symbolical as such things in dreams are symbolical: they veil an unconscious fantasy of the kind classically expressed in the myth of Uranus and Cronus. So at this level again—the
deeper level at which tragic drama tends to rehearse archetypal imaginative themes—Gloster's maiming is implicated with the play, cohering
with its primitive character as a whole and having a distinguishable relationship to yet more savage deprivations in analogous parent-and-
child stories.

We may feel, then, that Shakespeare turned to Sidney's story of the blinded Paphlagonian king both of intention and by radical dramatic instinct. . . .[265] Having seen both a conscious and an involuntary symbolical purpose expressed in the blinding can we go on to discover any aesthetic consideration which did in fact prompt Shakespeare to place it directly before his audience? And can we distinguish any particular reason he had for apprehending success from so drastic a show of violence?

The first of these questions is, of course, in part answered by a consideration of the dramatic structure. *King Lear* alone among the tragedies has two parallel plots, and this is a device of intensification. Two planes of torment, each with its own tempo, are built into the play. Lear's tragedy is progressive or incremental, and primarily spiritual; Gloster's tragedy is catastrophic, the blow coming in a single shattering frenzy of hate; and it is its awful physical finality that is at first predominant. The artistic purpose is clear enough: 'Gloucester is bound, and tortured, physically; and so the mind of Lear is impaled, crucified on the cross-beams of love and disillusion. . . . The Gloucester theme throughout reflects and emphasizes and exaggerates all the percurrent qualities of the Lear theme.' [3] Thus the single stroke of Gloster's blinding had to be set over against, and indeed overgo, the long torment, the progressive deprivations, of the old king. Somehow, and even at the play's pitch here in the third act, the thing had to be brought sharply home. No mere narration would stand out in the necessary relief. And so it was the stage or nothing.

This is, in a sense, a negative consideration: Shakespeare took the course he did because the alternative was ineffective. But we may, perhaps, add something positive by returning to the play's imagery and noticing its dominant character as described by Miss Caroline Spurgeon.[4] [Quotes passage pointing out bodily tension.] [266]

The blinding of Gloster represents a sort of crystallizing of this element of physical outrage which the imagery holds so massively in suspension throughout the play. For showing the blinding of Gloster there were reasons valid in drama; nevertheless considerations enough stood on the other side. Amid all this was there any overriding condition on which he might rest? Far in the future, again, the answer was to be given; and by one of the best of his readers.   *Keats*

On 19 December 1817, not very long after his twenty-second birthday, Keats saw Benjamin West's 'Death on the Pale Horse'; two days later he wrote to his brothers: *Quotation*

It is a wonderful picture, when West's age is considered; but there is nothing to be intense upon; no women one feels mad to kiss, no face swelling into reality—The excellence of every art is its intensity, capable of making

all disagreeables evaporate, from their being in close relationship with Beauty
and Truth. Examine 'King Lear,' and you will find this exemplified throughout; but in this picture we have unpleasantness without any momentous
depth of speculation excited, in which to bury its repulsiveness.

Is not this a true perception, which the flicker of immaturity in Keats's
response can by no means obscure? In *King Lear* Shakespeare contemplates his theme with intensity, and nowhere more so than in the
scene under notice. In Lear's family and in Gloster's the same passions
are operative,[267] and the twofold vision of intra-familial strife is terrible enough. Here the climax comes when Lear's daughters abandon
him to the storm and Edmund betrays his own father. But it is Regan
who plucks Gloster's beard and Cornwall who blinds him; it is Edmund who gives order for Lear's death. Such horrors broaden the
picture we must contemplate and make it more perplexing. For we are
aware that these new crimes are prompted by some extension or displacement of the unfilial passions already exhibited to us, and so we
obscurely apprehend that in the world about us the whole 'masse of
publique wrongs, Confusde and filde with murder and misdeeds,' is
but the overflow of evil from where it is most awful.

The blinding of Gloster . . . is, in fact, an eye-opener, and in
the issue 'a momentous depth of speculation is excited.' This sustains
something which under other conditions would be repulsive or intoler-
able. The quality of the poet's contemplation, the height of his argument: these enable him to reach far out into the territory of the hateful
and raise what he finds there to the level of the terrible and of his
tragedy.[268]

There is one condition which might falsify what is here advanced,
namely that the play is (what John Addington Symonds took it to be [5])
'a stony black despairing depth of voiceless and inexplicable agony';
that it was composed in a mood of overwhelming dejection in which
Shakespeare was capable of misusing his still splendid powers. But that
there is nothing of this in *King Lear*—which evidences, rather, a careful
craft in the service of a fine spiritual sanity—a noble essay on the play
has sufficiently shown.[6] In the only versions of the full story likely to
have been known to Shakespeare or his audience Cordelia is represented
as yielding to despair and taking her own life. This ending, which
would be unbearable in his play, Shakespeare rejects; and the text
shows him, moreover, going out of his way to ensure that his audience—
even the simpler or less attentive among them—shall be aware of this
departure from the familiar tale. The point is surely crucial. That Cordelia should to the last 'outfrown false Fortune's frown' elevates the
fable and enlarges the mind of the spectator; and this care of Shakespeare's to lead his audience up is hardly compatible with a willingness
to follow some brutal section down.[269]

1 *Shakespeare*, 1907, p. 27.[264]
2 *Prefaces to Shakespeare, First Series*, 1927, p. 179.[265]
3 G. Wilson Knight, *The Wheel of Fire*, 1930, pp. 186-8.
4 *Shakespeare's Imagery and What It Tells Us*, 1935, p. 338.[266]
5 *Shakspere's Predecessors in the English Drama*, 1884, p. 370.
6 R. W. Chambers, *King Lear*, 1940.[269]

$\times$

George Orwell

From "Lear, Tolstoy, and the Fool" in *Shooting an Elephant And Other Essays* by George Orwell, copyright 1945, 1946, 1949, 1950, by Sonia Brownell Orwell. Reprinted by permission of Harcourt, Brace and Company, Inc.

[Tolstoy's] examination of *King Lear* is not "impartial," as he twice claims. On the contrary, it is a prolonged exercise in misrepresentation. It is obvious that when you are summarizing *King Lear* for the benefit of someone who has not read it, you are not really being impartial if you introduce an important speech (Lear's speech when Cordelia is dead in his arms) in this manner: "Again begin Lear's awful ravings, at which one feels ashamed, as at unsuccessful jokes." And in a long series of instances Tolstoy slightly alters or colors the passages he is criticizing, always in such a way as to make the plot appear a little more complicated and improbable, or the language a little more exaggerated. For example, we are told that Lear "has no necessity or motive for his abdication," although his reason for abdicating (that he is old and wishes to retire from the cares of state) has been clearly indicated in the first scene. . . .[37]

. . . why did Tolstoy, with thirty or more plays to choose from, pick out *King Lear* as his especial target? . . . Is it not possible that he bore an especial enmity towards this particular play because he was aware, consciously or unconsciously, of the resemblance between Lear's story and his own? But it is better to approach this clue from the opposite direction—that is, by examining *Lear* itself, and the qualities in it that Tolstoy fails to mention.

One of the first things an English reader would notice in Tolstoy's pamphlet is that it hardly deals with Shakespeare as a poet. Shakespeare is treated as a dramatist, and in so far as his popularity is not spurious, it is held to be due to tricks of stagecraft which give good opportunities to clever actors. Now, so far as the English-speaking countries go, this is not true. Several of the plays which are most valued by lovers of Shakespeare (for instance, *Timon of Athens*) are seldom or never acted, while some of the most actable, such as *A Midsummer Night's Dream*, are the least admired. Those who care most for Shakespeare value him in the first place for his use of language,[38] the "verbal music" which even Bernard Shaw, another hostile critic, admits to be "irresistible." Tolstoy ignores this, and does not seem to realize that a poem may have a special value for those who speak the language in which it was written. However, even if one puts oneself in Tolstoy's place and tries to think of Shakespeare as a foreign poet it is still clear that there is something that Tolstoy has left out. Poetry, it seems, is *not* solely a matter of sound and association, and valueless outside its own language-group: otherwise, how is it that some poems, including poems written in dead languages, succeed in crossing frontiers? Clearly a lyric like "Tomorrow is Saint Valentine's Day" could not be satisfactorily translated, but in Shakespeare's major work there is something describable as poetry that can be separated from the words. Tolstoy is right in saying that *Lear* is not a very good play, as a play. It is too drawn-out and has too many characters and sub-plots. One wicked daughter would have been quite enough, and Edgar is a superfluous character: indeed it would probably be a better play if Gloucester and both his sons were eliminated. Nevertheless, something, a kind of pattern, or perhaps only an atmosphere, survives the complications and the *longueurs*. *Lear* can be imagined as a puppet show, a mime, a ballet, a series of pictures. Part of its poetry, perhaps the most essential part, is inherent in the story and is dependent neither on any particular set of words, nor on flesh-and-blood presentation.

Shut your eyes and think of *King Lear*, if possible without calling to mind any of the dialogue. What do you see? Here at any rate is what I see: a majestic old man in a long black robe, with flowing white hair and beard, a figure out of Blake's drawings (but also, curiously enough, rather like Tolstoy), wandering through a storm and cursing the heavens, in company with a Fool and a lunatic. Presently the scene shifts, and the old man, still cursing, still understanding nothing, is holding [39] a dead girl in his arms while the Fool dangles on a gallows somewhere in the background. This is the bare skeleton of the play, and even here Tolstoy wants to cut out most of what is essential. He objects to the storm, as being unnecessary, to the Fool, who in his eyes is simply a tedious nuisance and an excuse for making bad jokes, and to the death of Cordelia, which, as he sees it, robs the play of its moral. According to Tolstoy, the earlier play, *King Leir*, which Shakespeare adapted

terminates more naturally and more in accordance with the moral demands of the spectator. . . .

In other words the tragedy ought to have been a comedy, or perhaps a melodrama. It is doubtful whether the sense of tragedy is compatible with belief in God: at any rate, it is not compatible with disbelief in human dignity and with the kind of "moral demand" which feels cheated when virtue fails to triumph. A tragic situation exists precisely when virtue does *not* triumph but when it is still felt that man is nobler than the forces which destroy him. . . .[40] . . . In Tolstoy's impatience with the Fool one gets a glimpse of his deeper quarrel with Shakespeare. He objects, with some justification, to the raggedness of Shakespeare's plays, the irrelevancies, the incredible plots, the exaggerated language: but what at bottom he probably most dislikes is a sort of exuberance, a tendency to take—not so much a pleasure, as simply an interest in the actual process of life. It is a mistake to write Tolstoy off as a moralist attacking an artist. He never said that art, as such, is wicked or meaningless, nor did he even say that technical virtuosity is unimportant. But his main aim, in his later years, was to narrow the range of human consciousness. One's interests, one's points of attachment to the physical world and the day-to-day struggle, must be as few and not as many as possible. Literature must consist of parables, stripped of detail and almost independent of language. The parables—this is where Tolstoy differs from the average vulgar puritan —must themselves be works of art, but pleasure and curiosity must be excluded from them. Science, also, must be divorced from curiosity. The business of science, he says, is not to discover what happens but to teach men how they ought to live. So also with history and politics. Many problems (for example, the Dreyfus case) are simply not worth solving, and he is willing to leave them as loose ends. Indeed his whole theory of "crazes" or "epidemic suggestions," in which he lumps together such things as the Crusades and the Dutch passion of tulip growing, shows a willingness to regard many human activities as mere ant-like rushings to and fro, inexplicable and uninteresting. Clearly he could have no patience with a chaotic, detailed, discursive writer like Shakespeare. His reaction is that of an irritable old man who is being pestered by a noisy child. "Why do you keep jumping up and down like [41] that? Why can't you sit still like I do?" In a way the old man is in the right, but the trouble is that the child has a feeling in its limbs which the old man has lost. And if the old man knows of the existence of this feeling, the effect is merely to increase his irritation: he would make children senile, if he could. Tolstoy does not know, perhaps, just *what* he misses in Shakespeare, but he is aware that he misses something, and he is determined that others shall be deprived of it as well. By nature he was imperious as well as egotistical. Well after he was grown up he would still occasionally strike his servant in moments of anger, and somewhat later, according to his English biographer, Derrick Leon, he felt "a frequent desire upon the slenderest provocation to slap the faces of those with whom he disagreed." One does not necessarily get rid of that kind of temperament by undergoing religious conversion, and indeed it is obvious that the illusion of having been reborn may allow one's native vices to flourish more freely than ever, though perhaps in subtler forms. Tolstoy was capable of abjuring physical violence and of seeing what this implies, but he was not capable of tolerance or humility, and even if one knew nothing of his other writings, one could deduce his tendency towards spiritual bullying from this single pamphlet.

However, Tolstoy is not simply trying to rob others of a pleasure he does not share. He is doing that, but his quarrel with Shakespeare goes further. It is the quarrel between the religious and the humanist attitudes towards life. Here one comes back to the central theme of *King Lear*, which Tolstoy does not mention, although he sets forth the plot in some detail.[42]

. . . The subject of *Lear* is renunciation, and it is only by being wilfully blind that one can fail to understand what Shakespeare is saying.

Lear renounces his throne but expects everyone to continue treating him as a king. He does not see that if he surrenders power, other people will take advantage of his weakness: also that those who flatter him the most grossly: i.e. Regan and Goneril, are exactly the ones who will turn against him. The moment he finds that he can no longer make people obey him as he did before, he falls into a rage which Tolstoy describes [43] as "strange and unnatural," but which in fact is perfectly in character. In his madness and despair, he passes through two moods which again are natural enough in his circumstances, though in one of them it is probable that he is being used partly as a mouthpiece for Shakespeare's own opinions. One is the mood of disgust in which Lear repents, as it were, for having been a king, and grasps for the first time the rottenness of formal justice and vulgar morality. The other is a mood of impotent fury in which he wreaks imaginary revenges upon those who have wronged him. . . .

. . . the most impressive event in Tolstoy's life, as in Lear's, was a huge and gratuitous act of renunciation. In his old age he renounced his estate, his title and his copyrights, and made an attempt—a sincere attempt, though it was not successful—to escape from his privileged position and [44] live the life of a peasant. But the deeper resemblance lies in the fact that Tolstoy, like Lear, acted on mistaken motives and failed to get the results he had hoped for. According to Tolstoy, the aim of every human being is happiness, and happiness can only be attained by doing the will of God. But doing the will of God means casting off all earthly pleasures and ambitions, and living only for others. Ultimately, therefore, Tolstoy renounced the world under the expectation that this would make him happier. But if there is one thing certain about his later years, it is that he was *not* happy. On the contrary, he was driven almost to the edge of madness by the behavior of the people about him, who persecuted him precisely *because* of his renunciation. Like Lear, Tolstoy was not humble and not a good judge of character. He was inclined at moments to revert to the attitudes of an aristocrat, in spite of his peasant's blouse, and he even had two children whom he had believed in and who ultimately turned against him—though, of course, in a less sensational manner than Regan and Goneril. His exaggerated revulsion from sexuality was also distinctly similar to Lear's. . . .[45]

. . . what exactly is the moral of *Lear?* Evidently there are two morals, one explicit, the other implied in the story.

Shakespeare starts by assuming that to make yourself powerless is to invite an attack. This does not mean that *everyone* will turn against you (Kent and the Fool stand by Lear from first to last), but in all probability *someone* will. If you throw away your weapons, some less scrupulous person will pick them up. If you turn the other cheek, you will get a harder blow on it than you got on the first one. This does not always happen, but it is to be expected, and you ought not to complain if it does happen. The second blow is, so to speak, part of the act of turning the other cheek. First of all, therefore, there is the vulgar, common-sense moral drawn by the Fool: "Don't relinquish power, don't give away your lands." But there is also another moral. Shakespeare never utters it in so many words, and it does not very much matter whether he was fully aware of it. It is contained in the story, which after all, he made up, or altered to suit his purposes. It is: "Give away your lands if you want to, but don't expect to gain happiness by doing so. Probably you won't gain happiness. If you live for others, you must live *for others,* and not as a roundabout way of getting an advantage for yourself."

Obviously neither of these conclusions could have been pleasing to Tolstoy. The first of them expresses the ordinary,[46] belly-to-earth selfishness from which he was genuinely trying to escape. The other conflicts with his desire to eat his cake and have it—that is, to destroy his own egoism and by so doing to gain eternal life. Of course, *Lear* is not a sermon in favor of altruism. It merely points out the results of practising self-denial for selfish reasons. Shakespeare had a considerable streak of worldliness in him, and if he had been forced to take sides in his own play, his sympathies would probably have lain with the Fool. But at least he could see the whole issue and treat it at the level of tragedy. Vice is punished, but virtue is not rewarded. The morality of Shakespeare's later tragedies is not religious in the ordinary sense, and certainly is not Christian. Only two of them, *Hamlet* and *Othello,* are supposedly occurring inside the Christian era, and even in those, apart from the antics of the ghost in *Hamlet,* there is no indication of a "next world" where everything is to be put right.

All of these tragedies start out with the humanist assumption that life, although full of sorrow, is worth living, and that Man is a noble animal —a belief which Tolstoy in his old age did not share.

. . . If only, Tolstoy says in effect, we would stop breeding, fighting, struggling and enjoying, if we could get rid not only of our sins but of everything else that binds us to the [47] surface of the earth—including love, then the whole painful process would be over and the Kingdom of Heaven would arrive. But a normal human being does not want the Kingdom of Heaven: he wants life on earth to continue. This is not solely because he is "weak," "sinful" and anxious for a "good time." Most people get a fair amount of fun out of their lives, but on balance life is suffering, and only the very young or the very foolish imagine otherwise. Ultimately it is the Christian attitude which is self-interested and hedonistic, since the aim is always to get away from the painful struggle of earthly life and find eternal peace in some kind of Heaven or Nirvana. The humanist attitude is that the struggle must continue and that death is the price of life. "Men must endure Their going hence, even as their coming hither: Ripeness is all"—which is an un-Christian sentiment. Often there is a seeming truce between the humanist and the religious believer, but in fact their attitudes cannot be reconciled: one must choose between this world and the next. And the enormous majority of human beings, if they understood the issue, would choose this world. They do make that choice when they continue working, breeding and dying instead of crippling their faculties in the hope of obtaining a new lease of existence elsewhere.

We do not know a great deal about Shakespeare's religious beliefs. . . . at any rate he was not a saint or a would-be saint: he . . . is . . . noticeably cautious, not to say cowardly, in his manner of uttering unpopular opinions. Almost never does he put a subversive or sceptical remark into the mouth of a character likely to be [48] identified with himself. Throughout his plays the acute social critics, the people who are not taken in by accepted fallacies, are buffoons, villains, lunatics or persons who are shamming insanity or are in a state of violent hysteria. *Lear* is a play in which this tendency is particularly well marked. It contains a great deal of veiled social criticism—a point Tolstoy misses—but it is all uttered either by the Fool, by Edgar when he is pretending to be mad, or by Lear during his bouts of madness. In his sane moments Lear hardly ever makes an intelligent remark. . . .[49]

✝

Geoffrey L. Bickersteth

From "The Golden World of 'King Lear.' "
Proceedings of the British Academy, XXXII
(1946), 147-171. By permission.

. . . the medieval Church had . . . invented her own idea of the cosmic drama and given it expression in the cycle of miracle plays and, most conspicuously, in Dante's unique trilogy. But this was bound to take the form, not of tragedy, but of comedy. For the conflict it represented could not but end happily (except for the irretrievably wicked), since its hero, in the person of Christ, had, as a matter of historical fact—so the faithful believed—already defeated the villain once and for all by his victory on the cross. It was for this reason that the renaissance dramatists, Shakespeare included, when seeking to revive the art of tragedy, found nothing to their purpose in the religion, the philosophy, and the literature of Christianity, and therefore neglected it. They turned to pre-Christian sources of inspiration instead. . . . It followed that the type of character they took as the ideal of [164] tragic heroism was that endowed with the virtues of Roman Stoicism. Of these the most conspicuous was Patience, that is, the power of self-control shown in *suffering,* of putting up with the slings and arrows of outrageous fortune, and in *long-suffering,* or enduring with unbroken fortitude the pain inflicted by these, to the end. . . .

To exhibit a hero of this kind in his full splendour human life would have to be identified with its own long-suffering or patience of itself, symbolized dramatically in an actor not initiating action—note the paradox—but at all times, and always to his disadvantage, being acted upon, both from without and from within, since thus alone could he develop the virtue wherein precisely his heroism consists. His temperament, therefore, his age, and his social status must all be such as to make him by nature intolerant under affliction, a 'bad patient,' as the doctors say. . . . So long as he exists he endures and suffers without yielding to his own passionate inclination to rebel against his destiny or, rebellion proving vain, to seek escape in suicide. The beauty of a world so imagined would then no longer be felt to lie primarily in the vision of it as a moral cosmos automatically correcting by the operation of Nemesis its own internal anomalies with complete indifference to the claims, not of humanity (which, as the culprit, only gets what it deserves), but of individual human beings, to justice as justice is humanly understood. It would depend rather on the degree of suc-

cess with which the dramatist enables us to see in it the one and only
world ideally suited for engendering, developing, and perfecting the
supreme virtue of patience. . . .[165]

. . . if 'Nature' . . . be the first mighty word that tolls insistently
throughout the play, 'Patience' is no less emphatically the second, as
examples like the following show: 'Pray, Sir be *patient*' (Act I), 'I pray
you, Sir, take *patience*'—'I can be *patient*'—'you heavens give me that
patience, patience I need' (Act II), 'No, I will be the pattern of all
patience'—'Pour on, I will *endure*'—'Sir, where is the *patience* now/
That you so oft have boasted to retain?' (Act III), '*Patience* and sorrow
strove Who should express her goodliest'—'This world do I renounce
and, in your sights, Shake *patiently* my great affliction off'—'Bear free
and *patient* thoughts'—'Thou must be *patient;* we came hither crying'
—'You must *bear* with me' (Act IV), 'Men must *endure* Their going
hence, even as their coming thither'—'The wonder is he has *endured*
so long'—'The oldest hath *borne* most' (Act V). Plainly, then, from the
aesthetic point of view there can never be too *much* evil and consequently too *much* suffering in a world so imagined. Cordelias must die
in their innocence . . . since nothing short of this will test to the utter-
most the hero's patience, his power to endure even that extremity of
anguish without collapse. And Lear survives this final proof. At the
moment when, old though he is and afflicted as never before, he strides
on to the stage—I say 'strides,' for this is no occasion for realistic acting
—bearing lightly in his arms the symbol of all that has for him made
life worth living . . . we are overwhelmed with wonder—reduced to
awe-stricken silence by this majestic spectacle of man's 'unconquerable
mind.' [166]

✕

Harley Granville-Barker

From *Prefaces to Shakespeare*. Princeton, New
Jersey: Princeton University Press, 1946. By
permission of the publishers.

The scene in which Lear divides his kingdom is a magnificent
statement of a magnificent theme. It has a proper formality, and there
is a certain megalithic grandeur about it, Lear dominating it, that we
associate with Greek tragedy. Its probabilities are neither here nor
there. A dramatist may postulate any situation [271] he has the means
to interpret, if he will abide by the logic of it after.[272]

Shakespeare has . . . to carry us into strange regions of thought and passion, so he must, at the same time, hold us by familiar things. Lear, betrayed and helpless, at an end of his command of self or circumstance, is dramatically set above the tyranny and logic of both by being made one with the storm, and by his harmonizing with the homely fantasies of the Fool and the mad talk of Poor Tom, till his own "noble anger" breaks the bounds of reason too. Without some anchorage in simplicity, this action and these characters would range so wide that human interpretation could hardly compass them. Kent does something to keep the play's feet firm on the ground; Gloucester a little; the Fool was to Shakespeare's audience a familiar and sympathetic figure. But Lear himself might escape our closer sympathy were it not for his recurrent coming down from the heights to such moments as

> No, I will be the pattern of all patience;
> I will say nothing.

as

> My wits begin to turn.
> Come on, my boy. How dost, my boy? Art cold?
> I am cold myself. Where is this straw, my fellow?

as

> No, I will weep no more. In such a night
> To shut me out! Pour on, I will endure.
> In such a night as this!

or as

> Make no noise, make no noise; draw the curtains; so, so, so.
> We'll go to supper i' the morning; so, so, so.[280]

This final stroke, moreover, brings us to the simplest physical actualities; Lear's defiance of the elements has flickered down to a mock pulling of the curtains round his bed. Later, when he wanders witless and alone, his speech is broken into oracular fragments of rhapsody; but the play of thought is upon actuality and his hands are at play all the time with actual things; with the flower (is it?) he takes for a coin, with whatever serves for a bit of cheese, for his gauntlet, his hat, for the challenge thrust under Gloucester's blind eyes. Let us note, too, how one of the finest passages of poetry in the play, Edgar's imaginary tale of Dover cliff, consists of the clearest-cut actualities of description. And when Lear wakes to his right senses again, simplicity is added to simplicity in his feeling the pin's prick, in his remembering not his garments. The tragic beauty of his end is made more beautiful by his call for a looking-glass, his catching at the feather to put on Cordelia's lips, the undoing of the button. These things are the necessary balance to the magniloquence of the play's beginning and to the tragic splendor of the storm.[281]

. . . it would seem that for this massive fortress of pride which calls itself Lear, for any old man indeed of eighty and upwards, there could be no dramatic course but declension. Who would ever think of developing, of expanding, a character from such overwhelming beginnings? Yet this is what Shakespeare does, and finds a transcendent way to do it. So the actor's difficulty is that he must start upon a top note, at what must be pretty well the full physical stretch of his powers, yet have in reserve the means to a greater climax of another sort altogether. It is here, however, that the almost ritual formality of the first scene will help him. The occasion itself, the general subservience to Lear's tyranny (Kent's protest and Cordelia's resolution only emphasize this), Lear's own assertion of kingship as something not far from godhead, all combine to set him so above and apart from the rest that the very isolation will seem strength if the actor takes care to sustain it. There need be, there must be, no descent to petulance. Lear marking the map with his finger might be marking the land itself, so Olympian should he appear. The oath by the sacred radiance of the sun is one that only he may swear.[284]

He has doffed his kingship; free from its trappings, how the native genius of the man begins to show! It flashes on us as might the last outbursts of some near-extinct volcano. He is old and uncertain; but a mighty man, never a mere tyrant divested of power. He has genius, warped and random genius though it may be, and to madness, as will appear, very near allied. And Shakespeare's art lies in showing us this in nothing he does—for what he does now is foolish—but in every trivial thing that he is. All the action of the scene of the return from hunting, all his surroundings are staged to this end. The swift exchanges with the disguised Kent . . . his encounter with the pernickety jack-in-office Oswald, and with the frail, whimsical Fool who mockingly echoes his own [285] passionate whimsies; all this helps set in motion and sets off a new and livelier, a heartier Lear. Not that Shakespeare bates us one jot of the old man's stiff-necked perversities. He no more asks our sympathy on easy terms for him than will Lear yield an inch to Goneril's reasonable requests. A hundred useless knights about the house—even though, from their master's point of view, they were men of choice and rarest parts—must have been a burden. Lear's striking Oswald really was an outrage; after due complaint Goneril would doubtless have reproved his impertinence—for all that she had prompted it! Even with the petted Fool, and in the very midst of the petting, out there snaps

Take heed, sirrah, the whip!

We need look for no tractable virtues in him.[286] . . . This Lear is as quick on the uptake as it is his Fool's business to be. An unnatural quickness in an old man, is it, and some sign of a toppling brain! His silences are as pregnant. He listens and finds cheer in the Fool's chatter and song, throws him an answer or so to keep it alive, snarls now and then like an old lion if a sting goes too deep. Yet his thoughts, we can tell, are away. We must visualize this scene fully and accurately; the Fool caroling, his poor heart being heavy with Cordelia's loss he carols the more; the old king brooding; and Kent ever watchful, with a dog's eyes. Mark the effect of Goneril's appearance before her father, in purposed, sullen muteness; the Fool's speech points it for us, should we be unobservant; then her break into the prepared formality of verse, as this verse will seem, capping the loose prose of the scene and the Fool's rhyming. Mark, too, the cold kingliness of Lear's four words, all his response to her careful address:

> Are you our daughter?

He resorts to irony, the fine mind's weapon, which blunts itself upon the stupid—for Goneril is stupid, and she has stupidity's stubborn strength.[287]

If the play, with the invocation of the curse upon Goneril, entered an arena of anarchy and darkness, Lear himself is to pass now from personal grievance to the taking upon him, as great natures may, the imagined burden of the whole world's sorrow—and if his nature breaks under it, what wonder! And Shakespeare brings about this transition from malediction to martyrdom with great art, by contrivance direct and indirect, by strokes broad and subtle; nor ever—his art in this at its greatest—does he turn his Lear from a man into an ethical proposition.[289]

Lear's death, upon one ground or another, is artistically inevitable. Try to imagine his survival; no further argument will be needed. The death of Cordelia has been condemned as a wanton outrage upon our feelings and so as an aesthetic blot upon the play. But the dramatic mind that was working to the tune of

> As flies to wanton boys are we to the gods;
> They kill us for their sport.

was not likely to be swayed by sentiment. The tragic truth about life, to the Shakespeare that wrote King Lear, included its capricious cruelty. And what meeter sacrifice to this than Cordelia? Besides, as we have seen, he must provide this new Lear with a tragic determinant, since "the great rage . . . is kill'd in him," which precipitated catastrophe for the old Lear. And what but Cordelia's loss would suffice? [299]

. . . with regard to Goneril and Regan [Shakespeare] is quite content to assume—we shrink from the assumption nowadays—that there are really wicked people in the world. That admitted, these two exemplars of the fact are lifelike enough. Their aspect may be determined by the story's needs, but their significance does not end here; and, within the limits afforded them, they develop freely and naturally, each in her own way.

Likeness and difference are marked from the beginning. They are both realists. Their father wants smooth speech of them and they give it, echoing his very phrases and tones. They ignore Cordelia's reproaches; she is exiled and in disgrace, so they safely may. Left alone together (and the drop here from verse to prose seems to bring us with something of a bump to the plain truth about them), they are under no illusions at all, we find, about their own good fortune.

> he always loved our sister most; and with what poor
> judgment he hath now cast her off appears too grossly.

There are few things more unlovely than the passionless appraisement of evil and our profit in it. They are as wide-awake to the chances of trouble ahead; but while Regan would wait and see, Goneril means to go to meet it.

It will be a fatal error to present Cordelia as a meek saint. She has more than a touch of her father in her. She is as proud as he is, and as obstinate, for all her sweetness and her youth. And, being young, she answers uncalculatingly with pride to his pride even as later she answers with pity to his misery. To miss this likeness between the two is to miss Shakespeare's first important dramatic effect; the mighty old man and the frail child, confronted, and each unyielding.

> So young and so untender?
> So young, my lord, and true.

And they both have the right of it, after all. If age owes some tolerance to youth, it may be thought too that youth owes to age and fatherhood something more—and less—than the truth. But she has courage, has Cordelia, amazing courage. Princess though she be, it is no small matter to stand her ground before Lear, throned in the plenitude of his power, to stand up to him without effort, explanation or excuse. Nor does she wince at the penalty, nor to the end utter one pleading word. Nor, be it noted, does Kent, who is of her temper, ask pity for her. His chief concern is to warn Lear against his own folly and its consequences. It is her strength of mind he emphasizes and praises.

> The gods to their dear shelter take thee, maid,
> That justly think'st and hast most rightly said!

Nor would she, apparently, open her mouth again to her father but that she means her character shall be cleared. And even this approach to him is formal and uncompromising:

I yet beseech your majesty...

She does (Shakespeare keeps her human) slip in, as if it hardly mattered, a dozen words of vindication: [303]

> ...since what I well intend,
> I'll do't before I speak.

Yet, lest even that should seem weakness, she nullifies its effect for a finish. Nor does Lear respond, nor exonerate her except by a noncommittal growl. Still, she is not hard.

> The jewels of our father, with wash'd eyes
> Cordelia leaves you....

Shakespeare has provided in this encounter between Cordelia and Lear that prime necessity of drama, clash of character; that sharpest clash, moreover, of like in opposition to like. He has added wonder and beauty by setting these twin spirits in noble and contrasted habitations. Pride unchecked in Lear has grown monstrous and diseased with his years. In her youth it shows unspoiled, it is in flower. But it is the same pride.

The technical achievement in Shakespeare's staging of Cordelia is his gain of a maximum effect by a minimum of means. It is a triumph of what may be called "placing." The character itself has, to begin with, that vitality which positive virtues give. Cordelia is never in doubt about herself; she has no vagaries, she is what she is all circumstances apart, what she says seems to come new-minted from her mind, and our impression of her is as clean cut. Add to this her calm and steadfast isolation among the contending or subservient figures of that first scene—and the fact, of course, that from this very thrift of herself the broadcast violence of the play's whole action springs—then we see how, with but a reminder of her here and there, Shakespeare could trust to her reappearance after long delay, no jot of her importance nor of our interest in her bated.[304]

[Cordelia's]

> No cause, no cause!

when [Lear] would welcome her reproaches, is not at all the kindly, conventional, superior "Let's forget it" of the morally offended. It is but the complement of that "Nothing" which cost her a kingdom, and as true of her in its tenderness as the other was true. For the simple secret of Cordelia's nature is that she does not see things from the standpoint of her own gain or loss. She did not beg, she does not bargain. She can give as she could lose, keeping a quiet mind. It is no effort to her to love her father better than herself. Yet this supremest virtue, as we count it, is no gain to him; we must note this too. Her wisdom of heart showed her Regan and Goneril as they were; yet it was

an inarticulate wisdom and provoked evil in Lear, and could but hold
her bound in patience till the evil was purged. . . .[305]

[Kent] is another positive, absolute being; he, Lear and Cordelia
make a trinity of them. He has not Lear's perilous intellect nor Cordelia's peace of soul. His dominant quality is his unquestioning
courage; akin to this the selflessness which makes it as easy for him to
be silent as to speak. And he springs from Shakespeare's imagination
all complete; full-flavored and consistent from the first. Surer sign yet of
his author's certainty about him is the natural inconsistency of the
man as we see him. Through the first three acts there is never a stroke
in the drawing of Kent which is merely conventional, nor yet an uncertain one. But neither is there one which, however unexpected, need
perplex us. And for a small sign of Shakespeare's confidence in the
sufficiency of his creature, see the shrewd critical thrust which he lets
Cornwall have at him:

> This is some fellow,
> Who, having been praised for bluntness, doth affect
> A saucy roughness. . . .

Even though it be a Cornwall disparaging a Kent, the thrust is shrewd
enough for Shakespeare not to risk it unless he is confident that Kent's
credit with the audience is firm.[306]

Elizabethan acting did not inhabit the removed footlight-defended
stage of the theater of today, and all its technique and conventions and
the illusion it created differ appropriately in consequence; this is the
constant theme of these Prefaces, and must be of any study of the staging of Shakespeare plays. But certain effects, however gained, are common to all drama, certain problems recur. A problem in the writing
and acting of tragedy is the alternate creating and relaxing of emotional strain; the tenser the strain, the less long can an audience ap-
preciatively endure it. "Comic relief" has a crude sound; but, to some
degree and in some form or other, the thing it suggests is a necessity.
Greek tragedy had "choric relief"; emotion in the Greek theater was
magnified and rarefied at once, and sharp transitions were neither
wanted nor workable. Shakespeare had the constant shift of scene and
subject, usual in his theater, to help him; and his most strenuous
scenes, we may remark, tend to be short ones. We may suppose him
ever mindful of the difficulty of keeping the attention of a motley
audience fixed, but still alert; and in the body of a scene, if it needs
must be a long one, we shall always find what may be called "points of
rest and recovery."

But the problem can be stated in other terms. Tragedy, it may be
said, takes us out of ourselves; how else can it be enjoyed? A dash of
comedy will, by contrast, restore us to ourselves; yet, for the tragedy's

sake, the less conscious of the process we are the better. Here lay for Shakespeare, in this play, the histrionic value of the Fool. He wanted no comic relief in the crude sense; but this familiar stage figure, even though turned to tragic purpose, kept for that audience, if insensibly, its traditional hail-fellow quality. Only the dramatic and human value of the character is preserved us for today to the full. Of the effect of the snatches of song and rhyme, the lyric lightening of the epic strength of these scenes, we keep only the most manifest part. The things themselves are queer to us, and this is just what they should not be.[310]

Yet which of us must not feelingly protest that the Gloucester, who threads and fumbles his way so well-meaningly about the family battlefield his house is turned into (much against his will), is very harshly used indeed? Is this poetic justice? He does all that one who respects his superiors may do to save Kent from the ignominy of the stocks. He does his best to pacify Lear.

> I would have all well betwixt you.

How familiar is that heartfelt cry of the man who sees no sense in a quarrel! When he does take sides his reasons and his method are not heroic, it is true.

These injuries the king now bears will be revenged home; there is part of a power already footed; we must incline to the king. I will look to him and privily relieve him, go you and maintain talk with the duke, that my charity be not of him perceived. If he asks for me, I am ill and gone to bed.

No, truly, it is not heroic, when battle is joined, to be ill and go to bed. But caution is a sort of a virtue; and the keeping of a family foot in each camp has good sanction. Yet who can be altogether wise? In his next breath comes

> If I die for it, as no less is threatened me, the
> king, my old master, must be relieved.

And this his best impulse is his undoing. Unwittingly he is telling Edmund how best to betray him. He points the way; Edmund has but to follow it—just a little further. Irony deepens when later he calls upon Cornwall to spare him in the sacred name of that hospitality which, towards his king, he himself has so spinelessly betrayed. Yet, "tied to the stake," he can "stand the course" courageously enough; and he recovers self-respect in hopeless defiance of his tyrants. With just a little luck he need never have [315] lost it. Now he is blinded and turned helpless from his own doors. Is this poetic justice upon a gentleman, whose worst fault has been to play for safety, his worst blunder to think ill of a man without question and to believe a liar? Disquieting to think that it may be!

Edmund is, in wickedness, half-brother to Iago. Having no such great nature as Othello's to work on, Shakespeare has no need of such transcendent villainy; and he lessens and vulgarizes his man by giving him one of those excuses for foul play against the world which a knave likes to find as a point of departure. His first soliloquy is a complete enough disclosure. The fine flourish of

> Thou, Nature, art my goddess. . . .

(finer by its surprise for us in the mouth of the modest young man of the earlier scene), and the magnificent rejection of conventional morality narrow to their objective in

> Well, then,
> Legitimate Edgar, I must have your land.

And from this firm businesslike basis Edmund, except for pure pose, never soars again. The later

> This is the excellent foppery of the world. . . .

is enjoyable argument doubtless, and doubtless he chuckles over it. There is a sporting and imaginative touch, perhaps, in the trick that finally gets rid of Edgar; the stabbing his own arm, we feel, is to his credit. But for the rest, a strict attention to business, and a quick eye to one main chance after the other, suffice him. And this, really, is almost the loathliest thing about the man. He not only betrays his father to Cornwall, but he cants about loyalty the while. He accepts the attentions of Regan and Goneril without surprise or embarrassment (he is a handsome young fellow and he knows it), calculates which will be the more desirable connection, but will leave Goneril to get rid of her husband alone [316] if that risky task has to be undertaken. It even passes through his mind that she herself—if not Regan—may in her turn have to be "put away". . . .[317]

Edgar is a "slow starter" and shows no promise at all as a hero. . . .[318] What are the steps by which he passes from nobody to somebody?

His very reserve at the beginning can give him a stamp of distinction, and should be made to do so. And the notion of that strange disguise would not come, we may say, to a commonplace man. Through the ravings of Poor Tom we can detect something of the mind of Edgar with its misprision of the sensual life—of his father's life, is it? We can certainly see his pitiful heart; this Shakespeare stresses. But only in the soliloquies that end Act III, Scene vi, and begin Act IV do we discover the full mind of the man. . . .[319] . . . Edgar's philosophy of indifference to fortune, of patience with life itself, of the good comfort of fellowship, is now, certainly, to dominate the play. . . .[320]

A modern audience must lose almost as much of the flavor of Oswald as of the Fool; and more still must be lost if he is stripped of his doublet and hose, forbidden his swagger and his curtseys and thrust back into the dark ages. We cannot be expected to cheer—as I doubt not Shakespeare's audience did—when Kent breaks out with

> That such a slave as this should wear a sword,
> Who wears no honesty!

nor to take the precise point of Lear's

> How now, where's that mongrel?

that newfangled fellow, neither gentleman nor plain servant, mimicking the manners of the one, doing dirtier work than the other. Kent sizes him up when he dresses him down, with enjoyable completeness; so does Lear, later, in a dozen words: [324]

> This is a slave, whose easy-borrowed pride
> Dwells in the fickle grace of her he follows.

So does Edgar, having rid the world of him, as

> a serviceable villain;
> As duteous to the vices of thy mistress
> As badness would desire.

Oswalds have existed in every age and been good game for abuse, but the London of Shakespeare's day had evidently produced an unusually fine crop of them. . . .[325]

Johnstone Parr

From "Edmund's Nativity in *King Lear.*" *Shakespeare Association Bulletin,* XXI (1946), 181-185. By permission of the *Shakespeare Quarterly.*

The only natal horoscope in Shakspere's plays which has any "technical" significance is Edmund's nativity in *King Lear.* Nonchalantly and scoffingly Edmund tells us:

My father compounded with my mother under the dragon's tail, and my nativity was under Ursa major; so that it follows I am rough and lecherous. Tut, I should have been that I am had the maidenliest star in the firmament twinkled on my bastardizing.

We need not dwell upon that item in the horoscope known as the Dragon's Tail; many editors have noted its sinister influence. But Edmund's statement that his "nativity was under Ursa major" and the conclusion that this configuration supposedly made him "rough and lecherous" has been ignored by all critics of the play.

Ursa Major (known also as the Great Bear or the Big Dipper) is a group of fixed stars north of the zodiac whose astrological nature was reckoned as that of the planets Mars and Venus, with Mars predominating. Claudius Ptolemy, undoubtedly in the Renaissance the supreme authority in astrological matters, writes:

The constellations north of the zodiac have their respective influences, analogous to those of the planets, . . . *Ursa Major* is like Mars, but the nebula under the tail resembles . . . Venus in its influence.[1]

If we consult the works of the astrological authorities, we discover that these two planets which governed Ursa Major produced a character remarkably similar to that of Edmund.

Richard Saunders, in a huge compendium which reports a host of Renaissance physiognomists and astrologers, specifically calls the Martial man "rough." Says he

Those who are born Martial and under Aries are red or flaxen hair'd, a rough sort of people, rude and invincible; . . .[2]

Cornelius Agrippa describes the Martial man similarly: "A sour, fierce, cruel, angry, rough countenance and gesture [181] are ascribed to Mars." [3] And Ptolemy would ascribe many particulars of Edmund's character to the dominant influence of the War-planet:

Mars alone having dominion of the mind, and placed with glory makes men . . . irascible, warlike, versatile, powerful in intellect, daring, bold, . . . obstinate, . . . self-confident, contemptuous, . . . tyrannical, . . . , but, posited ingloriously, he makes men cruel, mischievous, sanguinary, tumultuous, . . . rapacious, pitiless, familiar with crime, restless, . . . hostile to their families, and infidels in religion.[4]

As we have seen, the constellation of Ursa Major exerted the *combined* influences of Mars and Venus. The astrologers do not leave us in doubt as to the dispensations of such a configuration. Ptolemy continues:

Should Mars be conciliated with Venus, and . . . if he have an inglorious position when thus conciliated, he makes men overbearing, lascivious, sordid, opprobrious, adultrous, mischievous, liars, fabricators of deceit, cheats of their own families as well as others, eager in desire, . . . debauchers of wives and virgins, daring, impetuous, ungovernable, treacherous, faithless, dangerous, . . .[5]

And Albohazen Haly, chief representative of the Arabian astrologers, agrees. . . .[182]

. . . the astrological authorities would presage that one born under the influence of Ursa Major would be "rough and lecherous," and destined to become a villain of the first order.

Now Edmund's career shows him to be in large measure the living embodiment of astral influences exerted by the malignant constellation of Ursa Major. He is recognized immediately as the villain of the play after his first soliloquy, in which he informs us of his religious infidelity, his audacious independence, and his "invention" whereby he shall dupe his legitimate brother out of the latter's inheritance. As he pursues his plan of maliciously playing upon Gloster's credulity, we see Edmund's scoffing and contentious attitude toward his old father's belief that the recent eclipses portend no good for the kingdom. His complete independence, egotism, and religious infidelity are seen again in his belittling remarks about astrology, a science in which Lear, Kent, and Gloster all had faith.[6] His treachery and his martial lack of sympathy are fully exhibited by his deliberate betrayal of his father into the hands of those who pluck out the old man's eyes and send him stumbling off to Dover. His skill in devising deceits and frauds is well attested by the manner in which . . . he dupes both Gloster and Edgar. But he is no coward; indeed, he possesses an unusual amount of military prowess, valor, courage, and strength of will. It is he who leads the "powers" of Albany and Regan, wins the battle against the invading French army, gives orders as to what should be done with the captives. He is bold enough to defy Albany and courageous enough to accept at once the challenge from Edgar. Doubtless the predominance of Mars in his nativity is responsible for such martial—such "rough"— qualities. For Edmund is, like the Martial man, a purposeful adventurer—determined to seize first his brother's possessions and then (through deceitful and unscrupulous conciliation [183] with Goneril or Regan) the crown. Also like the Martial man (to use Professor Bradley's phrasing), "he regards men and women, with their virtues and vices, together with the bonds of kinship, friendship, or allegiance, merely as hindrances or helps to his end." [7]

The planet Venus asserts her influence in Edmund's nature also, for there is no question but that he is (as Shakspere tells us) "lecherous." We learn of Edmund's adulterous proclivities when he accompanies Goneril from Gloster's castle to her own. And it is not long thereafter that we find Regan suspicious of his having been abed with sister Goneril. Such amorous depravity is indeed the sort attributed to the influence of Venus in conjunction with Mars; and to this astral configuration might also be attributed Edmund's nonchalance and faithlessness behind his frank confession:

To both these sisters have I sworn my love;

. . . .

Which of them shall I take?
Both? one? or neither?

At all events, an Elizabethan audience who perceived that Edmund was born under the "rough and lecherous" constellation of Ursa Major would have strongly suspected him sooner or later to "compound" with such women of the play as were assailable.

So, it seems to me, did Edmund appear to an Elizabethan audience: a Martial man with strong Venerian proclivities, because of the predominance of Ursa Major in his natal horoscope. And if this evil configuration appeared to the Elizabethans in any measure responsible for Edmund's preoccupation with fraud, deceit, perjury, contemptuousness, religious infidelity, and lechery, perhaps we need no longer wonder with Professor Bradley why it is that "a man so young as Edmund can have a nature so bad." [8] [184]

---

[1] *Tetrabiblos sive Quadripartitum*, Trans. J. M. Ashmand (London, 1822; Chicago, 1936). Bk.I, ch.x. Numerous editions of Ptolemy's *Quadripartitum* were published in the sixteenth century: in 1533, 1535, 1541, 1552, 1554, etc.

[2] *Physiognomie, Chiromantie, Metoposcopie* (London: 1653), p. 157. At the beginning of this work, Saunders lists almost two hundred authors as his authorities.

[3] Henry Cornelius Agrippa von Nettesheim, *De occulta philosophia*, or *Three Books of Occult Philosophy or Magic*, ed. W. F. Whitehead (New York, 1897), Bk.1, ch.lii, p. 156.

[4] Ptolemy, *op cit.*, Bk.III, ch.xviii. Similar statements may be found in Claudius Dariot's *A Briefe ... Introduction to the Astrological Judgement of the Starres*, trans. Fabian Withers (London, 1583, 1591, 1598), sig.D3r; John Indagine's *Briefe Introductions unto ... Natural Astrology*, trans. Fabian Withers (London, 1575, 1598), sigs. Plv, P2r; Augier Ferrier's *A Learned Astronomical Discourse of the Judgement of Nativities*, trans. Thomas Kelway (London, 1593), p. 14; and many others. (Copies I used are those in the Folger Shakespeare Library.)

[5] Ptolemy, *loc. cit.*

[6] *Cf.* Hardin Craig, "The Ethics of *King Lear*," PQ, IV (1925), 97-109, and his *Shakespeare* (New York, 1932), p. 851; Professor Craig maintains that "Edmund's denial of planetary influence must be set down as a sort of religious infidelity."

[7] A. C. Bradley, *Shakespearean Tragedy*, p. 301.

[8] Bradley, *op. cit.*, p. 301. [185]

✕

John Crowe Ransom

From "On Shakespeare's Language." *Sewanee Review*, LV (1947), 181-198. By permission of Alfred A. Knopf, Inc.

When Lear finds his Fool beside him in the storm, his thought suddenly turns from his own sufferings to the plight of the poor. It is a kingly thought, and leads him to apostrophize privilege everywhere:

> O, I have ta'en
> Too little thought of this. Take physic, pomp;
> Expose thyself to feel what wretches feel,
> That thou mayst shake the superflux to them
> And show the heavens more just.

There is a slight flurry of latinity in the *physic, pomp, expose*. But the key to the passage is *superflux*, a word that nobody had [186] used till now, and, to tell the truth, a word that even this usage did not fix securely in the language. It would mean overflow; in Schlegel the German is *das Überflüssige*. I judge that we all are reminded more or less consciously of Lazarus begging for the crumbs which fall—without being noticed because there is so much food—from the rich man's table. But I believe we should balk at speaking of them as an overflow. We are prepared to accept a bolder metaphor in the Latin than we can take in the English. Especially striking is the collocation of *shake* and *superflux*. All we can think of really shaking to the poor in this connection would be the tablecloth holding the surplus crumbs; which would not exactly be flowing. The whole image receives more notice and not less from our having these literal difficulties with it.[187]

>✠

R. C. Bald

From " 'Thou, Nature, Art My Goddess':
Edmund and Renaissance Free-Thought."
J. Q. Adams Memorial Studies. Washington,
1948. Pp. 337-349. By permission of the Folger
Shakespeare Library.

[Edmund's invocation to nature reflects opinions which an Elizabethan audience would have] regarded as heterodox and subversive.
. . . Edmund's words, therefore, which are spoken on the first occasion
on which he is alone and has an opportunity to reveal himself to the
audience, were deliberately intended to shock and startle. They proclaim him at once as an extreme and dangerous individualist who
scorns the conventional restraints and for whom the ordinary bonds of
society and morality have no meaning. The evil in Goneril and Regan,
gradually revealed as the play progresses, seems, though equally a violation of the bond between child and parent, to be instinctive and unreasoned. Edmund's, on the other hand, is from the outset calculated
and reasoned; anarchy is his creed.

Another manifestation of Edmund's individualism, which occurs
a little later in the same scene as his invocation of nature, is to be
found in his contemptuous rejection of his father's appeal to astrology.
Once again he is alone on the stage, and there can be no question that
his words represent his real thoughts:

This is an excellent foppery of the world, that when we are sick in fortune
—often the surfeit of our own behavior—we make guilty of our disasters the
sun, the moon, and the stars. . . .

Such sentiments find so ready an endorsement in the modern mind
that one scarcely stops to examine them or consider them in relation to
the speaker and the situation. Yet it is far from certain that these lines
represent Shakespeare's own attitude. It is true that Shakespeare puts
similar words into the mouths of some of his other characters; one
immediately calls to mind

> The fault, dear Brutus, is not in the stars
> But in ourselves, that we are underlings,[347]

and, from a very similar context,

Virtue, a fig! 'Tis in ourselves that we are thus or thus. Our bodies are our
gardens, to which our wills are gardeners . . . either to have it sterile with

idleness, or manured with industry; why, the power and corrigible authority of this lies in our wills.

But Cassius in the act of inveigling Brutus to join the conspiracy against Caesar and Iago subverting the feeble Roderigo to his purpose can scarcely be reckoned as the safest exponents of moral principles. Why is it that only Shakespeare's villains and conspirators express such ideas?

It is self-evident that the presentation of an idea by a speaker in a drama, particularly in one of Shakespeare's, must always be considered in relation to its context. . . .

The leading authority on Elizabethan astrology, Professor D. C. Allen, concludes that very few of the literary men of the period rejected it altogether; the weight of tradition was too strong. It was difficult to escape the feeling that the stars must have some influence on the characters and actions of human beings, but most intelligent men had a very natural distrust of the professional astrologer and almanac-maker, and probably agreed with those writers who maintained that the influence of the stars could be countered by education, climate, or the will. . . . There is little reason to doubt that we have here a fair summary of Shakespeare's attitude. While he would have hesitated to deny that [348] the stars could affect men's lives, there is nothing to suggest that he had so much faith in their influence as to deny the freedom of the will. Free-will is of the essence of tragedy, which cannot exist under determinism, and astrology is only a crude form of determinism. As an explanation of the tragic mystery, the inadequacy of Kent's

> It is the stars,
> The stars above us, govern our conditions

is patent even in the play in which it occurs. [349]

$$\times$$

Oscar James Campbell

From "The Salvation of Lear." *ELH* [*English Literary History*], XV (1948), 93-109. By permission.

. . . *King Lear* is, in my opinion, a sublime morality play, the action of which is set against a back-drop of eternity. Lear's problem and his career resemble those of the central figure in the typical moral-

ity play, who is variously called Genus Humanum, Mankind, or Everyman. And the action of Shakespeare's play is his greatly modified version of man's endless search for true and everlasting spiritual values,
rewarded, in this case, by the final discovery of them just before he
must answer Death's awful summons. *The Tragedy of King Lear*
differs however from the usual Morality first, in being cast in a much
deeper tragic mould and second, in presenting the salvation of Mankind not in orthodox theological terms nor even in strictly Christian
terms. For Lear is not so much an erring Christian as a completely
unstoical man and he is converted to a state of mind which is a mixture
of stoic insight and Christian humility. Furthermore the methods by
which his conversion and redemption are accomplished are similar to
those advocated by the great stoic philosophers.

I realize, of course, that stoicism was an eclectic philosophy which
changed at least in emphasis in the long course of its development from
the time of Zeno in the fourth century B.C.[94] to its adoption in
Rome. Roman stoicism is a development of the teaching of the roman-
ized Greek Panaetius, who was a close associate of Scipio Africanus.
Books I and II of Cicero's *De Officiis,* the first extant Roman exposition
of stoicism, are supposed to be a restatement of Panaetius' "Upon External Duty." The later stoics whose writings are of importance are
Seneca, Plutarch, Epictetus and Marcus Aurelius. It was the practical
moral philosophy of these stoics of the Roman Empire that influenced
the Renaissance and English thinkers of the sixteenth and seventeenth
century.

This is not the place to review even the major tenets of later
stoicism. It is sufficient to mention one or two of its controlling ideas
which will appear in our study of Lear. The stoics believed

1. That there are only two kinds of men, the completely wise and good
and the completely unwise and bad.
2. That no outward calamity is a misfortune, but a divine instrument for
the development and training of a man in virtue.
3. That the good man gives Reason his undivided devotion and rejects
passion and even emotion as a disease of the intellect.
4. That the good life must be sought in the soul (the God within) where
it can be untouched by those vicissitudes of Fortune which are beyond human
control.
5. That the good man must therefore (a) resign himself to the will of
the Universe, (b) treat his fellow men with forbearance and humility, and
(c) willingly accept his Destiny.[95]

Lear . . . in many respects resembles mankind of the traditional
sermon and morality play. Like him, the old king has finished his work
in the world, and can therefore devote all his attention to preparation
for death. He then seeks to discover who are his real friends, through
whose companionship he can face death without fear.[99] . . . he makes

the fatal mistake of thinking he can buy affection. But Goneril and Regan, representing worldly goods and those insubstantial human relationships which are precariously cemented only by favors granted, grievously disappoint him. He suffers shattering disillusionment when he sees that their love has been an illusion, that they have been attached only to his power and possessions. The discovery that as soon as he strips himself of these, his ungrateful daughters scorn and reject him, reduces him to anger and despair. . . .

Lear, then, is like mankind of both the Morality and homiletic tradition in that he has devoted his energies to the accumulation and worship of ephemeral possessions and to the pursuit of merely secular satisfactions. But he has erred not because he has deviated from the Christian's straight path to Heaven but because he has flouted all the stoic's rules for the attainment of wisdom.

When we first see Lear, he is the typical unwise man, for he has disobeyed all the stoic's rules for right conduct. He values his kingship not for the responsibilities it places upon him but for the possessions and outward shows which attend it. Indeed he has run so directly counter to the injunction to detach himself from the things of this world that he has come to value even love only as it can serve his vanity.

Moreover he is the complete slave of the most violent and uncontrollable of his passions—anger. . . .[100]

All of the clashes with his unfilial daughters which follow his abdication are . . . exhibitions of unstoical conduct. His wrath explodes at their every attempt to strip him of the hundred knights who form his body guard. Intemperate insistence on retaining these symbols of luxury and pride is a combination of impulses which the stoics stigmatized as evil. . . . Frustrated in his efforts to retain . . . things which the stoics despised, he violently turns from the satisfaction of these condemned appetites and begins his frantic search for the truth that will free him from his slavery to passion. Thereafter he shows his abhorrence of passion by the violence of his anathemas against lust, one of the impulses which most surely degrades man because it most completely submerges reason.

On his pilgrimage he is accompanied by two companions, and commentators, both of whom are creatures of Cynic-Stoic primitivism introduced into Elizabethan literature by way of Roman satire. These two are Kent, the stoic plain man, and the Fool, or the wise innocent—each a child of Nature. Kent follows the rules for the proper Cynic behavior, as defined among others by Epictetus; that is, "the exercise of the right and duty to rebuke evil in others". . . .[102]

Lear meets Gloucester's good son Edgar who is now disguised as Tom, a bedlam beggar, that is, a poor harmless insane fellow who has been allowed to beg on the roads in order to collect money to pay for his keep in the mad house. Lear asks this grotesque creature, "What is your study?" Edgar's answer is, "How to prevent the fiend and kill the vermin," a reply which means, as Joseph Wood Krutch once pointed out, how to attain comfort of body and peace of mind. Yet in the situation in which he finds himself, neither he nor Lear can attain either blessing. The rain continues to drench them both and the wind to lash them. "Tom's acold" and Lear's wits are crazed. Nature proves to be no kind fostering mother to unaccommodated man, but a relentless enemy. Lear's frantic search cannot end on the heath. To the will of the natural universe thus revealed Lear cannot resign himself. These scenes show that the pessimism of seventeenth-century England has superseded traditional stoic pessimism in Shakespeare's conception of the human situation.

Yet the suffering Lear is now enduring begins to show itself as purgatorial. It forces him to realize his own humanity and awakens the philanthropic disposition which was the attitude the stoics cultivated toward their fellow men. . . .[105]

The real redemption of Lear comes when he awakens from the delusions of his frenzied mind to discover Cordelia and her unselfish enduring love. The mere sight of her kills "the great rage" in him, the unstoical emotional turmoil from which all his sins and sufferings have sprung. Now he is calmly receptive to the healing power of Christian love. For he has not arrived at utter indifference to external events, at that complete freedom from emotion, the disease of the intellect, which produces true stoic content. On the contrary Lear finds his peace in an active emotion—in all absorbing love. That it is which at last renders him independent of circumstance. . . .[106]

$$\times$$

Robert Bechtold Heilman

From *This Great Stage: Image and Structure in King Lear*. Baton Rouge, La.: Louisiana State University Press, 1948. By permission of the publisher.

In some respects the relationship between Lear and Cordelia submits easily to definition: Cordelia is the side of Lear capable of tenderness, love, and insight. Yet in Cordelia is the best evidence that, as I

have already said, the children do not become mere allegorical equiv-
alents for isolated parental qualities. For if Cordelia is chiefly the part
of Lear which makes him capable of redemption, she also embodies
some of his proneness to error. I say "some of" because Lear makes,
as we shall see, a whole series of desperate mistakes, in most of which
Cordelia conspicuously does not share. He, for instance, misestimates
the protestations of Goneril and Regan, as she does not. But Lear's
abdication represents a flaw which *is* echoed in Cordelia. For the
abdication is a kind of refusal of responsibility, a withdrawal from a
necessary involvement in the world of action, and the effect of it is to
turn the kingdom over to Goneril and Regan. Likewise Cordelia's
rejection of Lear's distribution scheme—her nonjurancy, so to speak—
is a withdrawal from the [35] immediate world of action, and it leaves
the world of action entirely to her sisters. Perhaps her motive is entirely honorable, and there is for her no practical way of mediating
between two claims each with its own kind of validity; in that case
her situation is roughly analogous to Antigone's. But perhaps in her
refusal we are to see something of spiritual pride (of which Lear
accuses her in I.i.131). . . .[36]

The irony of Gloucester's final condition is exactly paralleled by
the irony of his earlier actions as a man with good eyes. Just when
he most fails to see where he is going, he feels, like Oedipus, most
shrewd and observant. The sight pattern points the issues for us. While
he is being made to see things as Edmund wishes Gloucester feels that
he is detecting the truth: "Let's see," he demands of Edmund three
times (I.ii.35,45)—and he does not see. Again, ". . . if it be nothing,
I shall not need spectacles" (35-36). Spectacles are a symbol of what he
does need: Shakespeare hits upon the characteristic human frailty by
which the denial of a deficiency actually announces the deficiency. It
is altogether [45] logical, then, that Edmund's next move against Edgar
takes place *at night* (II.i): the physical darkness betokens Gloucester's
failure to see into what is going on. The actors in the nocturnal setting,
indeed, represent more than one phase of a human plight: Gloucester
victimizes and Edgar is victimized—he flees at night—because of the
same kind of unseeingness. It is a meaningful, not merely a rhetorical,
irony when Edmund calls, "Light, ho, here! . . . Torches, torches! . . ."
(33-34): those who want light least can call for it most loudly. Then
Gloucester enters—how? ". . . with torches" (38)—the agent of light,
but a kind of light—a physical reality like his eyes—that does him no
good; it is inner illumination that he needs. It is at the end of this scene,
finally, that Regan and Cornwall come to Gloucester's castle. They
come, then, at night, a fact which we might easily pay no attention to
if Shakespeare did not twice remind us of it. Edmund tells Edgar that
Cornwall is coming, "now, i' th' night" (26); and then Regan's words

add emphasis, "out of season, threading dark-ey'd night"—a phrase full of suggestion of things not seen and things not meant to be seen. Regan's thus coming into the sight pattern nicely amplifies the moral context: Regan joins Edmund among those who utilize the dark. These must always have a Gloucester—the not-seeing, or, better, the late-seeing.

For gradually Gloucester comes to see—in practical terms, too late. The first glimmerings come to him in III.iii, when he tells Edmund of his decision to aid Lear. But even now, as we have seen, his motives are not altogether clear, and he is still in the dark about Edmund. In giving practical form to the allegiance to Lear upon which he has resolved,[46] Gloucester again acts in the darkness of the night. In III.iv he hunts up Lear in the stormy night, just as he hunted for Edgar at night in II.i. This time he finds what he is looking for, and at the same time, so to speak, finds himself. The scene of his arrival on the heath is full of imaginative connections with other scenes. Just before Gloucester enters, the Fool says: "Now a little fire in a wild field were like an old lecher's heart—a small spark, all the rest on's body cold. Look, here comes a walking fire" (III.iv.116-19). Since the play has opened with an account of Gloucester's lechery, it seems more than an accident that the Fool is given this particular simile just at the moment of Gloucester's entrance; we can hardly avoid reading it as a direct announcement of Gloucester. In another sense, too, the Fool's language is appropriate: Gloucester's heart has up until now been indeed but a "small spark," and, on the field of Lear's desolate situation, Gloucester's help is hardly more than "a little fire." Just at the moment when the Fool announces "a walking fire," Gloucester enters, significantly, "with a torch" (120). It is the only other time the play mentions lights. This time we feel that the torch is not ironic but symbolizes the first dim stage of enlightenment: Gloucester is no longer blindly confident as he travels the way of the world, and he exhibits a growing sympathy with Lear and a moderation of his attitude to Edgar, whom he once called villain repeatedly (II.i.79ff.) but of whom he now speaks in regret rather than anger (III.iv.171ff.). As I have said, he finds himself. In III.vi he warns Lear of the plot against his life. Just when Gloucester is at last taking a stand which can have very serious consequences, whether or not he can foresee them entirely, Edmund's plot against him matures. The very first [47] threat against him is Goneril's "Pluck out his eyes" (III.vii.5)—the eyes which have given Gloucester so limited a perception as to make him partially adjust himself to Goneril's own regime. He is arrested; then follows the "trial" scene; and his eyes are put out. He is deprived of the organs which he once used so superficially. Yet this happens just as he is at last coming to real insight.

The fifty lines of dialogue which accompany the gouging out of Gloucester's eyes are full of verbal commentary upon what is happening and its meaning. Cornwall is brutally direct: "Upon these eyes of thine I'll set my foot" (68). There is a minor tension between the horrifyingly fierce wit of Regan, "One side will mock another. Th'other too!" (71) and the dying sally of the Servant who has attacked Cornwall and has been stabbed from the rear by Regan, "My lord, you have one eye left/ To see some mischief on him" (81-82)—which is at once a reminder of Gloucester's torture and yet the proffering of such comfort as may come from a slender hope of requital for the torturer. Repeatedly Cornwall betrays a mad passion to cut off the seeing process (68,72), especially at the moment when, fatally wounded, he puts out Gloucester's second eye. "Lest it see more, prevent it" (83). Each remark of his picks up a *see* from the preceding speaker: he is frenzied by the thought, which hardly takes clear form in his mind, of what Gloucester has seen.

Cornwall's ferocity here is in excellent contrast with his bathetically considerate dismissal, a little earlier, of Edmund, who is almost equally callous. Even this dismissal is done in terms of the sight imagery. It is just after Goneril has called "Pluck out his eyes" that Cornwall speaks thus to [48] Edmund, "The revenges we are bound to take upon your traitorous father are not fit for your beholding" (7-8). Such considerateness sets off, also, the real, costly compassion which Gloucester has for Lear: and this is the heart of the scene—the growing insight of Gloucester. Gloucester is defensive at first, perhaps a little uncertain; but at last he recognizes the moment of decision. Questioned, he answers Regan, "Because I would not see thy cruel nails/ Pluck out his poor old eyes; . . ." (56-57), his words ironically anticipating his own fate. He even becomes consciously prophetic, "But I shall see/ The winged vengeance overtake such children" (65-66). The former peacemaker, once a little in awe of Gloucester, has thrown off his old character. Then Gloucester, "dark and comfortless" (85) as in the earlier night scenes, begs Edmund—who is physically absent now as he was spiritually deficient before, and whose physical absence Gloucester cannot see just as before he could not detect his spiritual shortcoming—to "enkindle all the sparks of nature" (86) to avenge him: Edmund is to be both a fire and a light. Instead, Gloucester ironically receives from Regan his climactic enlightenment: it was Edmund who "made the overture" (89) of Gloucester's treason, that is, laid it open to the eyes of Goneril and Regan. Yet the real climax comes in Gloucester's answer. Gloucester does not dwell on Edmund's treachery; in fact, he does not refer to Edmund at this moment or ever again. From now on, he is concerned about his own dreadful mistake and the wrong he has done Edgar. His words are,

O my follies! then Edgar was abus'd.
Kind gods, forgive me that, and prosper him! (91-92) [49]

Gloucester has leapt immediately to the truth about Edgar, as he might have done when Edmund first made his accusation. Then, he avoided the hard work of consulting Edgar's life—the true image of his character. Now, in his act of inference we see that his imagination—long dulled, or perhaps never active—is at work: insight comes to him. He whom Cornwall calls an "eyeless villain" (96) sees at last.

The blinding of Gloucester is at once an act of vengeance by the tyrants, an expiatory suffering by Gloucester, and an ironic commentary upon human experience. In this final character it transcends the concocted irony which at first glance the coincidence of Gloucester's coming to insight and his being blinded might be mistaken for. The irony is not a put-up effect but is inseparable from a profound writer's attitude to his materials. "Out, vile jelly!/ Where is thy lustre now?" (83-84)—Cornwall's words of triumph imply, as the speeches of Shakespeare's villains often do, more than he suspects. What Cornwall does not know is that Gloucester now sees better than he has ever seen; perhaps the final guarantee of his insight is his loss of outward sight. The vile jelly, the material seeing, had but caught reflections from the outer surfaces of life; as long as these were available to him, the seeing Gloucester was spiritually blind. The sisters and Cornwall cut him off from this outer world, which, as we know, circumscribed his vision; hence their fury is self-defeating, for they give him what their general conduct has already prepared him for—inward vision. His physical and material loss is spiritual gain: he who would find his life must lose it.

This is a basic paradox of the play. It is one of a series of paradoxes which, developed by the patterns, are the main [50] structural determinants of *King Lear*. To have eyes, and to see not, is to be at the mercy of evil, and thus to aid evil. . . .[51]

That the saving perspective, which brings evil into focus, is possible to man even after he has made serious mistakes, is the play's ultimate assertion.

Pessimism does not consist in seeing evil injure good; it is instead the inability to see good; or it is to conclude only that evil is mistaken for good; or to discover total depravity, but no grace. To find the play painful or shocking is to be unable to grasp quality as quality, and to substitute success for quality; it is to think in terms of the naïve expectation that longevity, as well as invulnerability to mortal ills, is the reward of virtue. This is the error of Lear at the beginning of the play —the introduction of irrelevant quantitative standards. Quantity of life or quantity of immunity to suffering has, alas, no relationship to moral integrity, or to quality of life which evokes admiration and which is the irreducible residuum after everything else is gone. To assume or seek such relationship is to substitute reward for merit, accident for substance; it is to move from tragedy to melodrama. Shakespeare stays firmly at the tragic level in his dramatic analysis of evil and of the fate of characters whom evil touches, of their ways of saving themselves even though subjected to deprivation and torture and death. . . .[290]

W. R. Keast

From "Imagery and Meaning in the Interpretation of *King Lear.*" *Modern Philology,* XLVII (1949), 45-64. Copyright 1949 by the University of Chicago. By permission of the publisher.

It is not accidental that Professor Heilman refers on several occasions to the similarities between his *King Lear* and *The Divine Comedy,* for the latter, though, as Dante said, quite opposite to tragedy, is precisely this kind of work. *King Lear,* so far as I am aware, has not been generally regarded, even by the more perceptive, as a joyful work; yet in the terms in which Professor Heilman describes it I do not see how it can be anything else. The whole tendency of his analysis—with its emphasis on salvation as the goal of Lear's actions, with its Christian "transvaluation" of a pagan world, with its placement of the climax of the play in Lear's reachievement of insight, with its treatment of the reversal as a passage from bad fortune to good—all this and much more makes it clear that Lear is a man who, after much suffering, which is expiatory and therefore in the proper sense deserved, achieves what he had all along been in search of, the vision in which is eternal life. That Lear dies, that he loses Cordelia at the moment of their reunion —these are incidental, parts of the play's superficial aspect, not of its inner reality, and serving at most to underscore paradoxically the magnitude of Lear's victory; for he that loseth his life shall find it. Only a person incapable, as Mr. Heilman says, of distinguishing between quality and quantity of life could feel anything but spiritual exaltation at Lear's triumph over himself and the world.

This interpretation . . . is preposterous. It violates the unmistakable signs of the play's effect which appear in the text, and it is founded upon a radical confusion of the feelings which a sensitive and inquiring reader might have *after* the play is over with those he has *during* the action itself. That Lear recovers or achieves penetrating insights into himself and the world is a commonplace of critical discussion of this play, as is the observation that the action suggests—or more properly, presupposes—a morally ordered universe. But do the concrete language and action of [62] *King Lear*, the particular details of its development as a drama, contain clear signs that Lear's career to the end of the play is to be thought of as having such insights and the affirmation of such a universe as its goal? Are we regularly reminded—indeed, are we reminded at all—that Lear's recovery of an imaginative synthesis, his earning the "realm of spirit," is what gives order and unity to the latter part of the play? Are we given in any way to understand that the attainment of "needful spiritual insight" is an ultimate end, or even a consolation? Why, if this is his end, does Lear cry out, over Cordelia's body:

> This feather stirs; she lives! If it be so,
> It is a chance which does redeem all sorrows
> That ever I have felt.

What, if some inner structure tending toward salvation is the unifying principle, is the sense of Kent's lines,

> That from your first of difference and decay
> Have followed your sad steps,

and his chilling words, "All's cheerless, dark, and deadly"? Why does Albany refer to Lear as "this great decay," and why does Kent, as Lear dies, say "Break, heart; I prithee break!"? And finally, not to prolong the list indefinitely, how is Mr. Heilman's etherealized conception of Lear's end compatible with the speech in which Kent adjures Edgar against attempting to revive the king:

> Vex not his ghost. O, let him pass! He hates him much
> That would upon the rack of this tough world
> Stretch him out longer.

Our present business, says Albany, is "general woe." Could Shakespeare have written a final scene—let alone the rest of the play—in which the comments of all the characters so obviously contradicted the effect he wished to produce? To suppose so is both to take a very low view of Shakespeare's art and to disregard completely the necessities of popular dramaturgy. Surely it is more consistent—with the text, with what we know of tragedy and of the conditions of Elizabethan theatrical practice, and with the mass of critical opinion about *King Lear*—to regard Lear's imaginative insights as occasioned by and directed toward his need for love and happiness with Cordelia, and to be moved by the awful irony of Lear's return to his original majesty, to an even greater majesty because it is now joined to a deep awareness of his humanity as well, precisely when it is too late for him to achieve that which alone makes majesty, authority, even humanity, meaningful and valuable to him. If, as we watch Lear's final agony over the body of Cordelia, we ascend to a higher level, on which the general woe becomes ineffable joy and the surcease of pain becomes the attainment of "the realities necessary to survival," what happens to Shakespeare's play? It recedes into the background, becoming not so much the concrete object which controls and dictates our emotions as the occasion for reflections and feelings embracing it and much [63] more besides. It may be that, in contemplation of the play as a whole, in mulling it over after it has done its work and after our emotions have returned from their painful excitement to an equilibrium, we shall decide, each according to his own philosophic or religious lights, that *King Lear* has for us a further significance, constitutes a spiritual affirmation, or even, as some have thought, is defective in the distance at which it lies from a realization of man's spiritual possibilities. But these are speculations occasioned by the reading of *King Lear* but in no way the effects peculiar to it—interesting, perhaps even valuable if they come from a sophisticated and philosophic mind—but not analyses of the play. . . .[64]

$$\times$$

Edith Sitwell

From " 'King Lear.' " *Atlantic Monthly,* CLXXXV (May, 1950), 57-62. By permission.

In this play, we see the upheaval of all Nature, the reversal of all histories.

In the beginning of the legend, Cronos devoured his own offspring. In *King Lear,* the brood devours the parent, in whom Age had become Time, and Time a fifth element. In the myth of Oedipus, son of Laius, King of Thebes, the Theban King, having learned from the oracle that he was doomed to die by the hand of his own son, exposed that son upon Mount Cithaeron immediately after his birth, with his hands and feet tied together. Here it is Lear, the father, who having first cast from his bosom his child Cordelia, is then shut from the gates to wander under the "extremetie of the skies," as an outcast. The eyes, not feet, of Gloucester, the father of Edmund, and the smaller echo of the great King, are pierced, and he is thrust outside the gates, to wander in blindness.

In the Fourth Scene of the Third Act, when Lear says "I'll talk with this same learned Theban," the outcast King has reversed his role. He is no longer Oedipus, but is the Sphinx, who must ask the great question. . . . And it is the naked man exposed upon the mountains— one more naked even than the questioner,—one who has nothing but his [58] bare humanity, who is now Oedipus the Theban, who can give an answer to the Riddle. No longer does the Sphinx, as in the ancient legend, put an oblique question, to which the answer is: "This is Man." Instead, bare and terrible, the question is put. Lear, the Sphinx, asks: "Is Man no more than this?"

But in this work of Night, no answer comes from the Naked Man, —no direct answer, only a few meaningless words, like dust from the ruins. But behind that huddle of meaningless words, lies the true answer: "Man is nothing."

The sounds of the words "Nothing" and "Patience" reverberate through the play.[59]

W. H. Clemen

From *The Development of Shakespeare's Imagery*. Cambridge, Mass.: Harvard University Press, 1951. By permission of Harvard University Press and Methuen & Co., Ltd.

. . . imagery is Lear's most characteristic form of utterance.

The reason for this becomes clear if we trace Lear's development during the early scenes. The first shows us Lear still in possession of his power; he is still a member of society. He makes decisions, gives orders and makes plans, addresses the other characters of this scene, his daughters, Kent, France, etc. But the very first scene gives us a hint of how Lear is going to lose contact with this natural relation to his environment. The dialogue which he carries on with his daughters is at bottom no true dialogue, that is, a dialogue based on a mutual will to mutual understanding. Lear determines in advance the answers he will receive; he fails to adapt himself to the person with whom he is speaking. Hence his complete and almost incomprehensible misunderstanding of Cordelia. . . .[134]

. . . Lear gazes within himself; he no longer sees people nor what goes on about him. In madness a man is alone with himself; he speaks more to his own person than to others; where he does not speak to himself, he creates for himself a new and imaginary partner. Lear speaks to people not present, he speaks to the elements, to nature, to the heavens. Men have forsaken him; so he turns to the non-human, superhuman powers. It is one of the functions of the imagery in *King Lear* to awaken these elemental forces and to open to them the way into the play.

The characters around Lear, too, the Fool, Edgar and Kent, speak a language rich in imagery. We shall discuss later the significance of the image in their utterances. If we glance, however, at the other group of characters, Edmund, Goneril, Regan, Cornwall, we note how seldom they employ images, how different is their whole language. In contrast to Lear and his followers, we never find that peculiar form of "mono-logic dialogue" between them. They speak rationally; they address their words to their partner, and converse in a deliberate and con-scious manner. They have a goal which they seek to attain and every-thing they have to say is bent upon this. Their language does not betray to us what is taking place within them—in the form of "imagina-tive visions"; it reveals to us solely their aims and attitudes, and how they intend to put these into practice. Thus their language scarcely changes throughout the course of the play, whereas Lear's, Edgar's and Kent's way of speaking is constantly varied. Goneril, Regan and Ed-mund are the calculating, cool and unimaginative people who are incapable of "creative" imagery. They have no relationship to nature, to the elemental powers. Their world [135] is the world of reason; they live and speak within the narrow limits of their plans, within the limits drawn by the plot and the given moment of the action. Lear's language continually points beyond these limits. Thus the dis-tribution of the images among the characters also gives us a hint as to their position within the play.

The middle acts of the tragedy, Acts II.-IV., are the richest in imagery. The outer action is less important here and is relegated to the background. The main emphasis does not fall upon the outer course of events, upon what Regan or Goneril are planning, or what Edmund is about, but rather upon what is passing in Lear himself. The outer drama has become an inner drama. Beneath the surface of the plot lies the deeper level of inner experience which gradually frees itself more and more from the sparse events of the action. The latter becomes a frame and an occasion in order that the former may take on living reality. In truth, Shakespeare has not treated this outer action with the same thoroughness and care as he usually employed in the construction of the plot. As Bradley has already pointed out, the plot displays a number of inconsistencies and is not carried out clearly. Goethe found the action of *Lear* full of improbabilities, and "absurd." But Shakespeare was concerned not with the "outer," but with the "inner" drama. . . . [136]

Lear's security is shaken for the first time by Cordelia's misunderstood renouncement. It is no mere chance that Lear at just this moment should turn to the non-human powers, call upon them and repudiate his fathership in their name. This reveals his relationship to the elemental powers; it is awakened when his relationship to the human world is shaken, and it is intensified, as if by a law of nature, by every further wound and repulse he receives from this quarter. On this first occasion we have not yet the form of the direct apostrophe, but the formula of the oath. When Goneril—some scenes later—expels him, Lear again turns to those powers of the underworld. We have a preparatory abrupt flash in "Darkness and devils! Saddle my horses;" (I.iv.274), and a few lines later, the first great explosion of this feeling in the apostrophe to nature (I.iv.297). When Goneril reappears, we hear: "Blast and fogs upon thee," and when finally his other daughter also rejects him, the elemental forces are called upon once again:

> You nimble lightnings, dart your blinding flames
> Into her scornful eyes! Infect her beauty,
> You fen-suck'd fogs, drawn by the powerful sun,
> To fall and blast her pride! (II.iv.167) . . .

When Kent in the first scene repeatedly takes the part of the unjustly treated Cordelia, Lear answers impatiently:

> The bow is bent and drawn, make from the shaft.
>
> KENT.   Let it fall rather, though the fork invade
> The region of my heart: (I.i.145)

This is the first independent image of the scene; the more excited Lear becomes, the more often do images appear in his language. The form of the comparison, such as we still have in the simile of the barbarous Scythian (I.i.118), is soon replaced by more direct and forceful metaphorical language in "Come not between the dragon and his wrath" (I.i.123). By the well-known image of the bent bow Lear [139] seeks to warn Kent of continuing in his contradiction; twenty lines later he seizes the sword. But beyond the significance of the moment, this image simultaneously contains dramatic irony: with the transfer of the crown to his daughters Lear has surrendered his own position and power; at this moment, without being aware of it, he has delivered himself up to his coming fate. Nothing can now recall the arrow.[140]

The figure in the play for whom the image is an even more characteristic form of expression than for Lear, is that of the Fool. The Fool never speaks in blank verse, indeed he never comes near the more conventional, measured and dignified manner of speech such as we find, for example, in the first part of the first scene. From the very beginning he has his own peculiar way of expressing himself, a manner which marks him as an outsider. In the speech of the Fool, Shakespeare has given the images wholly new functions. But what is the significance of the image in his case?

We have already stated that in the very first scene Lear loses the capacity for really understanding others in conversation; he cannot carry on a real dialogue. The words of the others no longer reach him or, if they do, in an ill-conveyed meaning. Lear shuts himself off; he becomes isolated in his speech, which from now on, even in the dialogue, bears the stamp of a monologue. The usual manner of speech can therefore no longer move him; such words can neither help nor heal Lear who, in his madness, needs help more and more. The Fool knows this from the very beginning, and he speaks to the King in simile, proverb and image and in rhymed adages and sayings which have the same purpose as his images. Much [141] of what the Fool says Lear neither hears nor grasps, for much is indeed spoken more to the audience than to the King. But part comes home to him and this he does comprehend. Even if Lear replies to only a few of the Fool's utterances, that is still no proof of what Lear may really have heard and understood. For much of the Fool's talk expects no answer. He inserts his sayings and comparisons between the speeches of the others, and he sings his little songs as an outsider, as it were—in this respect his position [1] is often similar to the chorus of the classical tragedy—and formulates most of what he says not as if it were coined to fit a particular case, or were directed at a particular person. "He that hath ears to hear let him hear!" It is the image which makes this unobtrusive parenthetical way of speaking possible. The image clothes the individual and particular case in a more general form; it may take away the sting. Between Lear and the Fool a new form of the dialogue develops which is no longer based upon rational communication, upon the simple play of question and answer, but which is a finer and more subtle interplay of shifting meanings and hints. [142]

. . . it is especially the little sayings and similes of the Fool pertaining to the triviality of every day which counterbalance the gigantic dimensions of Lear's feelings and ideas. The Fool understands how to reduce Lear's behaviour to the simplest, most uncomplicated images of actuality, so that the state of affairs becomes perfectly obvious. Thus, for example, by means of the trivial simile of the egg which Lear has divided to give away both halves (the two crowns) he shows how simple is the division of the kingdom and the relinquishment of the royal power (I.iv.173). . . . [143]

The dramatic quality of the imagery also becomes apparent in the way the dynamic presence of nature in the heath scenes is prepared for very early through allusions and hints; and the other hand, the raging

storm continues to sound in the words of the characters long afterwards in later scenes. As early as Edgar's monologue in II.iii. we have
an introduction to the great heath scene. Edgar's [144] language—from
the moment he begins to play the madman—is full of references to the
world of nature, and in this respect differs greatly from the unimaginative utterances characteristic of Edmund. His monologue displays many
a little touch which summons to the mind the picture of the heath-
landscape: happy hollow of a tree; pins, wooden pricks, nails, sprigs of
rosemary; poor pelting villages, sheep-cotes and mills—to select just a
few lines out of the scene. In the following act also his deliberately
confused talk greatly assists the creation of a powerful nature-atmos-
phere. To quote two examples:

> through ford and whirlipool, o'er bog and quagmire
> (III.iv.53)

or:

> who drinks the green mantle of the standing pool

When he says that he is ready "to outface/ The winds and persecutions of the sky" (II.iii.14), his words are parallel to, and anticipate
Lear's assertion in the next scene:

> No, rather I abjure all roofs, and choose
> To wage against the enmity o' the air;
> To be a comrade with the wolf and owl, (II.iv.211)

In Lear's language, too, the forces of nature make their appearance
before they become grim reality in the third act: "You nimble light-
nings" (II.iv.167). Especially the following line is already suggestive
of the atmosphere of the heath:

> You fen-suck'd fogs, drawn by the powerful sun.[145]

. . . even after this tempest scene is long past, it still lives on in the
memory. Thus Lear's recollection: "When the rain came to wet me
once, and the wind to make me chatter; when the thunder would not
peace at my bidding;" (IV.vi.102), or Cordelia's words in the next
scene:

> Was this a face
> To be opposed against the warring winds?
> To stand against the deep dread-bolted thunder?
> In the most terrible and nimble stroke
> Of quick, cross lightning? (IV.vii.32)

The elements of nature not only help to create the atmosphere,
but they also have symbolical significance and a definite "function."
This also holds true of the animal-imagery. . . . It is interesting to
note how these animal-images make their appearance in considerable
numbers from a definite moment in the play on. That is in the heath-

scenes of the third act. Nature, the landscape, the world of animals come to life after the world of man has failed; since his fellow-men have cast him out, the aged king turns to nature. . . .[148]

The fact that Lear meets with [Edgar] on the heath has symbolical meaning. Himself cast out and left defenceless to the untrammelled winds, he meets in Edgar the worst extremity of the outcast. His own condition, and above and beyond that, the insignificance of man in general, his similarity to the animal, become apparent to Lear: "unaccommodated man is no more but such a poor, bare, forked animal as thou art" (III.iv.111).

This comparison of man with the lowly animal finds its most significant expression in Gloucester's words, culminating in the well-known comparison:

> I' the last night's storm I such a fellow saw;
> Which made me think a man a worm: ...
>
> . . . .
>
> As flies to wanton boys, are we to the gods,
> They kill us for their sport. (IV.i.36)

Many animal comparisons of the Fool, too, are meant to stress the fact that men may fare no better than the animals; when he sees Kent in the stocks, he remarks: "Horses are tied by the heads, dogs and bears by the neck, monkeys by the loins, and men by the legs" (II.iv.7). Otherwise, however, most of the animal comparisons employed by the Fool are aimed to show how dumb animals, in spite of their want of reason, still fare better and act more sensibly than unintelligent human beings. . . .[150]

> Thou rascal beadle, hold thy bloody hand!
> Why dost thou lash that whore? Strip thine own
> back;

Lear, having experienced in his personal world the destruction of human right and order, thus gains insight into the common injustice and frailty of all mankind. His fancy now sees examples of this everywhere in the world. License appears to him in the form of animal-images (IV.vi.114) and in the vision of the "simpering dame" (IV.vi.-120); injustice and mendacity in the image of the railing judge (IV.vi.154), of the beggar running from the farmer's dog (IV.vi.158), of the hypocritical beadle, and of the magnificent robes which cover vice (IV.vi.168). In madness Lear has won eyes for reality.[152]

¹ In almost every Shakespearian tragedy there is the figure of the objective observer who interprets the action from a standpoint outside the dramatic action. In *King Lear* there is, in addition to the Fool, Kent, who serves as an objective observer, as does also in a certain manner Edgar.[142]

William Empson

From *The Structure of Complex Words*. Norfolk, Connecticut: New Directions, 1951. By permission of the publisher.

This speech to the heavens ["If it be you that stirs these daughters' hearts/ Against their father, fool me not so much/ To bear it tamely;"] has an important position because it touches off the storm; at least there seems no doubt that it would be taken so by the audience, who were accustomed to melodramas in which thunder comes as an immediate reply. The storm in Nature is no doubt partly the image of Lear's mind, but it is also an attack upon him, whether from the stern justice of God or the active malice of the beings he has prayed to. The use of the term *fool* acts as a strong support for the theory of malice. The N.E.D. quotes this example and makes it "4" "to make foolish, infatuate" as opposed to "3" "to make a fool of; impose upon, dupe, trifle with," but the decision is unsupported, because the N.E.D. apparently considers both these senses of *fool* as verb to be invented by Shakespeare. I think that the idea of stirring up his daughters against him makes the word here an obvious case of "3"; in fact I think the compilers of the dictionary deliberately invented their sense "4" to avoid the startling accusation against the heavens in this one passage. It is commonly the business of a clown to make fools of other people, and the heavens themselves, in this break-up of human order, are becoming fools like everyone else, and malicious ones. Every time Lear prays to the gods, or anyone else prays on his behalf, there are bad effects immediately.[134]

Fool [in Lear's "And my poor fool is hanged!"] has been taken as a kindly reference to the otherwise unrecorded fate of the clown, and this has a renewed attraction for our modern hard-boiled school, who regard it as a bit of tidying-up pushed in as a belated afterthought. The line breaks out as a wail after a tedious ten lines by Albany about rewards and punishments for the nobles, and even before that Lear was only dropping brief irrelevancies to Kent. His mind might have wandered to the clown; he believes that "Caius" is dead too. However, this interpretation of the word would make the sentence contradict the movement of [151] thought that it introduces, and must therefore be wrong; the passage is in verse, whereas random wanderings are always in prose. The argument is that other creatures are alive but not Cordelia, and the whole impulse of the speech is concentrated on her. On the other hand the N.E.D. theory that *fool* was used as a term of affection should not be carried to the point of thinking that this use excluded the normal meaning of the word. It seems extraordinarily out of place to describe Cordelia. In fact, the word seems likely to puzzle the audience whichever way round you take it. One must suppose, as Bradley did, that his mind has wandered so far that he no longer distinguishes the two; but this should not be softened into "a very old man failing to distinguish two of his children." The Fool has not been required after the storm scenes, because the mad king has taken over his functions completely. But Lear is now thrown back into something like the storm phase of his madness, the effect of immediate shock, and the Fool seems to him part of it. The only affectionate dependent he had recently has been hanged, and the only one he had then was the Fool; the point is not that they are alike—it is shocking because they are so unlike—but that he must be utterly crazy to call one by the name of the other. Presumably the audience was meant to accept it as mere raving and thereby get the right poetical effect; it is meant to recall the whole background of clownery, which is what he has discovered about the world. . . .[152]

$$\times$$

D. G. James

> From *The Dream of Learning: an Essay on the Advancement of Learning, Hamlet, and King Lear.* Oxford, England: Clarendon Press, 1951. By permission of the publisher.

. . . in *King Lear* [Shakespeare's] secular imagination is at its strongest and most determined. How determined it was, we can see if we look at the old play of *King Leir*. Here, for once, is a play, lately acted, as the 1605 Quarto declares, the tone of which is unmistakably one of Christian piety. Leir's dead Queen is 'possest of heavenly joys'; Cordella has a Christian sanctity; Leir himself acknowledges that he has offended against the majesty of God; and the blessing which he finally gives to Cordella is

> The blessing, which the God of *Abraham* gaue
> Vnto the trybe of *Juda*.

Now this biblical and Christian ethos is a new thing in the history of the story of Lear; it is not to be found in any of the earlier versions.

That Shakespeare knew this earlier play there can, I think, be no doubt whatever. Here, at least, I must take it for granted. What I wish to emphasize is that Shakespeare, in devising his version of the story, carefully declined to give it anything approaching a Christian setting: he puts the story back, where it had always earlier belonged, in a remote Celtic past; and the gods of the play become Apollo and Jupiter. I am not now concerned to argue, what I think would be extravagant, that there is nowhere in the play implicit Christian feeling; what seems certain is that it was Shakespeare's fully conscious decision not to give to the story any fraction of a Christian context. The play's action is terrible in all conscience; but there is no crumb of Christian comfort [92] in it.

There is a feature of Lear's personality which has always impressed me and which I cannot fail to feel is at the centre of Shakespeare's intention in this play. It is the sense, which Lear frequently conveys, that the source of his children's evil is in himself. This thought, which on occasion he pronounces clearly enough, he yet holds uncertainly; he falls away from it; and he falls away from it into violent expostulation and anger. Before speaking further of this, I give these quotations in illustration.

In the course of the great scene where Lear and Kent arrive at Gloucester's castle to find Kent in the stocks, Lear, having spoken tenderly to Goneril, goes on: [93]

> But yet thou art my flesh, my blood, my daughter;
> Or rather a disease that's in my flesh,
> Which I must needs call mine: thou art a boil,
> A plague-sore, an embossed carbuncle,
> In my corrupted blood.

And then he goes on, now tenderly, with

> But I'll not chide thee;
> Let shame come when it will...
> I do not bid the thunder-bearer shoot...

Again, in the storm on the Heath he declares that it is a judicious punishment that discarded fathers should come to this. ' 'Twas this flesh begot those pelican daughters.' Now this sense of guilt, sometimes clearly stated but then also forgotten, is an important power in the distress and conflict of Lear's mind; and it is something which, so long as it lasts, profoundly affects his attitude to Goneril and Regan. As I suggested in giving my first quotation, it mitigates his strong anger and causes him to desist from judgment:

> But I'll not chide thee...
> I do not bid the thunder-bearer shoot,
> Nor tell tales of thee to high-judging Jove.

This forbearance, or at least this wish to forbear, is something we must take account of; along with his violent anger and the still more violent curses he invokes upon his daughters, there goes a vague enough feeling of guilt and a sense, vague enough also, of a moral life and quality which he ought himself to come by. It is easy enough, and no doubt natural enough, to call Lear selfish, impulsive, and crass; but this is not the whole [94] truth about him; and Shakespeare makes clear that it is not. It is easy enough to say that when Lear speaks his words excusing Cornwall, on arriving at the castle of Gloucester, he is merely deceiving himself with wishful thinking. Again, it is easy to say that when Lear, on his journey to the castle of Gloucester, says 'I did her wrong,' he is referring to Cordelia; but it is, I suggest, better to think he is referring to Goneril on whom he had a little earlier called down a dreadful curse. For we cannot fail to remark how often he calls out for 'patience.' 'I can be patient,' he says in one place; in another, 'You heavens, give me that patience, patience, I need!'; and Kent mildly upbraids him with,

> Sir, where is the patience now
> That you so oft have boasted to retain?

He needs patience, and he knows it, however vaguely and intermittently. Now by 'patience' we mean, first, the power to suffer with calmness and composure; and secondly, forbearance with the faults of others; and it is these things which Lear has often boasted to retain. He has indeed 'boasted' to retain them; but he has at least felt the wish to retain them, and he is patient, or at least tries to be patient, when he is disposed to acknowledge that his daughters' evil is also his own.[95]

In the first scene Cordelia is led away by the King of France to become his Queen. It will be remembered that Cordelia has rejected Burgundy: 'I shall not be his wife.' France then speaks and declares, in a moving speech, that he will have her. Cordelia does not reply. It is Lear who replies: 'Thou hast her, France, let her be thine...'; and then, with Lear and the others gone, Cordelia and France remain behind with Goneril and Regan. But in the conversation that follows, Cordelia speaks to her [99] sisters; she speaks not a single word to France. France says, 'Come, my fair Cordelia'; and they are gone. There is not a word from Cordelia which expresses her feeling for the man she accepts for a husband. There is nothing here which even begins to correspond with the scene in the old play which shows the wooing of Cordelia by France and her loving acceptance of him. Whatever the role of Cordelia in the play is to be, we are not to see her as a lover and a wife. Then, late in the play, France and Cordelia come with their army; but, as everybody knows, and by what Mr. Granville-Barker called the clumsiest lines in the play, France is bundled back again home. But why? Because, again, Cordelia must not come in the role of a wife; her role is other, and wholly other, than this; Shakespeare has intentions which the presence of France would drastically interfere with. But why, in that case, did Shakespeare send over the King of France at all? The answer is not, I think, difficult to find. Shakespeare had to choose between two things: either the King of France (whom we certainly have been led to think of as a loving husband) must send Cordelia with an army to England and stay in France himself for reasons of state, or he must come over with her and be urgently recalled. Between these two there was little to choose. He decided so far to stick to the old story as to bring over the King of France, in that measure raise our expectations of a happy issue of the battle, and then to imagine a state of affairs in France which required his summary return. But what is certain is that Cordelia's life as a wife and queen are [100] strangely shut out from the play. It is her relation to her father which is alone relevant; and for this reason and in this measure, Cordelia is drastically simplified and, as we may say, dehumanized.[101]

Edgar, it will be remembered, declines to disclose himself to his father where the plot provides no obvious reason why he should not do so; and if the plot provides no reason why he should not do so, Edgar's compassionate human nature provides reason enough why he should. On meeting his blinded father, Edgar could well have disclosed himself, would in all nature have disclosed himself, given Gloucester comfort and succour, and saved his life. In Sidney's version there is no hiding of the son's identity; but in *King Lear* the reconciliation of father and son is withheld by what Edgar later acknowledged for a fault in himself; and we hear only from Edgar of how Gloucester died on hearing of the truth and after much terrible and unnecessary suffering. Edmund had deceived Gloucester; why must Edgar now also deceive him? What must now deny to father and son the joy they may have in each other, except for a last, heartbroken, fleeting moment? Why must common [106] human nature be so gratuitously and brutally outraged? For we must reflect that Gloucester, led by Edgar, and above all in the cliff scene, is an even more poignant and inexpressibly pitiable figure than when he staggered blinded from the knives of Cornwall; and this is not required by the plot and is strictly unnecessary: it only heaps misery on both Gloucester and Edgar. The natural flow of Edgar's love and forgiveness is brutally stopped to increase his and his father's suffering. Now if I am right in this, we can only conclude that this situation exhibits an intention essential to Shakespeare's imagination of the play.

Consider again now Kent. Here, if you will, is the common stuff of human nature: a man loyal, generous, rash; loving. But why does not Kent, at the opening of the storm and before Lear's madness sets in, disclose himself to Lear? Again, the plot does not at all forbid it; and again, Kent makes himself known to Lear only at the end when Lear is too far gone in grief and desperation to do more than take the barest note of him. Had Kent acted on what must have been his most natural impulse, he would not indeed have averted the main tragedy; but he could and would have brought comfort and companionship to the lonely and distraught Lear.

Now in the face of what I have said of Edgar and Kent, it is natural to say that we have to consider what, when we set ourselves to apprehend Shakespeare's masterpiece, we are undertaking to do. It is not, as I have said, a question of understanding an argument; [107] it is a question of rising to a difficult perception offered by Shakespeare's most mature tragic art. Now if we think so, we shall not put down these things I have spoken of as mere faults; . . . They were, we must suppose, integral to Shakespeare's intention when he wrote the play; they must become integral to ours when we read it or see it. Shakespeare will not allow us to imagine Cordelia in the human context of wifehood and queenship; he also will not allow the goodness of Edgar and Kent the comfort they may give and receive in the world's conflict. Against the pure wickedness of Cornwall and Edmund the beneficence of Edgar and Kent are not allowed to work with any mitigation; they are held firmly and unnaturally in much helplessness and suffering which are gratuitous and beyond the requirements of the plot.[108]

Why does Shakespeare suffer [Edmund] to speak only when he is expressly asked by Albany where Lear and Cordelia are? Shakespeare clearly gives us to understand that Edmund is changed, despite of his own nature; why do not common pity and compunction act in him? We may feel exasperation with Albany and Edgar at delaying at this time in a long colloquy; but we are more mystified by Edmund. Here too, then, a natural and generous impulse, even in Edmund, is forbidden; what good there came to be in him came to nothing in the plot's design. . . .[109]

. . . all three examples I have given, of Edgar, Kent, and Edmund, show Shakespeare removing virtue away from efficacy and power over the course of events. Lear must go on suffering uncomforted by the knowledge of Kent's presence, and Gloucester by the knowledge of Edgar's; and when Edmund at last repents, he is checked from influencing the course of the plot. On the one side, therefore, is surpassing good, and on the other extreme evil; but the scales are hopelessly weighted on one side; against the wickedness of Cornwall, Goneril, and Regan, what beneficence human nature is shown to possess is not allowed to issue in action; it is kept as far as may be in silence and suffering. Here, it will be seen, the simplification which Shakespeare conducts is not only in the characters themselves; it is, so to speak, in the control of the plot by the characters. The characters of Goneril, Regan, and [110] Cornwall are, indeed, simple. The characters of Edgar, Kent, and Edmund are not; but they are controlled by a plot which holds them, and therefore also Lear and Gloucester and Cordelia, in almost unrelieved suffering, and then brings them to their deaths.

Here, or so it seems to me, is the main abstraction which Shakespeare seems determined to conduct throughout the play: the forcing apart, I mean, of character from circumstance, of virtue from happiness and then of virtue from life itself. In the world which Shakespeare is now rendering, merit is made as powerless as possible and is then destroyed. . . . The play seems to be designed to exhibit suffering and helpless virtue, whether it be the virtue of a Kent, the uncertain virtue of a Lear, or the transcendent virtue of an Edgar and a Cordelia.[111]

The souls of Cordelia and Edgar are not in the stage figures who in battle and combat thus serve the purposes of a plot. . . . In Cordelia and Edgar Shakespeare is contemplating figures of spiritual perfection who cannot move, with [113] any substance of reality, at this level of the plot's working. Who can see Cordelia (or Lear, for that matter, in the state to which he has now come) at the head of an army, whether the army she leads be victorious or defeated? And the whole bent and direction of Edgar's spiritual bearing is away from this kind of thing; make him do this, and whether *he* be victorious or defeated, he is no longer Edgar. . . .[114]

Bradley is willing to believe, in the face of the play's improbabilities and therefore, as he thinks, carelessness of design, that the Fool was forgotten not by Kent and the others, but by Shakespeare. But if I have been at all right in what I have said, the Fool is at the centre of the play's imagination: his virtue is pitiable in its helplessness; he, like others, is an image of helpless and suffering love; he exerts no influence upon the course of events; the course of events passes him by.

For the truth is, or so it seems to me, that in this play Shakespeare is little enough concerned with strict dramatic plot or with character in the ordinary sense. He is, above all, concerned to exhibit certain moral ideas or states, imaginatively apprehended indeed, yet still ideas of evil and of good. His imagination sifts out these essences. To Evil he gives the initiative, the force, the driving power of the plot. Over against it he sets [116] Good; but he forbids it, so far as he may, to interfere with and control the action and consequences of Evil; it is made silent and patient; it is suffering love; it has little influence upon the executive ordering of the world; it merely *is* and suffers; it is not what it does but what it is, as it is shown in a Cordelia and an Edgar, that we contemplate. Evil drives on, dynamic and masterful, but to its own destruction; Good is still, patient, and enduring, but is also destroyed; no limit, not even that of death, is put to what it must endure.[117]

. . . in *King Lear* . . . the figures of patient merit have nothing of this fear of death [expressed in *Hamlet*]. The problems of living which Hamlet had posed seem not to be problems for them; they have come to a sense of life in which they do not occur; and similarly death does not come as a problem and as a source of fear. It comes differently as something somehow natural; and to endure it crowns the detachment and disinterestedness of their lives. 'Bear free and patient thoughts,' says Edgar:

> Men must endure
> Their going hence, even as their coming hither:
> Ripeness is all.[118]

This is the centre of Shakespeare's perception of life in his greatest play; and it will not do to speak of pessimism and gloom in the face of it; the crass opposites of pessimism and optimism have no relevance here. There could be no question of Cordelia's being brought, with the play, to some happy ending; to give her some thirty years of life in this world would have been as silly as to give us some assurance of temporal immortality for her in another. She, and through her Shakespeare, had come to a sense of life, and therefore of death, in which the soul makes no demand either of life or death. It is here, in all truth, that we may rightly say, The rest is silence.[119]

⟡

George W. Williams

From "The Poetry of the Storm in *King Lear.*" *Shakespeare Quarterly,* II (1951), 57-71. By permission.

In the first nine lines of scene ii the storm and the style rise to their greatest pitch. It is in fact only through the rise in the style that the audience comes to feel the full extent of the storm. In these lines Shakespeare reaches the point for which he has been preparing in the preceding two scenes. The report which the Gentleman makes in scene i first announces the condition of the king, at war with himself and the elements. This is followed by a digression of thirty-five lines during which the conversation shifts to the fortunes of Cordelia and the activities of the British dukes. Kent recalls the storm hastily before his exit and immediately in the person of the king it breaks in full fury. . . .

The phonetics in these lines is especially remarkable. Most notable is the frequency of fricatives and stops in clusters of onomatopoetic vernacular words chosen to suggest the roughness and harshness of the weather:[60]

blow, crack, cheek, blow, cataract, spout, drench'd, steeples, drown'd, cocks, thought-executing, oak-cleaving thunderbolts, singe, shaking thunder, strike (in the Qq. *smite*), thick, crack, spill, make.

The pattern of nasals—

winds, hurricanoes, drench'd, drown'd, vaunt, cleaving thunder, singe, thunder, rotundity, nature's moulds, germains, make, ingrateful man—

and the pattern of the sibilants—

winds, cheeks, cataracts, hurricanoes, spout, steeples, cocks, sulph'rous, executing, fires, couriers, bolts, singe, shaking, strike (in the Qq. *smite*), nature's moulds, germains, spill, once—

while not so spectacular are equally present. The combination of a low vowel with a nasal, honored from classical times, occurs most effectively in

> *Vaunt*-couriers to oak-cleaving *thund*erbolts
> Singe my white head! And thou, all-shaking *thunder*,
> Strike flat the thick *rotund*ity o' th' world.

Here the -*und*- group links the three lines inextricably together, providing the equivalent of the continued rumbling of thunder. But after the hissing, the crashing, and the thundering, the passage comes to rest as far as that is possible on the liquids, *mould, all, spill, ingrateful*.

The passage is one of those in Shakespeare extraordinary for what have been happily termed "amazing" words. Mr. John Crowe Ransom lately,[1] and others before him, have profitably studied etymologies, word origins, and the relationship which they bear to word-position in the line and the sentence and have demonstrated a productive and rewarding method of word-study. Shakespeare is a master of English and of foreign words in English. He is chief cook, and as has been suggested, he uses the same recipe as that recommended by Lear's Fool. Shakespeare does with his words what his "cockney did to the eels when she put 'em i' th' paste alive. She knapped 'em o' th' coxcombs with a stick and cried Down, wantons, down!" (II.iv.123-127). They behave; the concoction is unsurpassable. But noticeable at once in the passage, basically a paragraph of native or vernacular words, are the foreign importations. . . . Like the eels these words remain [61] alive, refusing to submit completely to being Englished; in their alien setting they raise their heads.

Cataract appears here in its only use in Shakespeare, though it was a common term throughout the sixteenth century. It was generally understood to refer to the "floodgates of heaven" regarded as holding back the rain or perhaps the waters above the firmament. In this passage, however, it is commonly considered by critics that its primary meaning is "waterspout," a rare though not original application, suggested by its conjunction with *hurricano* and *spout*. *Hurricano* is defined by its only other appearance in Shakespeare, in *Troilus and Cressida*, V.ii.171-173: "the dreadful spout/ Which shipmen do the hurricano call,/ Constring'd in mass by the almighty sun." The meaning as seen by this gloss is "waterspout," so that both these terms have the same significance, as it is thought, and are merely synonymous. Such a reading overlooks much in the pair, and there would seem to be good reason for accepting the more normal meanings "floodgates of heaven" and "sea storms." These latter interpretations are considerably richer since they contribute violence to the image, follow the familiar Bible story of the Flood, and evoke Jehovanistic overtones quite in keeping with the character of the protagonist. *Rotundity,* meaning evidently "roundness," is an instance of a rare Latinism taken over by Shakespeare and used only once. The active stem *rotund*- was well known in the late sixteenth century from the French or Italian; *rotundity*, however, is apparently directly from the Latin *rotunditas*. It is unusually effective in this passage. *Germain* is a word of Shakespeare's own coinage, from the Latin. It is an "inkhorn" term used with its Latin meaning, "seed," applying presumably to animal as well as to plant semenality. . . .[62]

It is not inappropriate to examine the relationship of the king and the elements at this point as it is revealed in these nine lines and in the following eleven. This tremendous nine-line speech can not be regarded as an accurate though frenzied meteorological report on the state of the weather. Such has already been given by the two faithful retainers at the opening of the Act. These lines are not the statement of one resigned to his fate, for the king is not yet in the purgative stage. If they are regarded as a prayer to the great gods for retribution,[2] serious difficulties are encountered in resolving the imprecations hurled at the elements in the second part of the speech, following the lines of the Fool, and including "I tax you not, you elements, with unkindness. . . ." and "But yet I call you servile ministers. . . ." If these lines again form a prayer they differ strikingly from the more easily recognized prayers, "O heavens, if you do love old men" and "Poor naked wretches." They are in fact much closer to the curses of barrenness which they parallel in thought as well as in tone and mood. The Gentleman explains finally the nature of the king's speech: "Bids the wind blow the earth into the sea,/ Or swell the curled waters 'bove the main" (III.i.5-6). This bidding can only be equivalent to the command of the king, as when he says: "bid them [Regan and Cornwall] come forth and hear me,/ Or at their [64] chamber-door I'll beat the drum/ Till it cry death to sleep" (II.iv.118-120). These wild lines then must be understood as direct orders to the winds, the waves, the thunder, and the lightning. Such an interpretation accords well with what has been seen of the character of the king. The commands of the first nine lines recall those given throughout the earlier part of the play; they are in the same vein. King Lear regards himself still as every inch a king, and shouting his orders to his subordinates, he reveals clearly his proud, arrogant, and stubborn authority. The elements are Lear's servants. But he has given to them, as to Cordelia, Kent, and the Fool, nothing. Here at last the reckoning is made: nothing comes of nothing. From these unfee'd servants Lear no longer receives toadying flattery, he no longer receives even obedience. To a royal philosophy of *quid pro quo* (or *quid pro nihilo*), the basis of Lear's erroneous sense of values, comes the awakening: "You owe me no subscription." *Nihil pro nihilo.* The first lines of the speech command general destruction in which Lear's white head must perforce be singed. The second group of eleven lines is anti-climactic; the destruction does not occur. The tempest continues, however, to beat down on Lear's unprotected head. The realization develops that the elements are no longer his servants; they are in fact his masters, now servilely and venally colleagued with his daughters. He is no longer a king. He discovers at this moment when the elements do not obey him that they, allies of his ungrateful daughters, have also thrown off the imperial yoke. Instead of responding to his commands immediately, as he remembers later, they turn on him. "When the rain came to wet me once and the wind to make me chatter; when the thunder would not peace at my bidding; there I found 'em, there I smelt 'em out" (IV.vi.102-105). It is the remarks of the Fool between the two sections of the speech that make this clear: "O nuncle, court holy-water in a dry house is better than this rainwater out o' door." That is to say, voluntary submission to your rebelling daughters is to be preferred to enforced submission to the rebelling of nature, which evidently has no longer any intention of obeying you.

Furthermore, in giving these orders to the elements, Lear is acting in conformity and parallel with Roman and Celtic tradition. These mythologies both state the ancient position of the king as the creator of the weather, especially of the stormy weather. . . .[65]

As the imagery of cataracts and hurricanes has evoked connotations of destruction comparable to that at the time of the Deluge, so the concluding images suggest the ruin of the Last Judgment. Bolts of thunder and lightning are to flatten out the roundness of the earth, Nature's moulds are to be cracked and shattered until they are useless, all germains are to be spilled. Such imagery can indicate only eschatological destruction. Bradley has suggested that the theme of the latter day may have been in Shakespeare's mind during the writing of this play, and Lear himself threatens to do undescribable things, the "terrors of the earth." Bradley cites specifically the passages in Matthew and Mark generally titled "the little apocalypse," and it may not be irrelevant to point out that in both these scriptural predictions there are descriptions of the time of the Final Judgment which would set it within the time scheme of this play: "the brother shall deliver the brother to death, and the father the sonne, and the children shall rise against their parents and shall cause them to die" (Mark xiii. 12). It is not improbable in the light of the importance of the themes of justice and injustice in the play that Shakespeare was thinking in the king's hectic speech in terms of the Day of Judgment when justice shall finally be accomplished in the world.

Moulds thus is to be regarded, with this interpretation of time in mind, as referring to the forms of Plato existent in the creator's mind in accordance with which everything was made that was made. . . .[67]

1 "On Shakespeare's Language," *Sewanee Review*, LV (1947), 181-198.[61]
2 As does G. Wilson Knight (*The Wheel of Fire* [Oxford, 1930], p. 201). It seems difficult to reconcile reviling with prayer.[64]

⤙⤚

Lily B. Campbell

From *Shakespeare's Tragic Heroes: Slaves of Passion*. New York: Barnes & Noble, Inc., 1952. By permission of Cambridge University Press.

The scene [between Kent and the Gentleman, IV.iii.44-49] contains almost the heart of the mystery. Cordelia is mistress over passion. Lear has been mastered by passion. It cannot be over-emphasized, I think, that Shakespeare's picture is of a Lear whose wrath has made him guilty of deeds both evil and foolish. It is not primarily ingratitude that has caused his downfall; rather it is his wrath over ingratitude. It must be remembered that his wrath over Cordelia's ingratitude was just as great as his wrath over the ingratitude of his other daughters.

If Lear had accepted the slight to his self-esteem as Cordelia or as Kent accepted the insults and injuries which he heaped upon them, there would have been no tragedy. And now we have Cordelia still bearing grief patiently, as she bore earlier wrongs, while Lear is paying with madness and shame the penalty of his continued wrath.[204]

The fifth act is a chaos of passion. The jealousy of the two sisters leads to an angry revenge that makes each slay the other. The fortunes of war go against Cordelia and Lear and put them in the power of Edmund. The interlude of their happiness in being reunited even in prison but interrupts the progress of horror momentarily. . . .

In his lust Gloucester begot his destroyer; in his anger he gave him power to destroy. His death came also from passion, for the recognition of his injured son as his guide overcame him finally. . . .[206]

King Lear as the tragedy of wrath, then, was planned as a tragedy of old age. In Lear and Gloucester Shakespeare represented old men bestowing benefits unjustly, led by flattery to give unwisely, led by anger to withhold unjustly and to seek revenge for imagined slights. Both the evil and the folly of their anger are brought out. The evil lay in their inflicting evil on others. The folly lay in the evil they brought upon themselves. Even Kent, the friend and loyal follower, is led in anger to go beyond the command of reason in his treatment of Oswald and hence to bring further misfortune on the King. Cornwall is killed in an angry fight with his servant, but the servant is also killed for his righteous anger. The whole is a welter of passion. But the picture is relieved by Cordelia, who cannot be moved by passion; by Edgar, who acts as reason dictates even in the guise of a madman; and by Albany, who at the last is the calm arbiter of the "gor'd state." [207]

✴

E. Catherine Dunn

From "The Storm in *King Lear.*" *Shakespeare Quarterly*, III (1952), 329-333. By permission.

The aptness of cosmic chaos in the Empedoclean sense to symbolize the effect of ingratitude can perhaps be seen again as the play draws to a close. In the cosmology of Empedocles the universe passes through a series of cycles in which first Love and then Strife predominates. Although Strife destroys the world, a new cosmos is born as Love returns. The reappearance of Cordelia, even for a short time, the victory of Albany, and the reinstatement of Edgar perhaps announce the return of Love, and create the "restoration of tranquillity" which is integral to the tragic effect. Lear and Gloucester have perished in the upheaval, but so also has the evil which destroyed them.[333]

William Haller

From " 'What Needs My Shakespeare?' " *Shakespeare Quarterly*, III (1952), 3-16. By permission.

The people who first saw *King Lear* upon the stage had been instructed time and again in the inseparable and inescapable but complementary duties of parents and children, and incidentally of husbands and wives and of rulers and subjects. As children they had been taught they must obey their parents. As parents they had been told they must love their children. But true obedience springs from love and only from love, and the true end of all love is obedience, that is to say, truly to serve the beloved, to submit willingly to that order of things which to know is to love and to love is to obey. Lear and his daughters have fallen into the first of all sins, namely pride, the love and worship of self, the beginning of all disobedience, deceit, hatred, hardness, enslavement to evil and disruption. What well-instructed man or woman in the audience could fail to see at once that Lear was a father who failed in his duty to his children while his children at the same time failed in theirs toward him? Who could not see that Cordelia loved her father but loved him less than she loved her own way and hated her sisters'? Or that the difference between Lear and Cordelia on the one hand and all the others is simply that through experience of evil, they came to know the good, to understand the great and mysterious law that in order to love we must be free but that to be free is to serve that which we love though we die for it.[14]

Leslie Hotson

> From *Shakespeare's Motley*. New York: Oxford University Press, 1952. By permission of the publisher.

For Shakespeare's audience it is plain that Lear's Fool, in his unobtrusive and humble robe of motley, was far from cutting any outlandish figure, or bringing in an atmosphere of romance or long-ago. He belonged to the contemporary scene, and his introduction by Shakespeare into tragedy was therefore a step towards realism, and away from what Sir Philip Sidney had reprobated as that gross absurdity of 'mingling Kings and Clownes,' of thrusting in crude rustic 'Clownes, by head and shoulders, to play a part in majesticall matters, with neither decencie nor discretion.' Rustics were not companions of kings, and were therefore out of place in tragedy. Fools or 'naturals,' on the other hand, belonged in the circles of high life, and might properly appear in 'majestical matters.' This consideration should have its weight in modern production and criticism, together with the realization, long overdue, that *motley* was not at all a gaudy parti-colour, but an undemonstrative vesture of humility.[100]

$$\displaystyle \not\Join$$

Arpad Pauncz

> From "Psychopathology of Shakespeare's *King Lear*." *American Imago*, IX (1952), 57-78. By permission.

[Pauncz outlines Lear's "attachment to his daughters, especially the third daughter."] Not fatherly affection, in the everyday sense of the word, is meant here, but rather a specifically erotic affection, which may readily be compared to the child fixation in the Oedipus Complex as described by Freud, except that it is reversed.

This reverse erotic fixation will be called the *adult* libido and more specifically, the *Lear Complex*. . . . The Lear complex endeavors to account for the specific erotic attachment of the father for his daughter. . . [58]

Lear not only loves his daughters; he is also in love with them, especially with the youngest one. The division of his land is not due exclusively to the weariness of his age and government. It is, in addition, a kind of love-suit for the favor of his daughters, and when he is rejected by his third daughter, he behaves like any temperamental, fiery, imperious suitor would have behaved in the same situation.[60]

In this sense he is actually "absurd." It is this rejection that really accounts for his boundless affectivity, his lack of insight and self-mastery and, to a very large extent, his future behavior as well.

The protestations of love of the two older daughters: "beyond all manners of so much I love you"; "I profess myself an enemy to all others joys"; "and find I am alone felicitate in your dear highness' love," go surely beyond the bounds of love which are due a father from his daughters.

These remarks, and perhaps even more the discreet and restrained utterance of the third daughter, make it quite clear that the daughters know their father's true interests rather well and that they are, with the exception of the third daughter,[61] also willing, at least ostensibly, to submit themselves to the wishes of the father.

Cordelia, "our joy" (I.i.86), the third and favorite daughter from whom Lear is expecting to receive the acme of all love declarations, does not exaggerate. She is aware of her real duties; she recognizes the impossibility of her father's demands; and while setting them back within their proper boundaries, she blasts at her sisters' adulation and offers which never can be fulfilled.[62]

It is interesting to note that as he disclaims his "paternal care," "propinquity" and "property of blood" for Cordelia, he uses words which significantly objectify "the barbarous Scythian" appetite for "his generation."

LEAR (I.i.119):
> The barbarous Scythian,
> Or he that makes his generation messes
> To gorge his appetite, shall to my bosom
> Be as well neighbor'd, pitied, and relieved,
> As thou my sometime daughter.

We see Lear's adult libido echoed again in the course of events, although it is sometimes ambivalently disguised. The favorite child who was nearest to his heart becomes a "little seeming substance" (I.i.201), a hateful being, "whom nature is ashamed almost to acknowledge hers" (I.i.216). However, something else that is very remarkable occurs. Lear, instead of making an effort to get rid of the hated being, almost dissuades the suitors of his daughter from an alliance with her. . . .[63]

The King of France is emotionally most involved and seems to sense the real meaning of the situation. [Quotes I.i.217-227 in support of this assertion.] [64]

Adultery, incest, fantastic erotic images seem to dominate Lear's mental life. Some of these images are unmistakably personally determined.[70] [Quotes IV.vi.113-133.]

We cannot fail to recognize that Lear's fantasies are increasingly earmarked by sexual coloring. And what is the meaning of Lear's following words?

> LEAR (IV.vi.166):
> Why dost thou lash that whore? Strip thine own back;
> Thou hotly lust'st to use her in that kind
> For which thou whip'st her.

Is it not that he himself wants to be vindicated, for his own lustfulness? And is not the essence of his remarks:

> LEAR (IV.vi.191):
> And when I have stol'n upon these sons-in-law,
> Then, kill, kill, kill, kill, kill, kill!

that he wants to get rid of his sons-in-law, that they have to be killed six times to be really eliminated? The direction of his lustful fantasies becomes even more specific when they find expression in the following statement:

> LEAR (IV.vi.206):
> I will die bravely, like a smug bridegroom.

With what purpose and meaning were these remarks expressed? Perhaps the answer is not so difficult to find if we know that they were addressed to the messenger of Cordelia, a gentleman whose job it was to conduct Lear to her and to safety.[71]

Huntington Brown

From "Enter the Shakespearean Tragic Hero." *Essays in Criticism*, III (1953), 285-302. By permission.

[Each of Shakespeare's] 'sympathetic' heroes except Lear is the same person at bottom when he dies that he was at the end of his first appearance on the scene, at least in the sense that of the halves of which he appears to consist, one is a critical half and holds the scales of judgment steady at all times, while the other pursues a calamitous adventure. . . . although Lear in disinheriting Cordelia seems to have no inner voice to warn him of the mistake, Kent supplies the deficiency, and in protesting uses expressions that suggest the same division between the hero and his true self that we have seen Romeo and Brutus aware of in their own minds. Kent says that 'Lear is mad,' and madness is always popularly defined as a kind of separation of the true from the outward man, as when we say that a mad person is 'not all there.' But we know that Kent speaks out of loyalty, love, and understanding, not hostility. He is indeed the voice [292] of Lear's own better self. We do not, however, warm to Lear until his misery has begun to strike sparks of illumination within his own mind, until, in short, some part of him becomes detached from the rest in his own eyes so that he can look at it squarely, even if, for a considerable time, with imperfect understanding. It is only gradually that he comes to see how extremely obtuse and selfish his conduct has been.[293]

The quarrel engaged thirty to forty years ago in Shakespeare criticism on the issue of the causal relation between character and action in the tragedies is still warm. The one school, as everybody knows, holds that action is everywhere the true expression and measure of character (so Bradley and other advocates of the prevailing nineteenth-century position, and latterly the Freudians), the other that action and character often present a contrast. The latter maintain that the interest of a play marked by contrast of this sort, instead of being the comparatively intellectual interest of a case history, such as would belong mainly to the plot considered as a whole, centres more in particular situations. They see both the character and the action as enlivened rather than weakened by the contradiction they present, and effects of pathos and horror as heightened beyond what is possible in the realm of realism. The most original and formidable authority for this view is E. E. Stoll, others include Schücking, C. S. Lewis and a growing number of younger critics.[301]

John Donnelly

emotional insecurity of Lear as parent
latent incestuous orientation of Lear
towards daughters, esp. Cordelia

From "Incest, Ingratitude and Insanity: Aspects of the Psychopathology of *King Lear*." *Psychoanalytic Review*, XL (1953), 149-155. By permission.

As the relatively mature individual grows from childhood through adolescence he passes from a position of complete submission to independence in living his own life. The mature parent recognizes this change and does not strive to maintain a hold thereafter. . . . Seldom in these circumstances is it relevant to think of "gratitude," since the child behaves as he does, not because he ought to, but because he wishes to do so. "Filial gratitude" is demanded in less healthy relationships, particularly when the parent is abnormal in one or more emotional spheres. . . . When adult years are approached and the adolescent strives for independence, the emotional security of the parent is threatened and recriminations of "ingratitude" commence. Moreover, it is this very type of father or mother who provokes behavior which is by normal standards actually unfilial, and who will produce charges of "filial ingratitude" even when the conduct is evidence of a healthy reaction.

On these factors to which in some degree every normally-reared [151] individual is exposed rests the appreciation of Lear's reactions to his daughters and the ability of the audience in turn to identify with the principal characters. The power of the play comes in large measure because the audience at first unconsciously identifies in part with the actions of Goneril and Regan. In the first few scenes the two sisters show a cool but rather accurate knowledge of their father's weakness, and until they practice overt cruelty the audience feels some justification for their attitude. Later the spectator has guilt feelings, but the retribution at the end assuages these.

From the outset Lear is portrayed as a parent such as those described above; his pride, his impetuousness, etc., are indications of the way in which he protects himself in his relationships with others. So insecure is he that when faithful Kent questions the extremity of his judgment he is banished, and, although Lear already believes that his daughters love him, he demands a public declaration of their affection, not only to show their gratitude for the gift they will receive, but really because he craves endless reassurance that they love him.[152] . . . Lear is not content with half the love of a wedded daughter.

But goes thy heart with this?
...So young and so untender?

This in itself makes clear that Lear expects his daughter to love him not only as a daughter but also as a lover. It has been suggested by Heilman that Lear "... rationalistically introduces a mensurational standard where there can be none." On the contrary, it is by no means a rational calculation on the part of Lear; rather it is the rational note in Cordelia's "half my love" that produces Lear's reaction—it is total, and therefore incestuous, love that he wants from her. True, he does not realize the incestuous nature of his attachment, but the violence of his curse illustrates the intensity of his feelings. . . . In Act V, when, the delirium having passed, Lear is re-united with Cordelia, his speech

...Come, let's away to prison:
We two alone will sing like birds i' the cage...

might well be made by a lover to his sweetheart, literally two against the world. Cordelia is the great love of his life and on the occasion of her betrothal and leaving his home, he has planned to give up his kingdom and retire ultimately to her,

I loved her most, and thought to set my rest
On her kind nursery. (I.i.122-123)

Evidence of the extent of Lear's sexual phantasies is readily found in the scenes in which he is insane. It is well established that the content of a delirium has a close connection with the unconscious drives and conflicts of the individual. On the outside world may be [153] projected the guilt unconsciously experienced.[154]

[Goneril and Regan's] lack of love for him is meaningful not only in their lack of gratitude for what he has given them but also in the sexual sphere. Not only does he show his rivalry to "Hot-blooded" France who took Cordelia but also he would kill all his sons-in-law (IV.vi.191-192). . . . With no male character in the drama does Lear have a good relationship, for Kent is banished and Gloucester does not seem close to him. All his affection is centered on his daughters and this appears to be linked with a latent incestuous orientation. For his emotional well-being he is dependent on them and on a return of their love in similar terms. . . .[155]

✕

Northrop Frye

From "Characterization in Shakespearian Comedy." *Shakespeare Quarterly*, IV (1953), 273-277. By permission.

The role of the vice includes a great deal of disguising, and the type may usually be recognized by disguise. A typical example is the Brainworm of Jonson's *Every Man in His Humour*, who calls the action of the play the day of his metamorphosis. Similarly Ariel has to surmount the difficult stage direction of "Enter invisible." In tragedy the vice has a counterpart in the type usually called the Machiavellian villain, who also often acts without motivation, from pure love of evil. Edmund in *King Lear* has the role of a tragic vice, and Edmund is contrasted with Edgar. Edgar, with his bewildering variety of disguises, his appearance to blind or mad people in different roles, and his tendency to appear on the third sound of the trumpet and to come pat like the catastrophe of the old comedy, seems to be an experiment in a new type, a kind of tragic "virtue," if I may coin this word by analogy.[274]

$$\nomsprec$$

✕

Lucyle Hook

From "Shakespeare Improv'd, or A Case for the Affirmative." *Shakespeare Quarterly*, IV (1953), 289-299. By permission.

[After the Restoration] Female characters continued to be subordinated, for the most part, to the male characters because of the tradition handed down by the early dramatists who had written feminine roles to be performed by young boys and whose real concern was to use the woman character as briefly as possible and get her off the stage. Since all drama was male drama, the woman was used as scapegoat, tool, or foil, as the case might be, for the larger masculine emotion on which the playwright was focusing his attention.

One has only to examine Shakespearian tragedy to realize the truth of this assertion. As fully rounded and boldly conceived as his great women appear, it must be conceded that his attention is not focused on them, because first, the position of woman in the Renaissance precluded the possibility that a feminine emotion or tragic flaw could result in true tragedy, and secondly, the exigencies of the times demanded that female characters be written so that young boys could play them convincingly. The emotional scenes in which women are involved *on the stage itself* are few. They develop off-stage, whereas the male characters develop in sight of the audience, and we are concerned primarily in the pride of Coriolanus, the ambition of Macbeth, the madness of Lear, the busy imagination of Hamlet rather than in the driving force of Volumnia or Lady Macbeth, the filial constancy of Cordelia, or the madness of Ophelia.[290]

The success of Otway in "rifling Shakespeare of half a Play" for his *Caius Marius* must have emboldened Nahum Tate to take "the Heap of Jewels Unstrung and Unpolish'd," as he explains in the dedicatory epistle to his *King Lear,* and make the play that held the stage spellbound till the middle of Garrick's career. No one has supplied a more persuasive explanation for the rewriting of Shakespeare for the Restoration audience. Among his objections to the original text are: "Lear's real and Edgar's pretended Madness have so much of extravagrant Nature" and "the Images and Language are so odd and surprizing." In all earnestness, he records in the prologue that he

> Yet hopes, since in rich Shakespear's Soil it grew,
> 'Twill relish yet, with those whose Tasts are true,

and more to the point,[297]

> Why shou'd these Scenes lie hid, in which we find
> What may at once divert and teach the Mind;
> Morals were always proper for the Stage,
> But are ev'n necessary in this Age.

As for the plot,

> 'Twas my good Fortune to light on one Expedient to rectifie what was wanting in the Regularity and Probability of the Tale, which was to run through the whole a Love betwixt Edgar and Cordelia, that never chang'd word with each other in the Original. This renders Cordelia's Indifference and her Father's Passion in the first Scene Probable ... The Distress of the Story is evidently heightened by it; ... This Method necessarily threw me to making the Tale conclude in a Success to the innocent distrest Persons. ...

An examination of the plot of Tate's version will bring to light several facts: one, that Nahum Tate was neither a Shakespeare nor an Otway, and second, that his re-hash shows even more than *Caius Marius* the growing female dominance in tragedy. The play in our eyes may be a travesty on Shakespeare's mad Lear and noble Cordelia. Its historical importance, however, lies in the fact that not Lear and his madness but the female figure, Cordelia, and her Tate-given love for Edgar constitute the core of the play. . . .[298]

G. Wilson Knight

From *The Shakespearian Tempest*. London: Methuen & Co., 1953. By permission of the publisher.

Observe Lear's 'ambitious' retort [III.i.] to tempests, recalling Nestor's speech; the words, 'swell,' 'rage,' 'fury'; the inhuman cruelty suggested by 'eyeless'; the 'little world of man' contrasted with the raging world of storm; 'contending' and 'conflicting'; 'curled,' a word met before; and finally, the ever-recurring lion, bear, and wolf. So starts our third act. We may observe, too, how sea imagery is twined with land-tempests; and how here the tempest is part of nature's universal roughness and cruelty, yet less cruel than man. . . .[195]

Notice the violent anthropomorphism of 'crack your cheeks,' 'bellyful,' 'spit,' and the usual oak-tempest association in relation to thunderbolts. Also the 'battle' metaphor and the thought that the tempest is leagued with Lear's daughters. The tempest here both points the tempest in Lear's mind and, more realistically, shows Lear as braving the cruelty of nature as an anodyne to human unkindness. As usual, the tempest is a thing of unique fury:

> . . . since I was man,
> Such sheets of fire, such bursts of horrid thunder,
> Such groans of roaring wind and rain, I never
> Remember to have heard: man's nature cannot carry
> The affliction nor the fear. (III.ii.45)

The storm is an instrument of divine judgment:

> Let the great gods
> That keep this dreadful pother o'er our heads,
> Find out their enemies now. (III.ii.49)

Let such cry 'these dreadful summoners grace' (III.ii.59). *Lear* is a play
which continually emphasizes 'justice'; and here the thunder, the
tempest, the conflicting wrath of winds and rain, all are as divine
summoners calling man to a dreaded acknowledgement of crime.
Thunder in Shakespeare is often thus an instrument of divine wrath.
So, earlier, Lear expressed a similar thought:

> I do not bid the thunder-bearer shoot,
> Nor tell tales of thee to high-judging Jove. (II.iv.230) [196]

A thought throwing back to *Measure for Measure* and forward to
Cymbeline. The fury of this storm is, indeed, tyrannical:

> KENT. Here is the place, my lord; good my lord, enter:
>   The tyranny of the open night's too rough
>   For nature to endure.   [*Storm still.*]
>   (III.iv.1)

Lear's answer is significant:

> Thou think'st 'tis much that this contentious storm
> Invades us to the skin: so 'tis to thee;
> But where the greater malady is fix'd,
> The lesser is scarce felt. Thou'ldst shun a bear;
> But if thy flight lay toward the raging sea
> Thou'ldst meet the bear i'the mouth. When the mind's free,
> The body's delicate: the tempest in my mind
> Doth from my senses take all feeling else
> Save what beats there. (III.iv.6)

Notice, again, the sea; the recurrent bear; the clear reference of the
physical to the spiritual, 'the tempest in my mind'; and the word
'raging.' Then, again, we are pointed to a stern realism. The tempest
will not give Lear leave to ponder on his own more agonizing mental
pain (III.iv.24). Then again the cruel storm draws noble charity from
Lear, replacing his ire. . . . All the sufferings of mortality, their pain,
and their redemption; all the enigmatic purposes of God, His justice,
His mercy, and His wrath; all are concentrated in this titanic tempest.
What reverberations of meaning echo in Lear's question to mad Tom
o'Bedlam: 'What is the [197] cause of thunder?' (III.iv.160). Such is
Lear's tempestuous purgatory. . . .

> *A tent in the French camp. Lear on a bed asleep, soft music playing.* . . .

Music and love; replacing for awhile tempest and mental agony, the
music of a daughter's love to heal the harsh unmusic of madness.

> O you kind gods,
> Cure this great breach in his abused nature!
> The untuned and jarring senses, O, wind up
> Of this child-changed father! (IV.vii.14) [198]

Sleep, music, nature's simples and Cordelia's love are the Doctor's medicines. Now the Doctor would have him wake; 'Louder the music there!'
(IV.vii.25). Cordelia kisses him, speaks those lines we have just quoted
recalling the tempest, so that recollection of that tempest is now divinely
enclosed in music. Lear wakes, and is redeemed into sanity, love, peace.
Again in *Lear* we have a powerful tempest-music opposition. Consider
the Shakespearian sonnet where child and father and happy mother
sing one note of family concord. That harmony is broken here in the
first act; the 'tempest' of division, anguish, and madness ensues; then
restoration is born for awhile on Cordelia's lips, and Lear wakes, as
a mortal man to immortality, wakes into music and love.

Throughout the play we have much animal-imagery. Very often the
beasts are fierce in the tempest-tradition. Some of these I have noticed
already; but a few more may be observed. There are Lear's words:

> Ingratitude, thou marble-hearted fiend,
> More hideous when thou show'st thee in a child
> Than the sea-monster! (I.iv.281)

Sea-monsters occur elsewhere. They are, clearly, like pirates, doubly
charged with sombre suggestion, with all the terrors of beasts and the
sea too. Albany is disgusted at Goneril's cruelty, and compares her to a
series of fierce beasts.

> Tigers, not daughters, what have you perform'd?
> A father, and a gracious aged man,
> Whose reverence even the head-lugg'd bear would lick,
> Most barbarous, most degenerate! have you madded. (IV.ii.40)

'Tigers,' and the 'bear': the usual tempest-beasts. Albany continues:

> If that the heavens do not their visible spirits
> Send quickly down to tame these vile offences,
> It will come,
> Humanity must perforce prey on itself,
> Like monsters of the deep. (IV.ii.46) [199]

Other fierce beasts are scattered throughout the imagery. And many
minor tempest-passages occur. Edgar, like Lear, determines to 'out-face
the winds and persecutions of the sky' (II.iii.11); and in his mock
lunacy he mutters, or sings, part of an old rhyme: 'Still through the
hawthorn blows the cold wind' (III.iv.102). Often he mutters 'Tom's
a-cold,' continually contributing to our sense of the bleak, wintry
effects, which so powerfully impregnate the middle scenes. . . . The
early action of the play is dominated by the tempest: it drenches everything, saturating the phraseology. . . .[200]

✳

Thelma Nelson Greenfield

From "The Clothing Motif in *King Lear.*" *Shakespeare Quarterly,* V (1954), 281-286. By permission.

In contrasting gorgeousness and nakedness, Shakespeare used a motif of [281] ancient and highly respectable lineage. It was a familiar symbol on the early stage in miracle and morality plays. It is in fact the dramatic center of the early part of the morality *Nature.* Off the stage, common in pictorial representation, were juxtaposed clothed and nude figures which carried symbolic meanings of a dramatic nature. Through a long and popular tradition the motif possessed various meanings that attach to its use in *Lear* and enrich the individual application there.

Erwin Panofsky has devoted part of his *Studies in Iconology* to a consideration of the use of contrasting draped and undraped figures in Medieval and Renaissance art.[1] He points out that in both periods the representation of these two figures together indicated conflicting principles, a *débat* in which one of the contestants was meant to be superior. However, the symbolic value of nudity was ambivalent. Especially in the Middle Ages, nudity could symbolize either the superior or the inferior quality.

This ambivalence, Panofsky shows, already existed in the Biblical and Roman traditions. In general, nakedness there represented something bad, such as poverty or shamelessness. However, it was also associated with truth—i.e., "the naked truth"—and so had favorable symbolic meaning, too. Medieval theological tradition likewise gave both favorable and unfavorable interpretations. Summarizing from P. Berchorius, Panofsky lists four theological meanings: "... *nuditas naturalis*, the natural state of man conducive to humility; *nuditas temporalis*, the lack of earthly goods which can be voluntary (as in the Apostles or monks) or necessitated by poverty; *nuditas virtualis*, a symbol of innocence (preferably innocence acquired through confession); and *nuditas criminalis*, a sign of lust, vanity and the absence of all virtues."[2] Along this line, nakedness was used to represent the lack of virtue in devils and vices, pagan divinities, and erring humans. But it also depicted our first parents, martyrs, and souls departing from the body.

However, in Medieval pictorial art, when the draped and undraped figures were set in deliberate contrast, the former symbolized a superior idea. For example, in one picture, a nude personification of Worldly Happiness appears inferior to the draped figure of Heavenly Life; in others Nature is nude in contrast to clothed Grace or clothed Reason.

Renaissance iconography reversed the symbolic values of these contrasting figures. In the Proto-Renaissance, nudity became the conventional representation of ecclesiastical virtues: temperance, fortitude, truth, chastity, etc. Clothing was used for personifications of vain, worldly, passing things. In the fifteenth century this symbolism was brought to a secular level. Botticelli's "Truth vs. Calumny" is one of numerous examples which depict, on a secular level, the superior quality as nude; and Titian's "Sacred and Profane Love" also shows something of the same reversal. Profane Love, instead of being a naked Venus, is richly dressed and holds a vessel of jewels; Sacred Love, undraped, bears a vessel of fire. Shakespeare, with his fine eye for double meanings and ironic [282] contrasts, exploited these complexities and contradictions of meaning in employing the motif in King Lear.[283]

Of the traditional aspects of the motif, the débat elements appear in various ways. Visually, there are opposed figures on the stage, represented in the extreme by the elegant Regan on the one hand and by the "looped and windowed" garments of "the naked fellow" poor Tom, on the other, and represented by Lear himself in his progressive dishevelment. Morally, the motif is used, as in a débat, to contrast inferior and superior values. And verbally, Lear "debates" with Regan and finally with himself on the matter of the meaning of garments.[284]

Like gorgeousness, nakedness has various implications. Regan is finely dressed but at the same time partially unclothed, wearing what "scarce keeps her warm." Regan's partial nudity reminds us that one of the meanings of nakedness, symbolically, is "lust, vanity and absence of all virtues." It prepares us for her savagery and her quick sensual passion for Edmund. Tom's nudity is a mark of his individual poverty and wretchedness, and it is his special mark of identification. He proclaims nakedness as his disguise (II.iii.11). The image of "poor naked wretches" exposed to the storm suggests to Lear a whole world of pitiful suffering of which he heretofore had taken too little heed. This image, soon to be manifested on the stage in the figure of Tom, inspires Lear, through pity, to dissociate himself from the "lendings" of royalty, "Take physic, pomp;/ Expose thyself to feel what wretches feel," (III.iv.33-34). Finally, Tom's physical appearance leads Lear to consider the essence of man and to seek for self-knowledge through identification with the "thing itself"; with man stripped of the attributes which accrue to him through external trappings of worm's silk and cat's perfume. (I am here considering Tom not as Edgar in disguise but as Tom of Bedlam, which he is to Lear and to the audience, also, except for the duration of a few small asides.)

Lear at the depths of his disillusionment and wretchedness and with the first onset of madness deliberately assumes the symbolic state of the nude figure: "Off, off you lendings! Come, unbutton here" (III.iv.113-114). He achieves wisdom by pitying, understanding and sharing this extremity of physical affliction. First bareheaded, now plucking off his garments, he achieves the symbolic condition which brings him self-recognition and the way to his salvation. The Christian analogy to Lear's psychological state and its relation to the use of the clothing motif provides familiar overtones. Man, in *Nature*, prepared for his heavenly salvation by casting off his garments. In fact, three of the theological meanings of the symbols of nudity are paralleled at this point in *King Lear:* "the natural state of man conducive to humility; ... the lack of earthly goods ... ; innocence (preferably innocence acquired through confession)." Lear's "innocence" becomes the exaggerated innocence of madness, a state which continues until Cordelia heals the sore spirit that has borne the shock of severance from its familiar condition in the world of human affairs.

The involvement of Lear with the motif of the garbed and ungarbed figures, used so emphatically in poetry and in action at this structural high point, reappears later. His preoccupation with clothing continues through his madness. He frets over Tom's garb (III.vi.84-86). In Act IV, he assumes a pathetic caricature of high office with his crown of weeds:

> rank fumiter and furrow weeds,
> With hardocks, hemlock, nettles, cuckoo-flow'rs,
> Darnel, and all the idle weeds that grow
> In our sustaining corn. (IV.iv.3-6)

When Lear is restored to his senses and to his friends, his new status is accompanied by new garments: "In the heaviness of sleep/ We put fresh garments on him" (IV.vii.21-22); and he notices these clothes very quickly upon his [285] awakening. At his death he reiterates on a quieter note but again physically and verbally the act of divesture: "Pray you, undo this button" (V.iii.308).[286]

---

1 Erwin Panofsky, *Studies in Iconology: Humanistic Themes in the Art of the Renaissance* (New York, 1939), pp. 154-157.

2 Panofsky, p. 156.[282]

Paul A. Jorgensen

From "Much Ado About *Nothing*." *Shakespeare Quarterly*, V (1954), 287-295. By permission.

The word *nothing* presents an interesting parallel [to the Elizabethan use of *honest*], for not only did its iteration stem from popular genres, but serious writers were using it for purposes other than verbal ingenuity. And there were further similarities. Like *honesty*, it had developed shadings just closely enough related to one another to prevent easy distinction. In its combination of one covert meaning with several respectable meanings—enough to make its use permissible, but never securely so—Shakespeare must have recognized one of his favorite opportunities. The fate of both words in modern exegesis also promises to be comparable. So enlightening, one fears, has been professorial clarification of the occasional pun on *honesty*, that many students have left the classroom believing that whenever Shakespeare said "honest" he meant "chaste." Less likely to emanate from classrooms, but not for that reason the less persuasive, are the results of Thomas Pyles' scholarly study of "Ophelia's 'Nothing,'" wherein he rescues the word (if not Ophelia) from a moderately respectable oblivion for a distinguished place in the "venereal vernacular of the day." [*Modern Language Notes*, XLIV (1949), 322-323.] Without meaning to sully what Professor Pyles rightly considers the "beautiful clarity" of his findings, I should like to restore some of the larger web of meaning which lay behind Shakespeare's remarkable insistence on the word.

"Can you make no use of nothing, nuncle?" asks Lear's Fool. The query strikes deeper into the King's impending tragedy than we at first realize. Certainly Lear's confident reply—"Why, no, boy, nothing can be made out of nothing"—would have struck original audiences as seriously, even ironically wrong. In its pagan doctrine it opposed a vital Christian tenet; it contradicted, in several other senses, the highly potential nature of the word and idea as demonstrated elsewhere by Shakespeare and his contemporaries; it had been [287] underlined by a previous dialogue (I.i.89-92) in which, after Lear and Cordelia exchange emphatic *nothing*'s, the King warns her, "Nothing can come of nothing"; and it is ironically echoed by the Fool's later pronouncement upon Lear himself: "Now thou art an O without a figure. I am better than thou art now: I am a fool, thou art nothing" (I.iv.211).

The audience which thus witnessed, in one sense, much growing tragically from nothing, and, in another, kings becoming things of nothing, had been familiarized with the pattern not only by De Contemptu philosophy but by two other well-known bodies of writing. The first consisted of theological treatises affirming the original nothingness surrounding creation and the essential nothingness of all temporal things. The second was part of the literary tradition which produced mock encomia like Erasmus' *Praise of Folly*. Both shared the purpose of defending the importance of nothingness.[288]

The Prayse of Nothing (1585), doubtfully attributed to Sir Edward Dyer, . . . not only claims for Nothing the distinction of being the origin and end of everything, but speculates upon how much better most things would be if Nothing had caused or influenced them. This exploitation of the word's ambiguity, especially when it is used as the subject of a sentence, is better illustrated in an anonymous ballad, apparently inspired by the tract and bearing the same title:

> Nothing was first, and shall be last,
>   for nothing holds for ever,
> And nothing ever yet scap't death,
>   so can't the longest liver:
> Nothing's so Immortall, nothing can,
> From crosses ever keepe a man,
> Nothing can live, when the world is gone,
>   for all shall come to nothing.

William Lisle's poem *Nothing for a New-Yeares gift* (1603) likewise uses the word, as in its title, in both a positive and negative sense. And in a manner reminiscent of the Queen's premonition in *Richard II*, Lisle pays tribute to the creative pains that come from meditating the subject:

> Excesse of studie in a traunce denies
> My ravisht soule her Angel-winged flight:
> Strugling with *Nothing* thus my bodie lies
> Panting for breath, depriv'd of sences might.
> At length recovered by this pleasant slumber,
> The straunge effects from Nothing, thus I wonder.[289]

In attempting a *dramatic*, rather than expository, elaboration, Shakespeare would give the playwright's equivalent of the poet's imaginative shaping. Out of a trifle, a misunderstanding, a fantasy, a mistaken overhearing, a "naughtiness," might come the materials for a drama—as happened, less deliberately perhaps, in *King Lear*.[295]

Keith Rinehart

From "The Moral Background of *King Lear*."
University of Kansas City Review, XX (1954),
223-228. By permission.

The character of Cordelia is so firmly fixed in Act I, scene i, that the audience cannot forget her nor the moral perfection with which she becomes increasingly identified. Like an arch, she spans the play. Disappointments and horrors fall on Lear and Gloucester in the interval between Act I, scene i, and her appearance in Act IV, scene iv, but they do not efface the impression which Cordelia has made. Her function as a symbol of morality is the more effective for her absence; she can be idealized more easily. Lear's foolish passion in rejecting her makes her wisdom all the more admirable.[223]

When one recalls Cordelia's qualities—wisdom, duty, measured affection, self-control, inner calm, her approval of the superiority of reason over will, her unwillingness to compromise her inner worth even for the most pressing motives of genuine affection and material gains, her benevolence and endurance—she evokes a familiar moral pattern indeed. She is a Stoic. There is no element in her character of Christian submission or humility. There is no reason to quarrel with Lear's assertion that she is proud. The Christian foolishness, of the type of St. Francis' Brother Juniper, is totally antithetical to her character. In *King Lear* folly leads to evil, wisdom to the good. The wise Cordelia exemplifies, as nearly as may be in drama, the attitude and behavior of the ideal Stoic, all of whose qualities she possesses. Her effect as the symbol of the good in the play is to fix its background of stoic morality.[224]

The essential unity and divinity of nature in its cosmic, moral and psychological aspects is again, as in the case of Cordelia, a familiar concept of stoic philosophy. Again the non-Christian element of *Lear's* moral background is emphasized; for, according to the stoics and contrary to Christian doctrine, nature is divine. The stoic emphasis on the prime importance of morality and the prime importance of universal order in securing the good, is preserved. The tragedy occurs when this order is violated.[225]

The clearest symbol of evil in the play is Edmund. He addresses Nature as a goddess (I.ii.1), but the Nature he honors is the nature of fierce and violent struggle, whose rewards are bestowed on the strong and crafty. She provides the key to Edmund's function in the play as a moral symbol. This dog-eat-dog idea of nature denies both moral order and any other sort of morality in nature. Edmund, therefore, seeks the first opportunity to destroy the order of his family and of the law to secure for himself the wealth and honors which are naturally denied him. His own evil he imputes to his brother, Edgar, for the purposes of fooling Gloucester who, taken in, denounces Edgar's unnatural behavior (I.ii.81). In dealing with Edgar to persuade him to avoid their father, Edmund echoes the word *unnatural* (I.ii.155) and, a little later, in a short soliloquy (I.ii.195-200), says that he plans to take advantage of Edgar's good moral nature. Edmund, following his own idea of nature, does not scruple to use hypocritically the concept of nature to which the "good" characters of the play subscribe.[226]

Justice is peculiarly the virtue of order in stoic philosophy; Gloucester, for pleasure's sake, has brought disorder, and with it his own ultimate downfall. Cordelia, Kent and Edgar, though separated spacially, are united morally and balance the spacial unity and moral discord of Edmund, Goneril, and Regan.[227]

$$\rightarrowtail\!\!\!\nmid\!\!\!\longleftarrow$$

L. C. Knights

From *"King Lear* and the Great Tragedies." *Penguin Guide to English Literature: The Age of Shakespeare* [1955]. Harmondsmith, 1956. Pp. 228-256. By permission of the publisher.

A consciousness of change and death, of a world subjected to time and appearance, of an inextricable mingling of elements in energies and passions that are at once the necessary condition of achievement and, apparently, self-destructive, is deeply embedded in plays as different as *Henry IV, Hamlet, Troilus and Cressida,* and *Measure for Measure.* The only way for Shakespeare to come to terms with those obstinate questionings was to probe still further into the nature of man, to expose himself yet more completely to 'the destructive element.' Exposure is the very essence of *King Lear,* which is one of the most profound attempts in the literature of the world to reach some bedrock certainty of affirmation concerning what it is that gives meaning and significance to human life.

In that excursion into no-man's-land Shakespeare was not, of course, entirely unaccompanied. He had behind him the humanistic and Christian tradition of the West, and in all the tragedies he made dramatic use of ideas, deriving from the medieval period, that were common to his age. Yet these ideas are never adopted uncritically; and in *Lear*, above all, there is a resolute refusal to *start from* anything that does not issue directly out of first-hand experience. (The symbolic significance of Lear's casting off his clothes in the presence of the virtually naked Poor Tom has often been observed.) The positives that emerge from this play are, indeed, fundamentally Christian values, but they are reached by an act of profound individual exploration: the play does not take them for granted; it takes nothing for granted but Nature and natural energies and passions.[232]

Lear's expression of revulsion and disgust is, I suppose, one of the profoundest expressions of pessimism in all literature. If it is not the final word in the play, it is certainly not because Shakespeare has shrunk from any of the issues. Pessimism is sometimes regarded as a tough and realistic attitude. Shakespeare's *total* view of human life in this play has a toughness and actuality that make most pessimism look like sentimentality. It is because the play has brought us to this vision of horror—seen without disguise or palliation—that the way is open for the final insights. In the successive stripping away of the layers of appearance, what remains to discover is the most fundamental reality of all. In the play it takes the form of the love and forgiveness of Cordelia. But that love has to be earned in the way in which all things most worth having are earned—by the full admission of a need, the achievement of honesty and humility, the painful shedding of all that is recognized as incompatible with the highest good, by, in short, making oneself able to receive whatever it may be.[237] It is because she is fully human—though there are also potent suggestions of divine grace—that she is 'natural' in a different sense from that intended in Edmund's philosophy. It is her sense of the bounty of [238] nature (of 'our sustaining corn' as well as of the 'rank fumiter and furrow weeds') that lies behind her invocation:

> All bless'd secrets,
> All you unpublish'd virtues of the earth,
> Spring with my tears! be aidant and remediate
> In the good man's distress! (IV.iv.)

In that 'spring' there is an identification of human nature and the wider Nature from which it is born. But it is because of her love and pity ('the good man' is the erring Lear) that she can invoke so wholeheartedly the 'unpublish'd virtues of the earth.' Her tenderness is

rooted in the same strength that enabled her to reject Lear's miscon-
ceived demands ('Corporeal friends,' said Blake, 'may be spiritual
enemies'). Her love is of a kind that, confronted with a real demand,
does not bargain or make conditions; it is freely given, and it represents an absolute of human experience that can stand against the full
shock of disillusion. When Lear, dressed in 'fresh clothes' and to the accompaniment of music (the symbolism is important), is awakened in
her presence, there follows one of the most tender and moving scenes
in the whole of Shakespeare. . . . [239]

The scene of Lear's final anguish is so painful that criticism hesitates
to fumble with it. Yet it may be said that there are at least two reasons
why no other ending would have been imaginatively right. We do not
only look at a masterpiece, we enter into it and live with it. Our
suffering then, and our acceptance of suffering, no less than Lear's, is
an intrinsic part of what the play is; for as with Lear and Gloucester
our capacity to see is dependent upon our capacity to feel. Now what
our seeing has been directed towards is nothing less than *what man is.*
The imaginative discovery that is the play's essence has thus involved
the sharpest possible juxtaposition of rival conceptions of 'Nature.' In
the Edmund-Goneril-Regan group the philosophy of natural impulse
and egotism has been revealed as self-consuming, its claim to represent
strength as a self-bred delusion. What Lear touches in Cordelia, on the
other hand, is, we are made to feel, the reality, and the values revealed
so surely there are established in the face of the worst that can be known
of man or Nature. To keep nothing in reserve, to slur over no possible
cruelty or misfortune, was the only way of ensuring that the positive
values discovered and established in the play should keep their triumphant hold on our imagination. . . .[240]

$$\times\!\!\!\!\times$$

Gerald Smith

From "A Note on the Death of Lear." *Modern
Language Notes,* LXX (1955), 403-404. By
permission of the Johns Hopkins Press.

The *Problems of Aristotle,* a pseudo-scientific text of 1597, speaks
of a death of joy as follows:

> Why have some men died through griefe and sadness,
> and some through joy, and none for anger?
> Is it because joy doth coole the very inwarde guts?
>
> (Sig. H)

When Strotzo, one of the villains of Marston's *Antonio's Revenge,* explains Andrugio's murder to Maria, he pretends that Andrugio had died a natural death of joy on hearing Piero's declarations of love and reunion:[403]

> The vast delights of his large sudden joyes
> Opened his pores so wide, that's native heate
> So prodigally flow'd t'exterior parts,
> That thinner [the inner?] Citadell was left unmand,
> And so surpriz'd on sudden by colde death.   (I.v.10)

As A. C. Bradley has always "fantastically" maintained, the deaths of Gloucester and Lear are from a combination of joy and grief on hearing that they will be joyfully reunited to their loved ones. Edgar says of his father:

> ... but his flaw'd heart,
>   Alack, too weak the conflict to support!
> 'Twixt two extremes of passion, joy and grief,
> Burst smilingly. (V.iii.196-199)

Likewise, it is this "large sudden joy" as Lear thinks he sees Cordelia's lips move that proves too great a contrast to his grief.[404]

⨉

E. M. M. Taylor

From "Lear's Philosopher." *Shakespeare Quarterly,* VI (1955), 364-365. By permission.

In the storm scene Lear speaks of Edgar as "this philosopher," "this same learned Theban," "Noble philosopher," "my philosopher" and "good Athenian"—all five phrases occurring in the space of less than thirty lines. Clearly, the king takes Poor Tom for a Greek philosopher come out of the storm to instruct him, and he refuses to be parted from his new-found teacher. . . . there is a straightforward association of ideas between the unaccommodated man who has dispensed with all lendings save a blanket, and Greek philosophy, and we are doubtless meant to follow Lear in making it. The Cynic philosophers were a byword for frugality and contempt for creature comforts, one mark of which—according to Diogenes Laertius, and other ancient authorities—was a preference for the single garment, a mere rag in winter and a heavy cloak in the heat of summer. One of the best known stories from ancient history is that of Diogenes and his tub; while another anecdote, perhaps better known to Elizabethan than to modern readers, is that concerning Crates of Thebes:

who to the intent that he might more quietly studie Philosophy, threw all his goods into the sea, saying, hence from me, you ungratious appetites, I had rather drowne you, then you should drowne me.[364]

Thomas Nashe tells this story in his *Anatomie of Absurditie* (*Works*, edited McKerrow, I, 34) in the course of a homily on youthful gallants and their love of finery, for any sixteenth-century moralizing on the virtues of the simple life easily shifted to an attack on extravagant dress, and to an identification of finery with sophistication. It would seem possible, then, even likely, that Shakespeare's audience would have caught the drift of Lear's address to Edgar as to a Cynical philosopher (indifferently Athenian and Theban, for leading thinkers of this school taught in both cities) and would have understood that the king's disordered mind was still teasing at the problems of Pomp and Poverty.

If this is accepted, it need hardly be stressed how germane Lear's delusion is to the rest of the play. The central theme of *Lear*, underlined again and again in the mercenary and in the schoolmaster images, is that a man who grossly overvalues material things and the outward trappings of state, virtue, and affection must be schooled by disaster and suffering into truer, more adequate, and more charitable assessments. . . .[365]

$$\gtrless\!\!\!\mid\!\!\!\lessgtr$$

Harry V. Jaffa

From "The Limits of Politics: An Interpretation of *King Lear*, Act I, Scene I." *American Political Science Review*, LI (1957), 405-427. By permission.

The negative view that Bradley and others have taken of the original plan has centered . . . on the love-test. The love-test has already been dismissed as a pretense, as far as the original division of the kingdom is concerned. The real objection has always been to the division of the kingdom itself. It has always been thought that, since the supreme object of monarchical policy in Shakespeare is the unifica tion of England, a British king who deliberately divides a united kingdom is committing the supreme act of monarchical folly. Yet reflection must make us cautious of accepting this view. . . .[410]

. . . we must note that Cornwall and Albany represent the geographical extremities of Britain. Cornwall clearly represents the south. Albany, according to Holinshed, originally was the northern part of the island, and included Scotland. In Act I, iv, 207 the Fool tells Lear "Thou hast pared thy wit o' both sides, and left nothing i' the middle," indicating that the two extremities (Goneril and Regan) have digested the center portion, which was to have been Cordelia's. Lear had married his two older daughters to two great lords whose estates (and hence, we may assume, whose power) lay at the opposite poles of the kingdom. Now, anyone who knows only so much of English history as is contained in Shakespeare's histories, knows that English kings found it impossible to exercise control in any region very remote from the center of the royal domains, without the support of the feudal potentates in those regions. The [411] selection of sons-in-law from the remote portions of his kingdom indicates, I believe, that Lear's unification of the kingdom was in part due to his ability to secure the adhesion of the lords of these outlying districts through marriage with the royal house. But the marriage of a daughter involves a dowry: Cornwall and Albany expected more than brides, and the possibility that a descendant might occupy the throne. What could be more natural than that they expected lands that lay in the neighborhood of their ancestral estates?

From this it would seem that Lear's action in dividing the kingdom was not arbitrary or foolish—it was an action predestined by the very means required to bring unity to the kingdom. Lear, it appears, delayed the division as long as possible, but he could not put it off indefinitely, any more than he could put off indefinitely his own demise.

In Lear's speech, announcing to the court the division of the kingdom into three parts, he gives two reasons for his action: first, that he wishes to shake all care and business from his age, conferring them on younger strengths; and second, "that future strife may be prevented now." There is a sense in which these two reasons may be regarded as a single one: that is, by devising a political arrangement whereby the peace of the kingdom could be assured without the adventitious factor of his personal ascendancy, Lear removed his chief present care by providing against future strife. However, if we view these two reasons more superficially, I think it would be correct to say that the second reason is the real one, and the first primarily an excuse for the latter. For it is difficult to believe that failing strength was a pressing motive for Lear's action: the old man was the most prodigious octogenarian on record, still spending his days hunting, and able, as the last act shows, to kill a man single-handed. The decisive consideration, however, is this: there is no evidence that, in the original plan, Lear intended anything resembling an abdication. On the contrary is the fact that Lear never abandoned the crown. What he divided between his sons-in-law, in the flush of his rage against Cordelia, was a coronet. He himself was to retain, even in the altered plan, "The name, and all th' additions to a king." Yet, as long as Lear retained the name of king, a name which he in no way shared with a successor, his delegation of authority to his sons-in-law remained fundamentally distinguished from an abdication. One may ask why Lear held [412] a coronet in his hand at all. The answer, I believe, is that the coronet, the symbol of ducal authority, was intended for Cordelia's husband. It must be remembered that the scene was intended to be one in which Cordelia received her husband and dowry. Her husband, whether Burgundy or France, would be a foreigner, whose British dukedom would be conferred along with Cordelia's hand. To sum up: Lear might have delegated much of his "business" to his sons-in-law in the original plan, but there is no sign of anything resembling an abdication. And as long as he did not abdicate he would, as King, remain the only personage capable of deciding the highest political questions. Since there is no explicit mention, anywhere in the scene, of a successor, the implication is that Lear would retain the power of naming a successor, and this in turn indicates an intention to retain decisive power.

Lear's original plan, I think, called for precisely equal shares to go to Albany and Cornwall, husbands of the two older daughters. But Cordelia was to receive a third "more opulent" than the other two. Lear divided his kingdom into "three," but the parts are not mathematical "thirds." Cordelia was not only to be situated in the middle, but to have the richest portion of the realm. Lear, as Bradley pointed out, intended to live with Cordelia alone. Living on as king with Cordelia, with Albany and Cornwall acting as his deputies in regions which he could not control without their loyalty anyway, does it seem that Lear was giving up anything that he could in any case have kept to himself much longer? Since Cordelia's husband would be a foreigner, living in the midst of Lear's long-time retainers, it is difficult to imagine any such conflict of domestic authority arising, as a result of the original plan, as arose in the altered plan. In the altered plan, the division of Cordelia's inheritance between Goneril and Regan left Lear's original retainers a minority among those owing primary fealty to Albany and Cornwall. But in the original plan any retainers the husband of Cordelia brought with him to England would in all likelihood have remained a small minority in comparison with those who had been brought up to regard Lear as their master. And all indications within the play are that Lear evoked the strongest loyalty from those who recognized him as their legitimate master.

Concerning the marriage of Cordelia, I think the evidence is overwhelming in favor of the view that she was intended as the bride of Burgundy. First, because [413] Lear offers her to Burgundy, although this is after her disinheritance. Second, because Burgundy has had previous knowledge of Cordelia's dowry. But such knowledge implies at the same time that he has been privy to some, if not all, of Lear's intended scheme. Such a confidential position certainly suggests the status of an intended son-in-law. Now France and Burgundy were traditional enemies. Their presence at Lear's court suggests that Cordelia's dowry would have been an important counter in the balance of power between them. Burgundy is the lesser power, as is shown by Lear's style in addressing him, and by the fact that Lear fears insulting France, but not Burgundy. Now Cordelia's marriage to France would have been a political blunder of the first magnitude, a blunder of which there is no reason to suspect the Lear who drafted the plan approved by Kent and Gloucester. For a French marriage would inevitably have given rise to the French claims to the British throne, such as actually led to the French invasion that occurs in the play. Lear would never have intended, nor would Kent have consented, that the King of France or his descendants, inherit the throne of Britain. In such a case there would have been the possibility, at least, that Britain would become the appendage of France. Moreover, such a marriage would have heavily unbalanced the system of powers, as that system is envisaged within the horizon of the play. France, commanding the fairest part of Britain, might easily have overmatched Burgundy, thereafter to hold the remainder of Britain in his power. On the other hand, however, Cordelia's dowry, added to Burgundy, might have aided the balance of power on the continent. And, conversely, Burgundy, added to Cordelia's part of Britain, would have neutralized any combination of the older sisters. A combination of the powers of Albany and Cornwall with France, against Cordelia and Burgundy, even apart from its geographical difficulty,[414] would have been unlikely. For the victory of Goneril and Regan over Cordelia, if achieved with the aid of France, would in all likelihood leave the elder sisters at the mercy of their great ally, to be overpowered and absorbed in turn. We may, however, ask why France, who was no doubt a political reasoner, wasted his time in a vain suit at Lear's court? The answer is, I think, in the first place, that the marriage was too important for him to be absent from the scene of its negotiation. We must remember that Goneril and Regan must have had an intense interest, not only in their younger sister's dowry, but in her marriage. And the moment of Cordelia's betrothal to Burgundy would be the precise moment for France to cultivate good relations with her older sisters. There remained, however, as a remote possibility, what actually came to pass. Just as the first Queen Elizabeth could always flirt with French dukes, as a threat to Spain, so could Lear use a French marriage for Cordelia as a threat to Goneril and Regan, and their husbands, should they fail to acquiesce in the preferred treatment given Cordelia in the division of the kingdom.

. . . the marriage of Mary Tudor to Philip was a "Burgundian" marriage. . . . The relevant point is that Mary, although married to a foreign prince who was nominally king of England, alone exercised the powers of the sovereign. Philip was never more than the consort of the queen, even though he was heir to a throne in his own right. A Burgundian marriage, in short, would have made the succession of Cordelia to the throne a viable political arrangement. Lear's scheme of marrying Cordelia to Burgundy gave good promise of leading to a stable international system, and a peaceful acceptance of Lear's will and testament at home.[415]

$$\times\!\!\!\!\times$$

Winifred M. T. Nowottny

From "Lear's Questions." *Shakespeare Survey*, X (1957), 90-97. By permission of Cambridge University Press.

Through the impact of the storm Shakespeare has effected one of the most difficult acts of communication necessary to the subsequent development of the play: he has brought home to us Lear's belief that all a man can know is what he knows through the flesh. Further, in Lear's defiance of the storm, his involvement with the problem of guilt has been brought to the fore. By a master-stroke, Shakespeare now establishes an intimate relation between Lear's several preoccupations, by using for them all the one symbol of the flesh: the flesh that suffers, knows, begets, is punished for its guilt. This is strikingly done when Lear first encounters Poor Tom. His first speech connects the idea of punishing the flesh with the idea of begetting:

> It is the fashion, that discarded fathers
> Should have thus little mercy on their flesh?
> Judicious punishment! 'twas this flesh begot
> Those pelican daughters.

His next speech connects the idea of the exposed and suffering flesh with the idea of real truth:

> Why, thou wert better in thy grave than to answer with thy un-covered body this extremity of the skies. Is man no more than this? ... here's three on's are sophisticated! Thou art the thing itself.... Off, off, you lendings! come unbutton here.[92]

Gloucester in the same scene furthers the power of the symbol with his words,

> Our flesh and blood is grown so vile, my lord,
> That it doth hate what gets it.

Henceforward the language takes on the function of binding more closely and exploring more deeply the connexions set up by Lear's experiences in the storm. It is the discovery of the metonymy, "the flesh," wherewith to advert to all the problems vital to the play which gives the language of the latter part of the tragedy its characteristic mark of simplicity charged with power, for within the metonymic structure made possible by the use of this common term, Shakespeare is able to sweep the strings of feeling whilst seeming to make no gesture at all.

The language of the play is further shaped for Shakespeare's pur-poses by a deliberate exploitation of the ambivalence of this term and of the aptness of the symbol for development through cognate terms such as "heart," "hand," "eyes," "brains," which also, in common usage, have both abstract and concrete significance. Much of the sombre power of the most memorable utterances in the mad scenes is due to the subtle interplay between the flesh as mere flesh and the qualities the flesh embodies, and to the interplay between the different members of that whole complex of ideas of which the flesh has been made the symbol. For instance, Lear's sudden demand,

> Then let them anatomize Regan; see what breeds about her heart.
> Is there any cause in nature that makes these hard hearts?

is macabre, not merely gruesome, because of the interplay between abstract and concrete, coupled with the interplay between the multiple references of the symbol: the flesh itself when dissected will reveal the truth, but an *intellectual* truth ("anatomize" meant not only to dissect but also to give a reasoned analysis or enumeration of qualities); this flesh is also the flesh in which evil things "breed" and the flesh subject to Nature's laws, the flesh in which the physical and spiritual are, according to Lear, so wholly united that the "heart" that breeds wick-edness is also the "heart" that can be dissected and its hardness probed to seek the final cause. And the form of this sudden demand is such that we can simultaneously accept it as natural to Lear's way of thinking, and reject it as unnatural to our own. . . . In the mad scenes Lear again and again has sombre utterances whose power to strike directly at the heart is due to the peculiar dexterity with which they walk the precipice between the figurative and the true, as in Lear's,

> Give me an ounce of civet, good apothecary, to sweeten my imagination. . . .

This technique is, I am convinced, deliberate, and it does much to produce that sense of inexplicable power which we feel in attending a performance of the play. . . .[93]

In the mad scene with Gloucester the dialogue deliberately inhabits a no-man's-land between truth and falsehood; it is this ("matter and impertinency mixed") that makes it the pregnant "reason in madness" it is. Lear's first remark sets the tone:

> No, they cannot touch me for coining; I am the king himself. Nature's above art in that respect.

This speech, whose immediate reference, no doubt, is to the imaginary press-money he is about to hand out, at once strikes the note of an uncertain relation between the true and the false, a note with many overtones: Lear is coining money, but is no coiner, since he is the King himself (and this phrase recalls his uncertainty about whether and in what sense he may be called king) and being by nature a king (if he is a king at all) his creations are true, unlike the feignings of art—but at the same time what he is now creating (the press-money) *is* a figment, with which he "pays" the other figments of his brain. . . . Then Lear in his fantasy asks for the password. A voice from the real world offers one at random. "Pass." Unnervingly, it is the right password. And, as Lear accepts Edgar as part of his fantasy, his voice reaches the dark world of the blind and deluded Gloucester: "I know that voice." Lear wheels upon him, not seeing him—"Goneril"—yet somehow seeing him—"with a white beard!"—and at once the white beard suggests white hairs as a figure of wisdom, and he recalls the deception of his daughters. . . .[94]

The grotesque picture of woman's sexuality (the extremest point of Lear's sense of the sinfulness of the flesh) is not only in itself a tale of false appearances, of monstrosity in nature and of a grotesque conjunction of gods and devils, but also it is in the end rejected as the vapour of an imagination itself in need of something to disguise its own stench. Hard upon this passage, both full of revulsion and provocative of revulsion in the hearer, come the words of Gloucester, charged with reverence and love:

> O, let me kiss that hand!

and, at this, Lear achieves the most sombre and powerful of those utterances in which the flesh and the spirit mingle in bewildering relations:

> Let me wipe it first; it smells of mortality.

It seems to me that, except for the last scene of all, there is no greater moment in the play than this. Here Lear is seen with that profound humanism which recognizes man as being at once wondrous and frail: supreme object of love and reverence, to whom one says, "O, let me kiss that hand!" and yet by his very condition, one who "smells of mortality"; in brief, the "ruined [master]piece of nature." This is a moment of complete truth, the more powerful because it comes as the climax of a dialogue fraught with ambiguities, with reason in madness, with lightning traversings and inversions of the familiar categories of the true and the false. This interchange between Lear and Gloucester is an epiphany of that idea of man by which the whole tragedy is informed. . . .[95]

$$\text{\Large $\rightarrow$}\!\!\!\times$$

Jonas A. Barish and Marshall Waingrow

From "Service in *King Lear.*" *Shakespeare Quarterly*, IX (1958), 347-355. By permission.

. . . a profound vision of life arises from the debris of the disaster. We are no longer able to view society as a rigid, absolute, or even wholly "real" structure. We, like Lear and Cordelia at the end of the play, have become "God's spies," and from this supreme vantage point recognize the hierarchical order for what it is: a system that expresses both more and less than the actualities of life. As servants of *God*, we discover the true and whole meaning of service: that by promoting concord between individuals of different rank, it ends by minimizing distinctions of rank. Witness Kent: the moral stature of the vassal raises him to a special plane of equality with his social superior. Returning to the stage to bid farewell to Lear, Kent is introduced to his master as "noble Kent, your friend" (V.iii.268). Through his very immersion in service (Edgar pays tribute to him as one "who in disguise/ Followed his enemy king and did him service/ improper for a slave" V.iii.219-221), he has transcended his status in the act of upholding it. On the other side, false service affects the structure of society in the opposite way: instead of progressing towards a uniquely human kind of solidarity, above the prevailing relationships of rank, it plunges society downwards into a bestial chaos where social distinctions are supplanted by the rule of tooth and claw.[348]

The conscious exponent of the service that leads to chaos is Edmund, whose malignance surpasses Oswald's by virtue of its greater self-awareness. Of all the characters Edmund is the one with the word "service" most often on his tongue. He offers his services on various occasions to Kent, Edgar, Gloucester, and Cornwall, as well as—in a more special sense—to Goneril and Regan. If, speaking to Kent in the opening scene of the play, he claims for himself the dual role of servant and pupil ("My services to your lordship. . . . Sir, I shall study deserving"), his first soliloquy notifies us that such professions are lip-service only. Even his vow of allegiance to his "goddess" Nature reduces itself to a tautology. Although the phrase "to thy law/ My services are bound" (I.ii.1-2) appears to recognize both the idea of obligation and the reciprocal character of the bond, in fact it is a negation of both, since what Edmund means by "Nature" and her "law" proves to be nothing but the anarchic principle of his own will and appetite, the absence of obligation to any one or any thing other than himself, the complete denial of reciprocity.[350]

If in Edmund we see the vicious servant posing as the genuine and making the world accept the imposture, in Edgar we see the true servant victimized, returning to enact a kind of purgatorial masquerade as the false servant. Edgar represents himself as a former courtier, proud, vain, and lascivious, who served the lust of his mistress' heart and the evil impulses in himself. But whereas in the "real" world of the play, false servants thrive, Edgar exhibits Poor Tom as outcast for his falseness. Poor Tom has become an archetype of degraded humanity, the victim of every humiliation inflicted on loyal followers—whipped, like the Fool, placed in the stocks, like Kent, imprisoned, like Cordelia, and, of course, banished. Here, because it occurs only in Edgar's fantasy, justice triumphs; the "undivulged crimes" of darkness are exposed and punished. Instead of "corruption in the place" and truth in exile, there is a meaningful relationship between crime and punishment. The madman, in a world itself gone mad, becomes a microcosm of the world gone sane, where malignant service, instead of being rewarded, is turned out of doors and pursued by vermin, dogs, and fiends.[351]

That the specific issue over which Lear becomes embroiled with his elder daughters should be his allowance of retainers is, needless to say, very much to the point in this discussion. Lear's impassioned defense of his knights represents his first attempt to grapple seriously with the meaning of service. If the relationship were simply a matter of ducats dispensed for chores performed, their dismissal would not matter. Others, as Goneril and Regan argue, could perform the same functions. But it is their personal loyalty to him that counts, their love; and it is this that Lear defends, and this that Goneril attacks. The very presence of honest and incorruptible service is a rebuke to her, whether it comes from the knights or from the keener-sighted and more articulate (and hence more hated) Fool. [353]

$$\rightarrow\!\!\!\leftarrow$$

William Frost

From "Shakespeare's Rituals and the Opening of *King Lear*." *Hudson Review*, X (1958), 577-585. By permission of the author and the publisher.

What can be said in defense of the [opening] scene?

In the first place, if it must be viewed as allegory, then as allegory, at least, it holds together extremely well. Its basic constituents are simply two contests of affection, the first among Goneril, Regan, and Cordelia, the second between France and Burgundy. That the second is a neat and ironic commentary on the first comes out in France's courteous lines to the reluctant Burgundy—

> My Lord of Burgundy
> What say you to the lady? Love's not love
> When it is mingled with regards that stand
> Aloof from th'entire point. Will you have her?
> She is herself a dowry.

concise statement ; maxim

The aphorism about the nature of love, though not so intended by France, who was absent from the earlier contest, sums up the moral issue involved in that contest, and prepares for the appropriately religious formality of France's ensuing proposal:

> Fairest Cordelia, that art most rich, being poor;
> Most choice, forsaken; and most lov'd, despis'd....

In the second place, the balanced ceremony of the scene accords well with the mythic, the folkloristic nature of the story as it came down from the old chronicles to Shakespeare: the story of an ancient king of Britain who had three daughters, of whom two were evil, and one was good. Such fairy-tale materials, of course, underlie more than one of Shakespeare's plots, and he has various ways of handling them; [582] here, his method is the simplest and boldest possible; all questions of motivation are bypassed at the outset, and we start with the naked myth. For given such a myth, to raise the question of motive would be to undermine dramatic effect in advance. As the earlier play *King Leir* surely demonstrates sufficiently, any conceivable rationalization is bound to be weak and inadequate.

In the third place, the machine-like quality of ritual produces, in the first part of the scene, precisely the effect of nightmarish inevitability most useful, I think, for certain sorts of tragedy. The driver is fully and terrifyingly in control of the car; every piston functions smoothly; and the road ends in a precipice just around the next corner. Any suggestion of deliberation, hesitation, or wavering between alternatives would but confuse and perplex the appalling spectacle. [583]

$$\rightarrow\!\!\!\!\!\!\times\!\!\!\!\!\!\leftarrow$$

G. R. Elliott

From "The Initial Contrast in *Lear*." *Journal of English and Germanic Philology*, LVIII (1959), 251-263. By permission of the author and the publisher.

[To emphasize the contrast between Lear's reason and subsequent passion in I.i.] Shakespeare endeavored to make Lear, before his outbreak against Cordelia, as reasonable and normal as possible. Certainly that task was difficult because of the conditions imposed upon the dramatist by the strange old story he was handling; moreover, in this crowded drama the Introduction—so to term lines 1 to 109—had to be extraordinarily brief and condensed. Hence the main intent of the Introduction, though no doubt apparent to the Elizabethan audience, is not unmistakably clear to the average modern reader; and he has been hindered rather than helped by the critics. They have made the mistake of reading back into the initial episodes the subsequent folly of Lear. They have ruined the great contrast described above by regarding him as, from the very first, unreasonable and abnormal. This view renders him unbelievably different not only from Shakespeare's other tragic heroes but also from what he himself is increasingly shown to be from the fourth scene onward, a very representative human being. That he is essentially such from the very start is shown by the dramatist in the Introduction.

Proponents of the contrary view are numberless. Mention of its two chief promoters, Coleridge and A. C. Bradley, will suffice. Coleridge declared that Lear's conduct at the first is "improbable"; and that his trial of his three daughters' love for him "is but a trick . . . a silly trick." [1] Bradley, fundamentally agreeing with Coleridge though more elaborate, speaks of Lear's "complete blindness to the hypocrisy" of Goneril and Regan; declares that his "original plan," the threefold division of the kingdom, is "foolish and rash"; and even goes so far as to assert that the very first lines of the play "tell us that Lear's mind is beginning to fail with age." [2] . . .[252]

. . . the play's first lines, far from telling us that "Lear's mind is beginning to fail with age," suggest exactly the opposite. In the past—with right intuition, as future events will demonstrate—he has had more fondness for the Duke of Albany than for the Duke of Cornwall; but he has refrained from showing obvious and impolitic favoritism: note Kent's "I *thought*" and Gloster's "It did always *seeme* so." And now, having weighed very carefully a difficult problem, he has finally decided that the shares of Goneril's husband, Albany, and Regan's husband, Cornwall, shall be so equal in value that neither couple shall be tempted to envy the other's "moiety." . . .[253]

Nor is there any suggestion of senile folly in his original plan considered as a whole. His tone from the first (ll.35ff.) is both masterful and sane. . . .[254]

The whole affair, particularly the declarations on the part of the three daughters, has been carefully "weighed" by Lear beforehand, with the full awareness of his intimate counsellors, Kent and Gloster; and the fact that they were mildly surprised by one feature of the scene (ll.1-7) suggests that they knew and approved all the rest of it. Kent's calm and cheerful mood, so fully displayed (ll.1-31) in the initial episode, persists when he listens silently to Lear's long opening [256] speech culminating in the command to his three daughters: Kent's mien in hearing that command is as casual as the king's tone in uttering it. He gives no sign of uneasiness here. Nor does the equally silent Cordelia. But she, unlike all the others present, on the stage and in the theater, is deeply disturbed by the ensuing speech of Goneril, so insincerely and ingeniously worded (ll.56-62). Aside she whispers intensely: "What shall *Cordelia* speak? Love, and be silent." That curt, tumultuous pentameter line is in striking contrast with Goneril's smooth finale—"Beyond all manner of so much I love you"—and also with Lear's ensuing stately passage, "Of all these bounds even from this Line, to this. . . ." And her intense agitation as indicated by her gravid aside (ll.78-80) after Regan's speech, constantly increases; unobserved by the rest of the company, notably Kent, who keeps watching with looks of deep devotion the old king intent upon the map of his beloved realm. Hence not only Lear but the good Kent and all the others are astounded when Cordelia refuses to play her part in the present great ceremony.

The words "a little," [in l.96: "Mend your speech a little"] prominent at the line's end, stress the obvious fact that she was not required to make an elaborate, emotional speech, to "heave/ My heart into my mouth" as she puts it with sullen bitterness. She was expected to utter her love briefly, simply, and sincerely, in happy contrast with her sisters. But instead of that right kind of plainness she has used the wrong kind: she has spoken, as Lear perceives and as every reasonable person must perceive, with "pride which she calls plainnesse" (1.131). The deep tenderness of her love for her father, equalling his for her, has been overcome for the time being by blind, unconscious, angry pride. . . .[257]

[Lear's] folly is not due to senile infirmity. Lear's mind, throughout the first scene, is remarkably active and powerful. His first division of the kingdom was carefully politic; and the new plan, announced in the remainder of his present long speech, is—so far as we now know— a shrewd second best. Presently Kent will term it "hideous rashnesse" (1.153); and such it will prove to be, in retrospect, when Goneril and Regan take over the rule of the kingdom; as they prepare to do in their private colloquy, carefully feeling each other out, at the close of this scene (ll.286-312). But that is not in accordance with Lear's design. In he whole course of the scene there is no indication that the "mad . . . old man," in Kent's brash terms, "bowes" to their "flattery" (ll.148-50). And now, disregarding them entirely, he assigns the supreme rule to their husbands, Cornwall and Albany (129-41). . . .[261] . . . his plan, though it has doubtful aspects, is very far from weakly irrational. It can be successful if Albany and Cornwall shall prove to be loyal, firm, and temperate. And such they appear to be when, using their new authority as joint heirs, they effectually restrain his violent gesture threatening the life of the violent Kent: together they exclaim, "Deare Sir, forbeare" (1.165). And that speech, their sole utterance in scene i, must be regarded as indicating their demeanor throughout the scene: they are not flatterers like their wives, nor emotionalists like all the others. Lear's final trust in them, prepared for in the Introduction (ll.1-7,42-46), is, so far as we now know, quite justifiable—unlike his final and utter repudiation of Cordelia.[262]

He [Lear] has our sympathy, not in the main because he is old, but, as I have tried to show, because he is a great person greatly provoked. Cordelia's fault is precisely the sort that is hardest for him to bear under the present circumstances. But her fault is immeasurably outdistanced, with supreme tragic irony, by the selfsame fault in himself. Proud obstinacy becomes in his case, as not in hers, the occasion of cruel, subhuman wrath, a wrath altogether deadly because, instead of exhausting itself in stormy outbreak, it assumes a rationalistic form—his careful plan whereby the two dukes shall govern under himself as titular king. He sinfully justifies and fixes his anger against Cordelia by converting it into a policy, a policy that is apparently almost, if not entirely, as statesmanlike as the threefold division of the kingdom originally planned. . . .[263]

[1] Thomas M. Raysor, *Coleridge's Shakespearean Criticism* (London, 1930), I, 55, 59.
[2] *Shakespearean Tragedy* (London, 1911), pp. 250, 281.[252]

⨉

Terry Hawkes

From " 'Love' in *King Lear.*" *Review of English Studies,* X (1959), 178-181. Reproduced by permission of The Clarendon Press, Oxford.

The first scene of *King Lear* has been described as improbable, Lear's question "How much do you love me?" has been called imponderable and improper, and his equation "so much love = so much land" is said to be immoral. Such epithets are without doubt justifiable, but their justification may well lie on firmer ground than "suspension of disbelief," or the traditional facts of the plot. What is certainly present in this first scene is a deliberate probing of the nature of love; a contrasting of love as a spiritual quality with the opposing material elements involved in money, land, and the division of a kingdom. Although this examination is carried out immaculately in terms of character, with the spiritual quality of Cordelia's love poised against the material gains for which Goneril and Regan vie, it is possible to suggest a further, subtler probing of the problem through the words used by these characters, particularly the word *love* itself. The two different, almost opposite meanings which this word could have at the time when Shakespeare was writing hint at, in miniature, the movement of the whole play.

O.E.D. gives as a developed meaning of *Love*, v.[2] (OE. *lofian* "praise") 'to appraise, estimate or state the price or value of.' This is

an entirely different word in origin and phonetic history from *Love,*
v.¹ (OE. *lufian*). . . .[178]

In his book *Words and Sounds in English and French* (Oxford,
1953), Professor John Orr, in the chapter "On Homonymics," writes of
a homonymic "collision" which took place between the Old French
verbs *esmer* and *aimer.* In the evolution of the French language, says
Orr, *esmer* "to reckon, calculate," although later replaced by the modern *priser,* nevertheless tended, in the final stages before *priser* supplanted it, to invade the "psychological field" of *aimer* "to love." To
illustrate his point he quotes from the *Roman de Brut* by Wace (one
of the sources of the *Lear* story and significantly very like Holinshed's
version). Cordelia, disgusted at her sister's flattery, answers, when asked
by her father how much she loves him:

> Mes peres iés, jo aim tant tei
> Com jo mun pere amer dei.
> E pur faire tei plus certein,
> Tant as, tant vals e jo tant t'aim.   (1739 ff.) [179]

The apparent translation of this last line is "so much you have, so
much you are worth, and so much I love you." But Orr goes on to
show that this line is a recognized proverbial saying, in the manner of
a pun, where the equivocation is between *aimer* "to love" and the
similarly pronounced *esmer* "to estimate the value of." So the punning
translation of this line is now "So much you have, so much you are
worth, *of such a price (or value) you are to me."*

It is generally accepted that Holinshed's *Chronicles* were among
Shakespeare's sources for *King Lear.* Holinshed's version of Cordelia's
reply to Lear in the 'division' scene is almost exactly taken from Wace:

> . . . I protest vnto you that I haue loued you euer, and will continuallie (while
> I liue) loue you as my naturall father. And if you would more vnderstand
> of the loue that I beare you, assertaine you selfe, that *so much as you haue,
> so much you are worth, and so much I loue you and no more.*

Whether the pun is intentionally implicit in this version of the line
mentioned above is not apparent; but linguistically it is implicit in the
two senses of *love* whether Holinshed meant it to be there or not.

Shakespeare's grasping of the pun upon *love,* whether or not from
Holinshed, can be detected without doubt in *King Lear.* Not surpris-
ingly, Goneril's *love* presents a fairly precise, tabulated catalogue in the
manner of an "estimate":

> Sir, I love you more than words can wield the matter,
> Dearer than eye-sight, space, and liberty;
> Beyond what can be valued rich or rare;
> No less than life, with grace, health, beauty, honour;
> As much as child e'er loved or father found; [180]

A love that makes breath poor and speech unable;
Beyond all manner of so much I love you.   (I.i.56ff.)

It is left to Regan to colour this estimate to one in terms of money,
which she does with an image of coinage:

Sir, I am made
Of the self-same metal that my sister is,
And prize me at her worth. . . .   (I.i.70ff.)

Cordelia's remark at a very early stage in the proceedings has indicated
her direct rejection of the whole immoral nature of *love* as an expressi-
ble "value." She seizes on the fact that the true sense of *love* implies
something which it is impossible to conceive of and "estimate or state
the value of" in any terms. Discarding the punning use of the other
verb *to love* which her sisters have offered to Lear she says, "What shall
Cordelia do? Love, and be silent" (I.i.63). Her reply to the King comes
with all the force of Wace's play:

. . . I love your majesty
According to my bond; not more nor less.   (I.i.93) [181]

>\<

William Elton

From *King Lear and the Gods*. San Marino:
Huntington Library Press, 1960. By permission of the author.

To sum up Lear's development is to rehearse the development of
the play, its gigantic inversions and complexities. From an opening
scene of maximal religious confidence of a heathen sort, we move towards a testing of that confidence—Lear's love-test of the opening scene
begins to involve an extra-familial, political, and cosmic love-test, one
which questions the heavens themselves. Human love betrayed reaches
into divine love betrayed; thus the question of providence obtrudes,
analogically, into the question of a daughter's affection.
Lear's polytheism impinges on an animism whose deities are ex-
tensions of nature, like the sun-god, Apollo. Hence, Lear's devout
polytheism, his adoring the Nature goddess, could yet embrace what
would seem, to a Renaissance Christian, symptoms of naturalism, and
therefore of skepticism. Living before the Christian revelation, as well

as outside it, Lear could not know or accept the basic paradox of Creation, that God created the world out of nothing. Thus Shakespeare's ascription to him, expositionally twice mentioned, that nothing could come of nothing, could signify, ambiguously, that Lear was a pagan, although a skeptic from a Christian standpoint; and that, although a pagan, Lear expresses his belief in such terms as might serve to foreshadow disbelief to come.

In Acts Two and Three, Lear's pagan devotion begins to undergo its trial, commencing that tension between belief and fear-not-to-believe that surcharges his already strained mind. Again, the failure in humanity parallels the failure in the heavens; the storm occurs on all levels at once, cosmic, familial, and personal. And Lear's questioning of man's state above the animals is a corollary of his questioning of divine providence and justice above men. Once more, from the Christian view of Shakespeare's audience, such denial of man's unique place was characteristic of skepticism; and, from a pagan view, Lear's doubtful defiance of the heavens is also a manifestation of a growing skepticism. This skepticism becomes even clearer when, at one point (III.iv.158-159), the King dares, in his madness, to question the divine source of thunder, which to Christians, and to many pagans, was ever the dread voice of the heavens. When Lear exclaims at the mid-point of the play, "I am a man More sinn'd against than sinning" (III.ii.58-59), we know we have proceeded to a point where a previous confidence in divine and poetic justice has become, in his own person, a bewildered sense of injustice. Ambivalence has overtaken faith. *attraction & repulsion at same time*

The storm is the test of the gods. Divine justice above, Lear hopes, will be shown by human justice and charity below (III.iv.33-36); their mutual dependence is the reason for the great significance of the religious level of this play. In Act IV the maddened Lear has given up his confidence in the sense of the thunder; "When the thunder would not peace at my bidding," and this cosmic debacle involves a human one, as he continues, "There I found 'em, there I smelt t'em out" (IV.vi.103-105). As Lear hints that the thunder, traditionally thought the voice of the gods, has a natural cause, so he hints at natural causation for a traditionally divine malady in humans, "hard hearts" (III.vi.76-79); Lear implies skepticism on the macrocosmic and microcosmic levels, operating here, as elsewhere, analogically, in thrusts which could have been evident to Shakespeare's audience, but which may be lost on our own. Indeed, the religious change between Shakespeare's time and the present is perhaps a measure of the incomprehensibility to modern spectators of his most cosmic tragedy.

By the end of Act IV, Lear's madness has run its course, as have also the tension and breakdown caused by the failure of belief on all levels; and he is ready for "belief" of some kind, though not for anything resembling his previous tenets. Lear's new "belief" is negative and exclusive, one of abnegation, *contemptus mundi*, and forfeit; it is not simply one of "salvation" which recent commentators have sought to fasten on him. It is, ironically, one whose fixity will, Lear vainly hopes, transcend all mutability; but that fixity is immediately to be undermined. Lear's new-found "faith" is pathetically and suddenly withdrawn from him by the murder of Cordelia.

His laments against divine providence, his repeated "why?", his sense of man's reduced place in the scheme of things beneath the lowly animals, his offering of violence to heaven's vault, are in large part motivated by a view that death, excluding Resurrection, ends all. The view of death, which is the premise of the play, implicit in its beginnings, and never contradicted, is by definition a skeptical-pagan, not a Christian, attitude. It thus explains the funereal chorus at the end of the play, which, syncretically, also invokes the Last Judgment (V.iii.263-264), while, at the same time, heathenishly, denies that immortality is possible; here syncretism intensifies Lear's despair, implying the disparity between pagan hopelessness and Christian possibility. The pagan attitude in the final scene also disposes of modern contentions that Lear is saved, or that the hope of salvation operates in the denouement. For we have the evidence of a Renaissance English bishop that Lear's attitude was the pagan attitude towards death, with the grief consequent upon an awareness that death ends all; Bishop Jewell admonishes that "to mourn in such sort as the heathen did we are forbidden. They, as did neither believe in God nor in Christ, so had they no hope of life to come. When a father saw his son dead, he thought he had been *dead for ever,*" as Lear exclaims of his daughter, "now she's *gone for ever.*"

PART TWO
BIBLIOGRAPHY

BIBLIOGRAPHY

The following list of works concerning *King Lear* is largely confined to pieces written in English since 1900. Items marked with an asterisk are excerpted in this book, and are not annotated. The following abbreviations are used:

CE	*College English*	PQ	*Philological Quarterly*
ELH	*English Literary History*	RES	*Review of English Studies*
ES	*English Studies*	SAB	*Shakespeare Association Bulletin*
Expl.	*Explicator*		
JEGP	*Journal of English and Germanic Philology*	SB	*Studies in Bibliography: Papers of the Bibliographical Society, University of Virginia*
KL	*King Lear*		
L	*Lear*		
MLN	*Modern Language Notes*	SE	*Studies in English* (University of Texas)
MLQ	*Modern Language Quarterly*		
MLR	*Modern Language Review*	SP	*Studies in Philology*
MP	*Modern Philology*	SQ	*Shakespeare Quarterly*
N&Q	*Notes and Queries*	SR	*Sewanee Review*
PMLA	*Publications of the Modern Language Association*		

I. *King Lear* and the Scholar

A. TEXT AND DATE

Adams, J. Q. "The Quarto of *KL* and Shorthand." *MP,* XXXI (1933), 135-163. A thorough study to prove that the Quarto derived from a shorthand report.

Bowers, Fredson. "An Examination of the Method of Proof Correction in *KL.*" *Library,* 5th Ser., II (1947), 20-44.

Cauthen, I. B., Jr. "Compositor Determination in the First Folio *KL.*" *SB,* V (1952), 73-80. Argues that a single compositor set the type.

————. "Shakespeare's *KL:* An Investigation of Compositor Habits in the First Folio and Their Relation to the Text." *Univ. of Va. Abstracts of Diss.,* 1951, pp. 13-18.

Cunnington, R. H. "The Revision of *KL.*" *MLR,* V (1910), 445-453. Argues that the Folio shows Shakespeare's revision of the Quarto.

Doran, Madeleine. *The Text of KL.* Palo Alto, 1931. Argues that the Folio derives from a revision of the Quarto version, which was set up from a MS of a revised first draft.

————. "The Quarto of *KL* and Bright's Shorthand." *MP,* XXXIII (1935), 139-157. A reply to Adams' article noted above.

179

Fleay, F. G. "The Date and Text of *KL.*" *Robinson's Epitome of Literature,* 1 August, 1879.

Greg, W. W. "The Function of Bibliography in Literary Criticism Illustrated in a Study of the Text of *KL.*" *Neophilologus,* XVIII (1933), 241-262. Reviews various arguments concerning the copy followed by Quarto and Folio version, incorporating Miss Doran's study.

Hubler, Edward. "The Verse Lining of the First Quarto of *KL.*" *Parrott Presentation Volume,* ed. Hardin Craig, Princeton, 1935, pp. 421-441. Shows that the mislineation of the first quarto might have been caused by a careless compositor trying to save space rather than by stenographic transcription.

Jazayery, Mohammed Ali, and Robert A. Law. "Three Texts of *KL:* Their Differences." *SE,* XXXII (1953), 14-24. Compare the Globe, Neilson, and Kittredge editions, find Globe poorest.

Kies, Paul P. "On the Dating of *Othello* and *KL.*" *Research Studies of the College of Washington,* III (1936), 72f. Corroborates 1605-06 date for *KL.*

Kirschbaum, Leo. "The True Text of *KL.*" *SAB,* XVI (1941), 140-153. Chiefly on bibliographical technique. Assumes the Quarto is based on a reporter's memory.

————. "How Jane Bell Came to Print the Third Quarto of Shakespeare's *KL.*" *PQ,* XVII (1938), 308-311.

————. Review of Duthie's edition. *RES,* II (1951), 168-173.

Merriman, R. B. "On the Date of *KL.*" *Athenaeum,* 23 May, 1908, 648. Argues that the names of Edgar's devils need not have come from Harsnett.

Small, S. A. "The *KL* Quarto." *SAB,* XXI (1946), 177-180. A short review of past scholarship.

Tannenbaum, Samuel A. "An Emendation in *KL.*" *SAB,* XVI (1940), 58f. Reads "Edmund the base/Shall to' th' Legitimate" as meaning "toe" Edgar.

Williams, Philip. "The Compositor of the 'Pied Bull' *L.*" *SB,* I (1949), 59-68. Uses spelling consistency test to argue for one compositor only.

————. "Two Problems in the Folio Text of *KL.*" *SQ,* IV (1953), 451-460. Argues against the single compositor theory, and that the Folio was not set from a corrected quarto copy.

B. ELIZABETHAN BACKGROUND

*Bald, R. C. " 'Thou, Nature, Art my Goddess': Edmund and Renaissance Free-Thought." *J. Q. Adams Memorial Studies* (1948), 337-349.

*Darby, Robert H. "Astrology in Shakespeare's *L.*" *ES,* XX (1938), 250-257.

*Draper, John W. "The Occasion of *KL.*" *SP,* XXXIV (1937), 176-185.

Farnham, Willard. *The Medieval Heritage of Elizabethan Tragedy.* Berkeley, 1936. Not specifically on *KL,* but very valuable to a study of the play.

Haller, William. " 'What Needs My Shakespeare?' " *SQ,* III (1952), 3-16. Explains Elizabethan notions of parental authority on p. 14.

Harrison, G. B. "The Background to *KL.*" *Times Literary Supplement,* 28 December, 1935.

*Hotson, Leslie. *Shakespeare's Motley.* New York, 1952.

*Jaffa, Harry V. "The Limits of Politics: An Interpretation of *KL,* I, i." *Amer. Pol. Science Rev.,* LI (1957), 405-427.

Rosier, James L. "The Lex Aeterna and *KL*." *JEGP*, LIII (1954), 574-580. Finds themes of the play in Hooker's *Laws of Ecclesiastical Polity*.

Taylor, George Coffin. "Two Notes on Shakespeare." *Renaissance Studies in Honor of Hardin Craig*. Stanford, 1941, pp. 179-184. Quotes Edmund's views on astrology next to comparable Elizabethan statements.

Tillyard, E. M. W. *The Elizabethan World Picture*. New York (n.d.). Vital to a study of Shakespeare. Discussion of Edmund's astrology in chapter five.

Wendell, Barrett. *William Shakspere*. New York, 1893. One of the first to argue for the importance of Elizabethan conventions concerning madness.

Wistanley, Lilian. *Macbeth, KL and Contemporary History*. Cambridge, 1922. Six chapters on *KL*, chiefly on relations to Darnley murder and the massacre of St. Bartholomew.

C. ON *KL* CRITICISM

Graham, Paul G. "Hebbel's Study of *KL*." *Smith College Studies in Modern Languages*, XXI (1939-1940), 81-90. On Friedrich Hebbel's preference for *KL*.

*Hook, Lucyle. "Shakespeare Improv'd, or A Case for the Affirmative." *SQ*, IV (1953), 289-299.

Kane, Robert J. "Tolstoy, Goethe, and *KL*." *SAB*, XXI (1946), 159f. A brief reminder of Goethe's and Tolstoy's reactions to *KL*.

*Keast, W. R. "Imagery and Meaning in the Interpretation of *KL*." *MP*, XLVII (1949), 45-64. Reprinted in Crane's *Critics and Criticism*.

*Orwell, George. "Lear, Tolstoy and the Fool." In *Shooting an Elephant and Other Essays*. New York, 1945.

Weisinger, Herbert. "The Study of Shakespearian Tragedy Since Bradley." *SQ*, VI (1955), 387-396. Classifies the chief kinds of criticism and their limitations.

Zandvoort, R. W. "*KL*: The Scholars and the Critics." *Mededelingen der Koninklijke Nederlandse Akademie van Wetenschappen*, XIX (1956), 229-244. Traces trends in *Lear* criticism since Bradley.

II. *King Lear* and the Critic

A. SOURCES

1. *Montaigne*

Collins, Churton. *Studies in Shakespeare*. London, 1904. Chapter on Montaigne's influence (pp. 277-296) questions extensive influence. Only brief reference to *KL*.

Harmon, Alice. "How Great Was Shakespeare's Debt to Montaigne?" *PMLA*, LVII (1942), 988-1008. Shows where else Shakespeare might have found ideas thought to be derived from Montaigne.

Henderson, W. B. Drayton. "Montaigne's Apologie of Raymond Sebond, and *KL*." *SAB*, XIV (1939), 209-225.

—————. "Montaigne's *Apologie* and *KL*." *SAB*, XV (1940), 40-54. A thorough study of Montaigne's ideas in *KL*. Concludes the article begun in vol. XIV.

Hodgon, Margaret T. "Montaigne and Shakespeare Again." *Huntington Library Quarterly*, XVI (1952), 23-42. Concerns evidence in *The Tempest* chiefly.

Hooker, Elizabeth. "The Relation of Shakespeare to Montaigne." *PMLA*, XVII (1902), 312-366.

Robertson, John M. *Montaigne and Shakespeare*. London, 1909. Sensible weighing of evidence; little specifically on *KL*.

Smith, Robert M. "Shakspere, the Montaigne of England." *SAB*, XXII (1947), 155-162. Not specifically on *KL*.

Taylor, George C. "Montaigne—Shakespeare and the Deadly Parallel." *PQ*, XXII (1943), 330-337. Reply to Miss Harmon's article. Examines methods of proving influence.

————. *Shakspere's Debt to Montaigne*. Cambridge, Mass., 1925. Prints similar passages from Florio's Montaigne and *KL* side by side, pp. 9-13.

2. *Other Sources*

Ekeblad, Inga-Stinas. "*KL* and Selimus." *N&Q*, CCII (1957), 193f. Suggests parallels with Greene's *The First Part of the Tragicall Raigne of Selimus*.

Law, Robert Alger. "*King Leir* and *KL*: An Examination of the Two Plays." Baldwin *Festschrift* (1958), pp. 112-124.

————. "Holinshed as Source for *Henry V* and *KL*." *SE*, XIV (1934), 38-44. Finds no "convincing evidence that Shakespeare ever read a single line of Holinshed's account of King Leir."

————. "Holinshed's Leir Story and Shakespeare's." *SP*, XLVII (1950), 42-50.

McKeithan, O. M. "*KL* and Sidney's *Arcadia*." *SE*, XIV (1934), 45-49. Argues that Edmund's vilification of Edgar in *KL* mirrors the Queen of Iberia's treatment of Plangus in the *Arcadia*.

Muir, K. "Samuel Harsnett and *KL*." *RES*, II (1951), 11-21. Quotes many parallels.

————, and J. F. Danby. "*Arcadia* and *KL*." *N&Q*, CLXLV (1950), 49ff. Suggest previously unnoted parallels between Sidney's *Arcadia* and *KL*.

Musgrove, S. "The Nomenclature of *KL*." *RES*, VII (1956), 294-298. Suggests Camden's *Remaines* as a source.

Perkinson, Richard N. "Shakespeare's Revision of the Lear Story and the Structure of *KL*." *PQ*, XXII (1943), 315-329. A thorough and acute study.

Perrett, Wilfrid. *The Story of KL from Geoffrey of Monmouth to Shakespeare*. Berlin, 1904, *Palaestra*, XXXV. Describes various versions of the Lear story.

Pyle, F. "*Twelfth Night, KL* and *Arcadia*." *MLR*, XLIII (1948), 449-455. Sees an influence of Sidney's *Arcadia* on the main as well as on the Gloucester plot.

Ribner, Irving. "Sidney's *Arcadia* and the Structure of *KL*." *Studia Neophilologica*, XXIV (1952), 63-68. Argues that Sidney's story of the Paphlagonian king relates to the main plot of *Arcadia* as the Gloucester story does to the main plot of *KL*.

————. "Shakespeare and Legendary History: *L* and *Cymbeline*." *SQ*, VII (1956), 47-52. Argues that Elizabethans would have regarded *KL* a history play.

Rollins, Hyder E. "*KL* and the Ballad of 'John Careless.'" *MLR*, XV (1920), 87ff. A source for the Fool's "Then they for sudden joy did weep" in I.iv.

Salter, K. W. "*L* and the Morality Tradition." *N&Q*, CXCIX (1954), 109f. Shows a parallel between a speech of Albany and a speech of God in *Everyman*.

Smith, Roland M. "*KL* and the Merlin Tradition." *MLQ,* VII (1946), 153-174. Suggests that some details in the play may well derive from Renaissance works on King Arthur and Merlin, and indicates resemblances between *KL* and Richard Johnson's Arthurian prose romance, *Tom a Lincolne.*

Traver, Hope. "*KL* and *Isaiah.*" *SAB,* IX (1934), 181-185. Argues for several thematic parallels.

Whitaker, Virgil K. "Shakespeare's Use of His Sources." *Renaissance Studies in Honor of Hardin Craig.* Stanford, California, 1941, pp. 185-197. Discusses *KL* briefly on pp. 190f.

B. IMAGERY

Bradbrook, M. C. Review of W. H. Clemen's *Development of Shakespeare's Imagery. SQ,* III (1952), 125.

*Clemen, W. H., *The Development of Shakespeare's Imagery.* Cambridge, Mass., 1951.

*Greenfield, Thelma N. "The Clothing Motif in *KL.*" *SQ,* V (1954), 281-286.

Hankins, John E. "*L* and the Psalmist." *MLN,* LXI (1946), 88ff. Notes resemblances between Lear's invocation of the storm and *Psalms* 144:4.

Kreider, P. V. "Gloucester's Eyes." *SAB,* VIII (1933), 121-132. An exhaustive description of sight imagery in *KL.*

Provost, George F., Jr. "The Techniques of Characterization and Dramatic Imagery in *Richard II* and *KL.*" *Dissertation Abstracts,* XV (1955), 1615f.

*Spurgeon, Caroline F. E. *Shakespeare's Imagery and What It Tells Us.* New York, 1936.

C. RELIGION AND ETHICS

Brooke, Tucker. "*KL* on the Stage." *SR,* XXI (1913), 88-98. On the moral lessons of the play.

*Campbell, Oscar J. "The Salvation of Lear." *ELH,* XV (1948), 93-109.

Craig, Hardin. "The Ethics of *KL.*" *PQ,* IV (1925), 97-109. Argues that ethical beliefs fundamental to *KL* are those stated by Plato in *The Republic,* by Aristotle in the *Nichomachean Ethics,* and by Wilson, Shakespeare's contemporary, in the *Art of Rhetoric,* and that the main outlines of the play suggest Shakespeare's use of these beliefs as they must have been reflected in the thought of his time.

*Dowden, Edward. *Shakspere: A Critical Study of His Mind and Art.* New York, 1875.

*Elton, William. *KL and the Gods.* San Marino, 1960.

French, Carolyn S. "Shakespeare's 'Folly': *KL.*" *SQ,* X (1959), 523-529. Argues that *KL* contrasts worldly wisdom and Christian folly, a higher form of wisdom.

*Freud, Sigmund. "The Theme of the Three Caskets." In *Complete Psychological Works,* Vol. XII. London, 1958.

*Lewis, Wyndham. *The Lion and the Fox.* London, 1927.

Maxwell, J. C. "The Technique of Invocation in *KL.*" *MLR,* XLV (1950), 142-147. On Christian and pagan elements in *KL.*

Mutschmann, H., and K. Wentersdorf. *Shakespeare and Catholicism.* New York, 1952. Evidence from *KL* used on pp. 227, 249, 337, and 372f.

Nosworthy, J. M. "*KL*—The Moral Aspect." *ES,* XXI (1939), 260-268. Brief comment on the importance of moral ideas in *KL.*

Parrott, T. M. " 'God's' or 'gods' in *KL*." *SQ*, IV (1953), 427-432. Argues that *KL* does not refer to God.

Ribner, Irving. "The Gods Are Just: A Reading of *KL*." *Tulane Drama Review*, II (1958), 34-54. Reads *KL* as a Christian morality.

Rinehart, Keith. "The Moral Background of *KL*." *University of Kansas City Review*, XX (1954), 223-238. On Stoicism in *KL*.

Siegel, Paul N. "Adversity and the Miracle of Love in *KL*." *SQ*, VI (1955), 325-336. Outlines the play with stress on adversity and love.

Spaulding, K. J. *The Philosophy of Shakespeare*. New York, 1953. Discusses *KL* only glancingly.

Thaler, Alwin. "The Gods and God in *KL*." *Renaissance Papers*, ed. A. H. Gilbert. Columbia, S. C., 1955, pp. 32-39. Reply to Parrott (*see* above).

D. CHARACTER

1. Madness

Ashton, J. W. "The Wrath of *KL*." *JEGP*, XXXI (1932), 530-536. Discusses Lear's anger leading to madness in terms of Elizabethan psychology.

Bucknill, John Charles. *The Mad Folk of Shakespeare*, 2nd ed. London, 1867. A fourth of the book is devoted to *KL*.

Campbell, Oscar James. Review of F. L. Lucas, *Literature and Psychology*. *SQ*, IV (1953), 467f. Attacks psychoanalytical interpretation of *KL*.

*Donnelly, John. "Incest, Ingratitude and Insanity: Aspects of the Psychopathology of *KL*." *Psychoanalytic Rev.*, XL (1953), 149-155.

Kahn, Sholom J. " 'Enter Lear mad.' " *SQ*, VIII (1957), 311-329. A general discussion of the growth of Lear's madness.

*Kellogg, A. O. *Shakspeare's Delineations of Insanity, Imbecility and Suicide*. New York, 1866.

*Mackenzie, Henry. *The Mirror: no. 100 (April 22, 1780). 9th ed., London, 1793, 327-334.

McCullen, Joseph T., Jr. "Madness and the Isolation of Character in Elizabethan and Early Stuart Drama." *SP*, XLVIII (1952), 206-218. Brief comment on Lear on pp. 217f.

MacLean, N. "Episode, Scene, Speech and Word: the Madness of Lear." In *Critics and Criticism*, ed. R. S. Crane, Chicago, 1952, pp. 595-615. A many-sided discussion of *KL*, with Lear's madness as focus.

*Pauncz, Arpad. "Psychopathology of Shakespeare's *KL*: Exemplification of the Lear Complex (A New Interpretation)." *American Imago*, IX (1952), 57-78.

*Ray, I. "Shakespeare's Delineations of Insanity." *Am. Journal of Insanity*, III (1847), 289-332.

Ribner, Irving. "Lear's Madness in the Nineteenth Century." *SAB*, XXII (1947), 117-129. Traces 18th and 19th century views in detail.

*Warton, Joseph. *The Adventurer*, 1778.

2. Old Age

Cox, Ernest H. "Shakespeare and Some Conventions of Old Age." *SP*, XXXIX (1942), 36-46. Shows that Shakespeare's descriptions of old age correspond to conventional medieval ones.

Draper, John W. "The Old Age of King Lear." *JEGP*, XXXIX (1940), 527-540. A thorough reading of the play in terms of Lear's age.

Miles, L. Wardlaw. "Shakespeare's Old Men." *ELH*, VII (1940), 286-299. A glance at Lear's and Gloucester's age on pp. 295ff.

3. Other Problems of Character

Block, Edward A. *"KL:* A Study in Balanced and Shifting Sympathies." *SQ*, X (1959), 499-512. Maintains that the play establishes an "equilibrium of balanced sympathy" for its characters.

Brown, Huntington. "Enter the Shakespearean Tragic Hero." *Essays in Criticism*, III (1953), 285-302. Argues that the play gathers sympathy for Lear only gradually (pp. 292f.).

Craik, J. W. "Cordelia as 'Last and Least' of Lear's Daughters." *N&Q*, CCI (1956), 11. Suggests that Stephen Batman's *The Doome Warning all Men to the Judgement* (1581) corroborates Cordelia being "least," meaning either *small* or *young.*

*Frye, Northrop. "Characterization in Shakespearian Comedy." *SQ*, IV (1953), 271-277.

Goldsmith, Robert Hillis. *Wise Fools in Shakespeare.* East Lansing, 1955. Argues (pp. 60-67) that the wisdom of Lear's Fool takes him out of the class of "natural" fools. Notes provide extensive bibliography.

Hammond, E. P. "Lear and His Daughters." *Poet Lore,* XXIV (1913), 110ff. Argues that the cruelty of Goneril and Regan is motivated and believable rather than gratuitous.

Isenberg, Arnold. "Cordelia Absent." *SQ*, II (1951), 185-194. Renews the old discussion on Cordelia's small part in the play, arguing that during her absence the audience remains aware of her for various reasons.

Mackail, J. W. *The Approach to Shakespeare.* Oxford, 1930. Emphasizes (on pp. 78-81) the importance in the play of Albany's prevailing sanity.

Morris, Aron. "Cordelia and Lear." *SQ*, VIII (1957), 141-158. Argues that Cordelia's "Nothing" is a conscious but futile attempt to educate Lear.

*Parr, Johnstone. "Edmund's Nativity in *KL*." *SAB*, XXI (1946), 181-185.

Pogson, Beryl. *In the East My Pleasure Lies.* London, 1950. Comments on Lear's blindness.

Smith, Robert M. "A Good Word for Oswald." *A Tribute to G. C. Taylor* (1952), pp. 62-66. Notes Oswald's courage and loyalty.

Spivack, Bernard. *Shakespeare and the Allegory of Evil.* New York, 1958. Sees Edmund as a descendant of the typical villain in Elizabethan allegorical drama, pp. 413f.

Stoll, E. E. "Kent and Gloster." *Life and Letters,* IX (1933), 431-445. Comparative character sketches.

Strindberg, A. "King Lear's Wife." *Poet Lore,* XXIV (1913), 108f. Argues counter-indications to Shakespeare's misogyny in *KL.*

*Taylor, E. M. M. "Lear's Philosopher." *SQ*, VI (1955), 364f.

Van Doren, Mark. *Shakespeare.* New York, 1939. Chapter on *KL* (pp. 238-251) explores Lear-Gloucester parallels in detail.

E. EXPLICATION AND DISCUSSION

1. Explication of Words and Limited Areas of the Play

Arms, G. W. "Shakespeare's *KL*, V, iii." *Expl.*, III (1944), Item 3.

Baldwin, T. W. "On *KL*." *MLN*, XXXVII (1922), 504. Corroborates Tamblyn's argument (*see* below) that Burgundy represents the King of Spain.

————. "Nature's Moulds." *SQ*, III (1952), 237-241. Compares the use of this image in III.ii. to its use in other plays.

Bradley, A. C. "The Locality of *KL*, Act I, Scene ii." *MLR*, IV (1909), 238ff. Reply to Hunter's article (*see* below).

Camden, Carroll. "An Absurdity in *KL?*" *PQ*, XI (1932), 408f. Answers S. A. Tannenbaum's article (*see* below) by reference to Elizabethan notions.

————. "The Suffocation of the Mother." *MLN*, LXIII (1948), 390-393. Identifies Lear's symptoms as hysteria.

Cauthen, I. B., Jr. "The 'Foule Fibbertigibbet,' *KL*, III.iv.113; IV.i.60." *N&Q*, CCIII (1958), 98f. Finds the devil's name used before Harsnett, with meaning of *chatterer* or *gossip*.

Clarke, G. H. "The Catastrophe in *KL*." *Queen's Quarterly*, XII (1934), 369-382. On eighteenth century revisions of Shakespeare, and the necessity for Cordelia's death.

*Dunn, E. Catherine. "The Storm in *KL*." *SQ*, III (1952), 329-333.

*Elliott, G. R. "The Initial Contrast in *L*." *JEGP*, LVIII (1959), 251-263.

*Empson, William. "Fool in *L*." *SR*, LVII (1949), 177-181. Reprinted in his *The Structure of Complex Words*, New York, 1951.

*Frost, William. "Shakespeare's Rituals and the Opening of *KL*." *Hudson Review*, X (1958), 577-585.

Hankins, John E. "Shakespeare's *KL*, V.iii." *Expl.*, III (1945), Item 48.

*Hawkes, Terry. " 'Love' in *KL*." *RES*, (N.S.) X (1959), 178-181.

Hazen, A. T. "Shakespeare's *KL*, IV, i." *Expl.*, II (1943), Item 2. Also comment by Monroe M. Stearns.

Heilman, Robert R. "Shakespeare's *KL*, IV, vi, 169." *Expl.*, VI (1947), Item 10.

Heninger, S. K., Jr. "Shakespeare's *KL*, III, ii, 1-9." *Expl.*, XV (1956), Item 1.

Hoepfner, Theodore C. " 'We that are young.' " *N&Q*, CXCIX (1954), 110. Finds it logical to give the final speech to Edgar rather than to Albany.

Hulme, Hilda. "Three Shakespearean Glosses." *N&Q*, CCII (1957), 237f. Discusses "accommodate" in IV.vi.91.

Hunter, Mark. "A Note on *KL*." *MLR*, IV (1908), 84ff. Shows that I.ii. may be assigned to Gloucester's castle by error.

*Jorgensen, Paul A. "Much Ado About *Nothing*." *SQ*, V (1954), 287-295.

Kelcy, A. "Notes on *KL*." *PQ*, XI (1932), 359-373. Discusses several difficult passages.

*Kernodle, G. R. "The Symphonic Form of *KL*." *Elizabethan Studies and other Essays*. Boulder, 1945, pp. 185-191.

Kirschbaum, Leo. "A Detail in *KL*." *RES*, XXV (1949), 153f. A note on Lear's "Come, unbutton here" and "Pray you undo this button."

Major, John M. "Shakespeare's *KL*, IV. ii. 62." *Expl.*, XVII (1958), Item 13.

Martey, Herbert. "Shakespeare's *KL*, IV. vi. 1-80." *Expl.*, XI (1952), Item 10. Brief note on Gloucester at Dover.

McKenzie, James J. "Edgar's 'Persian attire'." *N&Q*, CCI (1956), 98f. Believes Lear's reference to Edgar's clothing a pun on "perishing."

Musgrove, S. "*KL*, I. i. 170." *RES*, VIII (1957), 170f. Argues for the plural "sentences."

Noyes, Edward S. "On the Dismissal of Lear's Knights and Goneril's Letter to Regan." *PQ*, IX (1930), 297-303. Conjectures that Goneril dismisses 50 of Lear's knights in I.iii.

Pancoast, H. S. "Note on *KL*." *MLN*, XL (1924), 404-408. On Edgar's "Ripeness is all."

*Parr, Johnstone. "Edmund's Nativity in *KL*." *SAB*, XXI (1946), 181-185.

————. "A Note on the 'Late Eclipses' in *KL*." *SAB*, XX (1945), 46ff. Cites a prediction like that in *KL* from Himbert de Billy, 1603.

Perkinson, Richard N. " 'Is This the Promis'd End?' " *ES*, LXIII (1939), 202-211. Argues that Shakespeare had to make the tragic ending acceptable to an audience expecting a happy ending.

Raven, A. A. "A Note on *KL*." *MLN*, XXXVI (1921), 187. Suggests that Lear's failing sight allows him to think Cordelia lives at the end of the play.

Sledd, James. "Hause and Slaves in *KL*." *MLN*, LV (1940), 594ff. Gloss on the use of these two words.

Smith, Gerald. "A Note on the Death of Lear." *MLN*, LXX (1955), 403f. Cites Elizabethan notion that extreme joy may cause death.

Spevack, Marvin. "Shakespeare's *KL*, IV.vi.152." *Expl.*, XVII (1958), Item 4.

Stewart, Charles D. "Four Shakespeare Cruxes." *CE*, IX (1948), 187-191. Three passages from *KL*.

*Stewart, J. I. M. "The Blinding of Gloster." *RES*, XXI (1945), 264-270.

Tamblyn, W. F. "Notes on *KL*." *MLN*, XXXVII (1922), 346-349. On four problems of acting or interpretation.

Tannenbaum, Samuel A. "An Absurdity in *KL*." *Saturday Review of Lit.*, VIII (8 Aug., 1931), 46. Argues that Gloucester's eyes could not be pulled out without resulting death.

Taylor, George C. "Two Notes on Shakespeare." *PQ*, XX (1941), 371-376. A note on Edmund's skepticism of astrology.

*Williams, George W. "The Poetry of the Storm in *KL*." *SQ*, II (1951), 57-71.

————. "A Note on *KL*, III. ii. 1-3." *SB*, II (1949), 175-182. On Quarto and Folio versions of the "Blow winds, and crack your cheeks" passage.

2. *Discussion of Other Aspects of the Play*

*Barish, J. A., and M. Waingrow. " 'Service' in *KL*." *SQ*, IX (1958), 347-355.

Doran, Madeleine. "Elements in the Composition of *KL*." *SP*, XXX (1933), 34-58. Discusses sources and ideas in terms of her *The Text of KL*.

Draper, John W. "Patterns of Humor and Tempo in *KL*." *Bull. Hist. Medicine*, XXI (1947), 390-401.

Greg, Sir W. W. "The Staging of *KL*." *RES*, XVI (1940), 300-303. On the furniture needed on stage.

Hobday, C. H. "The Social Background of *KL*." *Mod. Quart. Misc.*, I (1946), 37-56. On class struggle reflected in the play.

Hockey, Dorothy C. "The Trial Pattern in *KL*." *SQ*, X (1959), 389-395. Shows that the idea of a trial occurs repeatedly in *KL*.

*Jaffa, Harry V. "The Limits of Politics: An Interpretation of *KL*, Act I, Scene I." *Am. Pol. Science Rev.*, LI (1957), 405-427.

McCloskey, John C. "The Plot Device of False Report." *SAB*, XXI (1946), 147-158. Discusses Edmund's slander of Edgar in relation to similar situations in other plays.

Muir, Edwin. "The Politics of *KL.*" In his *Essays on Literature and Society,* 1949, pp. 31-48. Argues that Goneril, Regan, and Edmund represent an order of society opposite to the old order of Lear.

Price, T. R. *"KL.* A Study of Shakspere's Dramatic Method." *PMLA,* IX (1894), 165-181. On the structure of *KL,* especially the double plot.

*Ransom, John Crowe. "On Shakespeare's Language." *SR,* LV (1947), 181-198.

Schulz, Max F. *"KL:* A Box-Office Maverick among Shakespearian Tragedies on the London Stage, 1700-01 to 1749-50." *Tulane Studies in English,* VII (1957), 83-90.

Vandiver, Edward P., Jr. "Longfellow, Lamir, Boker and *KL.*" *SAB,* XIX (1944), 132ff. References to *KL* by three American poets.

Watkins, W. B. C. "The Two Techniques in *KL.*" *RES,* XVIII (1942), 1-26. Finds in *KL* "a combination of psychological realism and symbolical stylization."

3. General Discussions

*Bickersteth, Geoffrey. "The Golden World of *KL.*" *Proc. Br. Acad.,* XXXII (1946), 147-171.

Blunden, Edmund. *Shakespeare's Significances.* London, 1929. Excellent on some details not discussed elsewhere. Reprinted in his *Mind's Eye,* 1934.

Boas, Frederick J. *Shakspere and His Predecessors.* New York, 1906. Argues that only with the appearance of Mad Tom does Lear finally go mad.

*Bradley, A. C. *Shakespearean Tragedy.* London, 1904.

Bransom, J. S. H. *The Tragedy of KL.* Oxford, 1934. A very thorough study, chiefly devoted to character.

*Brooke, C. F. Tucker. *The Tudor Drama.* Boston, 1911.

*Coleridge, Samuel Taylor. *Lectures and Notes on Shakspere,* collected by T. Ashe. London, 1890.

Craig, Hardin. *An Interpretation of Shakespeare.* New York, 1948. Considers authority the principal subject of *KL.*

Danby, John F. *Shakespeare's Doctrine of Nature: A Study of KL.* London, 1949. Discusses all the chief characters in detail.

*Dowden, Edward. *Shakspere: A Critical Study of His Mind and Art.* 3rd ed., New York, 1881.

*Granville-Barker, Harley. *Prefaces to Shakespeare.* Princeton, 1946.

*Hazlitt, William. *Characters of Shakespear's Plays.* London, 1817.

*Heilman, Robert B. *This Great Stage: Image and Structure in KL.* Baton Rouge, 1948.

Holzknecht, Karl J. *The Backgrounds of Shakespeare's Plays.* New York, 1950. A succinct explanation on p. 260 of the occasions which call for prose or verse.

*Hudson, H. N. *Lectures on Shakespeare.* New York, 1848.

*Jacox, Francis. *Shakspeare Diversions.* New York, 1875.

*James, D. G. *The Dream of Learning.* Oxford, 1951.

*Johnson, Samuel. "Notes on the Plays." London, 1765.

*Knight, G. Wilson. *The Shakespearian Tempest.* London, 1953.

————. *The Wheel of Fire.* London, 1930. Two notable chapters on *KL,* and a chapter on Tolstoy's criticism.

*Knights, L. C. "KL and the Great Tragedies." In The Age of Shakespeare. Harmondsworth, 1955.

*Lamb, Charles. "On Shakespeare's Tragedies." In The Complete Works in Prose and Verse of Charles Lamb. London, 1875.

*Lennox, Charlotte. Shakespear Illustrated. London, 1754.

Lloyd, William Watkiss. Critical Essays on the Plays of Shakespeare. London, 1894. Chapter on KL deals with sources, structure, and character.

Lothian, John M. KL: A Tragic Reading of Life. Toronto, 1949. Six introductory and interpretive lectures.

*Mackenzie, Henry. The Mirror, no. 100. In The Mirror: A Periodical Paper. 9th ed., London, 1793.

*Masefield, John. William Shakespeare. New York, 1927.

Moulton, Richard G. Shakespeare as a Dramatic Artist. London, 1885. Especially strong on the structure of the play. Allegorical interpretation.

*Murry, John Middleton. Shakespeare. London, 1936.

Nicoll, Allardyce. Studies in Shakespeare. London, 1927. Chapter on KL (pp. 136-164) criticizes weaknesses, especially of the opening scene. Extensive comparison to the chronicle King Leir.

*Nowottny, Winifred M. T. "Lear's Questions." Shakespeare Survey, X (1957), 90-97.

*Sitwell, Edith. "KL." Atlantic Monthly, CLXXXV (May, 1950), 57-62.

*Snider, Denton J. The Shakespearian Drama: The Tragedies. Boston, 1887.

Spencer, Benjamin T. "KL: A Prophetic Tragedy." CE, V (1944), 302-308. Finds lessons for our time in KL.

*Spencer, Theodore. Shakespeare and the Nature of Man. New York, 1942.

*Stoll, Elmer Edgar. Art and Artifice in Shakespeare: A Study in Dramatic Contrast and Illusion. New York, 1933.

*Swinburne, Algernon Charles. A Study of Shakespeare. 4th ed., London, 1902.

*————. Shakespeare. London, 1909.

Tamblyn, W. F. "Tragedy in KL." SR, XXX (1922), 63-77. Excellent discussion of extent to which characters cause their own tragedies.

*ten Brink, Bernhard. Five Lectures on Shakespeare. London, 1895.

*Thaler, Alwin. Shakspere's Silences. Boston, 1929.

Theobald, Lewis. The Censor. London, 1715. Outlines the play in no. 7, discusses it in no. 10.

*Thorndike, Ashley H. Tragedy. Boston and New York, 1908.

*Tolstoy, Leo. "Shakespeare and the Drama." Fortnightly Review, LXXXVI (Dec. 1906), 963-983; LXXXVII (Jan. 1907), 62-74. Also in Tolstoy on Art. London, 1925.

Traversi, D. A. "KL." Scrutiny, XIX (1953), 43-64, 126-142, 206-230. A full-length study of characters, themes, structure.

White, Richard Grant. Studies in Shakespeare. Boston, 1899. A discussion of variorum texts (pp. 183-210) followed by a general appreciation of the play.

TOPICAL INDEX

TOPICAL INDEX

The index lists pages on which indirect as well as direct references to a topic occur. It omits mere passing and wholly insignificant references to the main characters.